Terrorism

Terrorism

Origins and Evolution

James M. Lutz
and
Brenda J. Lutz

TERRORISM
© James M. Lutz and Brenda J. Lutz, 2005.

All rights reserved. No part of this book may be used or reproduced in any manner whatsoever without written permission except in the case of brief quotations embodied in critical articles or reviews.

First published in 2005 by
PALGRAVE MACMILLAN™
175 Fifth Avenue, New York, N.Y. 10010 and
Houndmills, Basingstoke, Hampshire, England RG21 6XS
Companies and representatives throughout the world.

PALGRAVE MACMILLAN is the global academic imprint of the Palgrave Macmillan division of St. Martin's Press, LLC and of Palgrave Macmillan Ltd. Macmillan® is a registered trademark in the United States, United Kingdom and other countries. Palgrave is a registered trademark in the European Union and other countries.

ISBN 1-4039-6646-X

Library of Congress Cataloging-in-Publication Data

Lutz, Brenda J., 1957–
   Terrorism : origins and evolution / James M. Lutz and Brenda J. Lutz.
     p. cm.
   Includes bibliographical references and index.
   ISBN 1-4039-6646-X
    1. Terrorism—History. I. Lutz, James M. II. Title.

HV6431.L87 2005
303.6′25—dc22   2005042972

A catalogue record for this book is available from the British Library.

Design by Newgen Imaging Systems (P) Ltd., Chennai, India.

First edition: September 2005

10 9 8 7 6 5 4 3 2 1

Printed in the United States of America.

To Tessa and Carol, our two lovely daughters
and
Alasdair, Bessie, Elsie, and Dryfus their loyal
Saint Bernards and Sadie, our pet Newfoundland

CONTENTS

Preface		viii
Chapter One	Terrorism Today and Yesterday	1
Chapter Two	Definitions, Classifications, and Causes	6
Chapter Three	Terrorism in the Ancient World	19
Chapter Four	The Middle Ages to the Renaissance	28
Chapter Five	Terrorism in the Age of Revolutions	35
Chapter Six	The End of the Napoleonic Wars to World War I	47
Chapter Seven	Terrorist Groups between the Wars	66
Chapter Eight	The End of Empires and Terrorism	84
Chapter Nine	The Rise of the New Left and the Failure of Communism: Increasing Terrorism on a Global Scale	99
Chapter Ten	From Marxism Back to Communalism	129
Chapter Eleven	Conclusions	158
Notes		169
Bibliography		195
Index		214

PREFACE

This book is a continuation of our work and interest in global terrorism and the issues surrounding it. The genesis for this work began with our concern that too much attention was being paid to terrorist actions in the Middle East and terrorism rooted in Islam. In point of fact terrorism is much more complex, and it has been a technique that is more widely present in the world. It is vitally important to understand the broader patterns of terrorism in today's world, and to begin to explore the significance of these patterns. Of course, to understand the present and think about the future, we also have to look to the past even if not exclusively. This volume is just a step in the continuing study of one of the most important phenomena in the world today.

We acknowledge with thanks the help of a number of people. We acknowledge in particular Barbara Blauvelt, the secretary in the Department of Political Science at Indiana University-Purdue University at Fort Wayne. If she were not so good at her job, Jim's job as chair would have been much more difficult and time-consuming, and this book would not have been finished on schedule. Jim's students have provided insight and sometimes a different perspective that has been helpful to us in our writing. The questions they have asked in class have directed some of the research whose results appear in the following pages. Many of our friends and colleagues have been very supportive of our work providing encouragement and suggestions. David Pervin at Palgrave was instrumental in supporting the idea behind the book, and the copyeditors and others at Palgrave have been responsible for a much better product.

The dedication acknowledges our two beautiful daughters, Carol (now 10) and Tessa (now 9). They really do not help us directly on writing projects like this one, but they provide inspiration as well as fascination for us in all that we do. They never cease to amaze us by all that they are. When all is said and done, they are the reason why we write.

Preface

Our Saint Bernards (Alasdair, Bessie, Dryfus, and Elsie) and our Newfoundland (Sadie) are magnificent companions who provide unquestioning loyalty. They are welcome distractions and provide the balance that we sometimes need. They do not care whether we are working on a book or not. They will lay at (or on) our feet waiting to be petted or begging for tummy rubs. They also never cease to amaze us. Moreover, we would like to take this opportunity to acknowledge our special friends, who are family to us and our daughters—Dick and Jane Thomas. They have been very interested as well as extremely supportive in the writing of this manuscript.

Of course, even with all this help and inspiration, we remain responsible for the final product and any errors of omission or commission contained within. We sincerely hope that this book broadens the perspective and enhances the understanding of global terrorism to all who read it.

JML and BJL
Fort Wayne, Indiana
November 26, 2004

CHAPTER ONE

Terrorism Today and Yesterday

Terrorism has become today's hot topic since the attacks of September 11, 2001, the defeat of the Taliban in Afghanistan, the war on terrorism, and the events in Iraq; consequently, terrorism is often seen as a recent phenomenon. One view is that modern terrorism began with the Munich Olympics in 1972, when Israeli athletes were taken hostage.[1] For many Americans the starting point would be later with the 1995 bombing in Oklahoma City, while citizens of other countries might well choose other events to signify the beginning point for modern terrorism. Analysts have also tended to view terrorism as a relatively recent phenomenon even though they look somewhat further into the past than many ordinary citizens. One earlier volume dealing with terrorism starts the discussion with the French Revolution.[2] Others suggest that except for a few special cases from the remote past, terrorism really began with the anarchists in the late nineteenth century.[3] Whether the real beginning is placed with the French Revolution or with the anarchists, the general view appears to be that terrorism is a relatively recent phenomenon. Terrorism, however, ultimately needs to be viewed in a historic context rather than just as a recent occurrence or even an occurrence that began in the late nineteenth century. What is probably more important than picking a point as the starting point is a realization of the fact that terrorism today is a continuation of a basic idea that goes back millennia. Terrorism has endured for over 2,000 years because its practitioners have been able to adapt to changing circumstances and to exploit vulnerabilities in targets.[4] Terrorism as a technique of political influence has not been limited to specific weapons or specific political causes or specific time periods. It is a tactic that all political contenders may be tempted to use if it seems likely to be effective.[5] Terrorism has existed for a long time, and it has periodically resurfaced as a means that groups use to attempt to attain important political objectives. It can be better understood with systematic analysis and comparisons over time.[6]

As is obvious from even a cursory scan of the literature, much has been written about terrorism in recent years. Much of it, of course, has dealt with Islamic terrorism as a direct consequence of the Al-Qaeda attacks on September 11, 2001 in New York and Washington DC, as well as the problems involving the Israeli–Palestinian dispute and other difficulties in the Middle East, although focusing on September 11 (or any other singular event) tends to concentrate on the unique rather than the general nature of the phenomenon of terrorism.[7] Such a focus is justified in many respects, but there is the danger that a concentration on these recent events will reinforce public and government perceptions as to what terrorism is and where it can occur—and, therefore, how it will be dealt with. It is essential that current terrorist activities and analyses of these activities are put in a broader and more accurate context. The following chapters will make certain points very clear. First, while terrorism has been around for a long time, it is possible that it may have become more common in recent times, but that is a question to be addressed, not an answer to be assumed. Second, terrorism is not just a type of violence practiced by any one religious group or just by religious groups. While religious beliefs have spawned terrorism, there are other causes that have generated such activity. Similarly, terrorism has not just been a phenomenon primarily associated with political activity in the Middle East. The Middle East is currently a center of concern (as it has been in the past), but other areas have seen this violent form of political activity appear with some regularity.

The chapters that follow will trace the evolution and use of terrorism for over two millennia. One of the reasons that so many believe that it is a relatively recent phenomenon is that there are much better records for the last hundred years of this millennium than are available for the centuries before that. It is important to be aware of the earlier events for which we do have reliable information, even though our information from earlier times is hardly systematic or uniform. We know that the Aztecs and other states in pre-Colombian America made human sacrifices. Some of the Aztec sacrifices were prisoners taken during military campaigns, but did other sacrifices involve the use of terror by the government to control the population? Did dissident groups resort to terror against their governments in this region during this time or did they rely on civil insurrections? Archeologists can tell us that people died violently, but not whether it was in the service of some cause or whether the death was at the hands of a terrorist or a soldier. Monuments and records from Assyria, Egypt, or Babylon detail the victories of kings and pharaohs with little information on the losers of battles, and such monuments hardly ever refer to violent dissident groups in these states that were forced to rely on terrorism to seek political objectives or did they use revolts relying on conventional weapons? The same is true for ancient civilizations in China and the Indus Valley as was true in the Middle East and pre-Colombian America. The victors, as is all too often stated, write history, and in early eras the losers were often ignored completely. The poor and the powerless, including unorthodox groups or violent ones, have rarely achieved literary mention.[8]

The terrorist movements analyzed in the following chapters cannot be systematic in one sense. In the very earliest years of recorded history, we are much more likely to know about only the most successful movements that relied on terror because they were far too important for contemporary commentators to ignore. The movements that were quickly defeated or those that failed to mount meaningful threats to governments in power have been largely forgotten with the passage of time. Similarly, those groups that were quickly discovered and dealt with by government forces hardly earned any historical comments that have survived. Only those groups that persisted and had some successes are most likely to be known in the current time from historical records. Historians will need to re-analyze the earliest events to determine whether or not they correspond to terrorist activities or whether or not they constitute rebellions or spontaneous mob violence. The current volume will give somewhat greater attention to the earlier examples because they are less often considered as part of the continuing phenomenon of terrorism. More recent organizations, such as Al-Qaeda, the Palestinian groups, and the Red Brigades need much less of an introduction.

The following chapters except for chapter two, which deals with definitions and key concepts and the concluding chapter, are arranged chronologically. The use of time periods as an organization device is not only one of convenience but it also provides some analytical advantages. A number of analysts of modern terrorism have argued that different types of terrorism occur in distinctive time periods.[9] Use of a chronological approach permits a consideration of technological factors and changes in weaponry. Targets could not be attacked at a distance with primitive weapons. Knowledge and use of poisons occurred later in time. Bombs became safer and more effective with the invention of dynamite. Fears of biological terrorism had to await the advancement of the scientific knowledge of disease to the point where toxins could be used to threaten governments and populations. Nuclear terrorism requires nuclear devices. The availability of modern communications has enabled terrorist groups to utilize different forms of organization.[10] As a consequence, the patterns that terrorism could take were constrained in different eras by technological possibilities. Similarly, the technology and weaponry available in a particular time period has influenced the abilities of governments to deal with dissidents and terrorists. The interaction of government capabilities and options available to violent dissident groups helps to explain the course that terrorism followed in different periods. A chronological approach, therefore, has distinctive analytical advantages, especially when attempting to follow the evolution of such a major political phenomenon over time.

Chapter two introduces basic concepts and definitions, including a definition for terrorism. There will be a discussion of three broad categories or types of terrorism. The three are communal (religious and ethnic), ideological (both left and right), and instrumental (power for its own sake). While state support for domestic terrorists operating against its own citizens could be considered a distinct type of terrorism, its underlying rationales are also communal, ideological, or instrumental. Chapters three through ten deal with the different time periods: the ancient world; the Middle Ages, the Reformation, and the Renaissance; the revolutions of the 1600s and 1700s; from 1815 to World War I; the interwar period; the breakup of empires after World War II; the revolt from the left beginning in the 1960s; and finally the more recent terrorism, much of it based in religion. The chapters deal with the various groups in broad strokes. A detailed analysis of the hundreds of groups that have existed is not possible in a single volume. There are groups omitted because it is not clear whether the violence associated with them was terrorist in nature. At the end of each of these chapters there is a table summarizing the terrorist groups discussed, which of the categories they fit best, their objectives, their weapons and casualties inflicted, and whether or not they were successful. Success will largely be defined by whether the groups using terrorism accomplished any of their stated or apparent political objectives. Of course, most violent dissident groups will have had a mixture of objectives—short-term and tactical as well as long-term or strategic. Terrorist campaigns may also generate some changes in the political system that are acceptable at some level to the dissidents. Thus, success is defined by the stated goals of the terrorists, what others have found to be unstated goals, and by external evaluations as to whether or not political changes occurred that were in accord at least in part with the objectives of the violent dissidents. Chapter eleven summarizes the results of this analysis of terrorism over time and attempts to arrive at some conclusions as to whether it has become more prevalent, how it has changed, and what the future may be likely to hold.

CHAPTER TWO

Definitions, Classifications, and Causes

There are a number of key issues for any analysis of terrorism, including a consideration of terrorism in a historical context. First, there has to be a useable definition of terrorism that clearly distinguishes between the practice of terrorism and the presence of terror. Second, categories to separate and distinguish the different groups that practice terrorism—and their objectives—need to be established and refined for the purposes of analysis. Third, some consideration of the potential causes of terrorism is necessary to provide any framework for analysis. It will be important to determine if there are common threads in the historical fabric of terrorism or whether certain periods of time have been characterized by different manifestations of terrorism or different causes.

Terrorism Defined

There have been a multitude of definitions of terrorism. One relatively *early* study of the topic found over one hundred different definitions.[1] The major terrorist attacks of recent years have generated even more attention and definitions—and disagreements—among analysts. Some of these differences exist because the terminology is designed for different purposes. In some circumstances the analysts are attempting to provide a legal definition that will be used in a court of law. Other definitions seek an international consensus with all the limitations inherent in such an ambitious and ambiguous task. International accepted definitions are difficult to achieve because some countries have attempted to make sure that national liberation movements are not included in the category while other countries attempt to exempt dissident movement fighting dictatorial regimes or police states.[2] While such flexibility is often necessary in terms of international diplomacy and international politics, it does not contribute much to the creation of a working definition.

A useful definition needs to be selective enough to be useful while not excluding relevant actions. For the present study, a reasonably broad definition will be used that has been culled from a number of studies and is as follows:

> Terrorism involves political objectives and goals. It relies on violence or the threat of violence. It is designed to generate fear in a target audience that extends beyond the immediate victims of the violence. The violence involves an organization and not isolated individuals. Terrorism involves a non-state actor or actors as the perpetrator of the violence, the victims, or both. Finally, terrorism is violence that is designed to create power in situations in which power has previously been lacking (i.e., the violence attempts to enhance the power base of the organization undertaking the action).[3]

The most obvious part of this definition is that the violence is directed toward political ends, a key factor that separates it from other forms of violence.[4] The political objectives that violent dissidents seek may be changes in policies, a change of leaders, changes in the government structure, or even changes in the territorial extent of the state. Violence for financial gain such as kidnappings for ransom or payments in exchange for protection against criminals is not terrorism even though it is designed to induce terror among those paying the ransom or the extortion. Many dissident organizations levy revolutionary taxes or collect "voluntary" contributions when they can, but the funds go to support the political cause rather than for personal enrichment.

The second element of the definition of terrorism is equally obvious—there must be violence or the credible threat of violence.[5] The presence of actual violence is usually obvious, but threats of violence can also be quite effective at times. For threats to be effective, however, the dissident group involved will normally already have demonstrated its ability to use violence. A group that has yet to use violence may threaten to do so, but the threat will not be effective in most cases if the group has no record of previous successful attacks. While some dissident groups may attempt to perpetuate hoaxes as a means of disrupting the political and economic systems, only a group with a record of violence will be able to use threats to gain political objectives or to achieve short-term tactical advantages such as freedom for imprisoned members of the group.

Terrorism requires an audience beyond the immediate targets or victims. An assassination of an official only constitutes terrorism if it is intended to warn or intimidate other officials. In this approach, one member of a group can be substituted for another.[6] If the assassination is simply intended to remove an individual from a position of power, it is not a terrorist act.[7] Similarly, the intent of bombings or other kinds of terrorist attacks is often to strike fear into the general public and to demonstrate that the government is no longer capable of protecting its own citizens and supporters.[8] What appears to be random are acts actually designed to indicate to any citizen or a member of a group of citizens that he or she is also at risk. Terrorism is ultimately a form of psychological warfare, and it is designed to induce fear.[9] The violence is designed to break the spirit of the opposition and the immediate victims of the violence are the means of sending a message.[10] The fear is intended to lead the audience to adopt a different course of action.[11] The target audience thus could be politicians, government officials, supporters of the government, opponents of the government if the state is supporting terrorism, members of an ethnic or religious groups, and so on. Many definitions include the stipulation that civilians and noncombatants are the principal targets of violence.[12] This addition is a very useful one in many cases, but it adds a great deal of complexity for analyzing the phenomenon since it requires defining civilians and acceptable and unacceptable targets. Suffice it to say that civilians are often the targets, but there can be other audiences as well. Effective terrorism also requires that the target audience be aware of the attacks. If no one knows that a terrorist action has even occurred, then the dissidents have already failed in one key area. The need for publicity for an action, in fact, will often lead terrorists to choose targets where media attention will be greater since the psychological effects will be increased as a consequence.[13] The political objectives of the terrorists, however, require that the violence or threat of violence be directed against a particular audience and not be truly random in order to be effective.

Organization is an essential element for terrorism even though individuals can engage in terrorist acts. For terrorism to have any chance of achieving political objectives, repetition and systematic action is required so that any demands for changes are credible.[14] A single individual would lack the resources to maintain a consistent campaign of actions. An organization is needed to give individual efforts sufficient weight for there to be any chance of change. Solitary individuals, however, can act as part of a broader, loosely organized movement. Although loosely organized groups existed before modern communications technology, it has greatly facilitated the development of the leaderless resistance form of organization. Leaders use the internet or other media to suggest the types of targets or the kinds of activities that individuals sympathetic to the cause might undertake as part of a movement even though the leaders do not actually issue orders to these followers.[15] The individuals have relative freedom in making tactical decisions regarding specific operations.[16] While this network of individuals is harder for intelligence agencies to penetrate, it still has an element of central direction and organization so that campaigns of activities rather than isolated attacks are possible.

For violence to fall within the area of terrorism, a non-state actor is involved as either the perpetrator of the violence, the target, or both. State to state violence is excluded even though some state actions directed against other states are designed to cause terror. During wartime, governments and soldiers frequently undertake horrific military actions that are intended to terrorize target enemy populations. Governments also undertake actions against other states during cold wars and peacetime, such as sabotage, assassinations, and similar activities, with the goal of inducing terror. Governments will even support existing dissident groups in enemy countries. These dissidents are not, however, controlled by the foreign government and would continue to exist if foreign support were withdrawn. When governments support or condone the use of terror against their own citizens, it does constitute terrorism and is considered later.

The final component of the definition is that terrorism is a weapon of the weak.[17] Dissident groups resort to terrorism when they are unable to win elections in a democracy or otherwise gain access to the centers of political decision-making in any kind of political system. If the dissidents are strong enough, they can stage a coup, undertake an armed insurrection, or attempt to secede. If they lack the strength for a direct assault on the government, the dissidents will be forced to resort to those violent methods that are open to the weak—terrorism, guerrilla warfare, or a combination of the two. Terrorism is an inexpensive method that generates results "giving a low cost/high yield potential."[18] Ultimately, terrorists hope that they can cause enough distress and dissatisfaction so that they can either force the government to change its policies or set the stage for a popular uprising.

Another major issue for defining terrorism involves the use of terrorism by states. Political scientists have long studied authoritarian regimes and totalitarian ones, as well as the mechanisms that these forms of government have used to maintain control. It is not necessary, however, to consider all abhorrent activities by governments to be terrorism. They may be exceedingly violent and evil without being terrorism. The above definition of terrorism, however, does not eliminate government actions from consideration in all circumstances. Government activities that encourage violence against its own citizens by paramilitary groups or death squads do fall within the definition of terrorism in many cases since the targets are not a state actor. State-supported terrorism can be especially violent and result in heavy casualties because the power of the state is behind the terrorists or at least permits the terrorists to operate without hindrance.[19] One important distinction is between state terrorism and repression. Many governments have actively practiced or actively practice repression, and perhaps even more frequently, groups in societies see themselves as disadvantaged and repressed by their government. One very important difference between the two is that when governments use repression, individuals in society know the rules of the system (unfair as they may be) and thus can avoid negative sanctions and punishment (barring a mistake by state authorities).[20] Citizens in a group do not become random targets that serve as a means for sending a message to wider audiences with repression. For this reason death squads frequently leave their victims to be found in public places as a horrific warning to others.[21] When regular security forces or the police are involved in actions, it can sometimes be difficult to distinguish between government repression and state reliance on terrorism to achieve political objectives. The use of extraordinary measures such as death squads and paramilitary organizations are likely to indicate the presence of terrorism. The use of outside groups provides cover for a government that cannot openly deal with dissidents, that is, plausible deniability. Death squads may appear because the regular judicial apparatus is ineffective or domestic or foreign opinion makes a crackdown difficult. The use of death squads could indicate that the government is weak and is forced to rely on terrorism in an attempt to survive.

Governments can also tolerate actions by private groups that seek to spread terror in support of government objectives. The groups may also appear to be effective in dealing with dissidents or even countering anti-government terrorism with pro-government terrorism. Government support in these cases can be overt or tacit. Support might include supplying arms or information, or of government officials looking the other way when these groups operate, or failing to make arrests of the persons involved. A variety of actions or lack of actions can be helpful, but again the reliance on these kinds of groups is usually a sign of government weakness. In some areas vigilante groups appear precisely because the officials of the state are unable to govern effectively. The activity of vigilantes is a vote of no confidence in the efficiency of the state.[22] Frequently, vigilante groups have appeared to provide law and order and to deal with criminal activity, but some vigilante violence can have more obvious political objectives and seek to intimidate an audience that is not engaged in criminal activity.

Types of Terrorism

For purposes of classification in the chapters to follow, terrorist activities will be grouped into three categories. The first category is communal terrorism, the second is ideological, and the third is instrumental. All the three types of terrorism can be practiced by groups antagonistic to a state, by groups in conflict with each other inside a state, and in some cases by groups that have the support of the government against another group of its own citizens.

Communal terrorism, whether by the state or dissidents, targets on the basis of ethnicity, religion, or both. Sometimes, only one element is present to divide groups and in other cases one element dominates and the other reinforces the division. Colonial struggles often involve situations where dissidents rooted in communalism use terrorism. In other circumstances, communal groups may be seeking greater rights from the majority community in a country—such as recognition of their language or religion within the framework of the existing state. Communities within a state may even resort to violence and terrorism against each other in efforts to achieve particular political goals, virtually ignoring the state in the process. The communities involved in the violence can be self-defined ones. Swedes have considered themselves separate from Danes for centuries even though they have shared the same religion and have spoken similar languages.

Ideological terrorism is political violence designed to achieve political goals that are determined by some patterns of political beliefs or theories. Left-wing groups usually seek a more inclusive governing system and greater rights and equality for individual members of society; right-wing groups seek a more elitist form of government where the appropriate persons govern, and they accept inequality as a principle of nature.[23] The two groups clearly have divergent, even antithetical, goals, even though both have ideological bases. The placement of dissident groups or government groups with ideological goals is often determined by their targets and goals. Left-wing ideological groups attack right-wing or democratic governments, while right-wing groups attack leftists or democratic governments. A democratic movement using terror would be considered right-wing if it were attacking a leftist dictatorship and left-wing if battling a right-wing dictatorship. Groups on the left frequently seek a change in the type of governments (and associated changes in policy and personnel). Leftist dissidents may seek to inspire a popular uprising in some situations. In other cases they hope that terrorist violence will lead a government to become excessively repressive, thereby alienating the population and driving the people to revolt. Right-wing groups also use terrorism to challenge governments. They hope that the violence causes enough disorder so that the government feels forced to become more authoritarian, and then have to rely on the appropriate groups in society to survive. Interestingly enough, both the left and the right may be seeking to create a more authoritarian government by the use of terrorist violence, although they expect different final outcomes.

The last type of terrorist violence is pragmatic or instrumental. All terrorist violence has elements of pragmatism involved. Targets are chosen because they are vulnerable. One official or building is replaced by another official or building because of circumstances. Some groups using terrorism, however, choose this course of action for overwhelmingly instrumental reasons. For example, the goal for the terrorist violence may be the attainment of power for its own sake or because of associated economic rewards. Ultimately, the successful use of terrorism with pragmatic goals would be a different distribution of government rewards, but there would be little attempt to change government political policies or structures. Governing elites using state terror may also have the largely instrumental goal of keeping themselves in power, but they use communal or ideological justifications for their actions.

Communal terrorism can sometimes reach genocidal proportions, but genocide and terrorism are not the same thing. Unfortunately, the term genocide has been used to refer to a variety of situations where there are a large number of deaths. The official UN definition refers to situations in which there are a large number of deaths *or* attempts to completely eliminate a particular group. As a consequence, the term has lost some of its meaning since the two situations can be different in terms of the goals of those carrying out the killing. When the goal is the complete elimination of a group, genocide does not constitute terrorism since there is no target audience. Genocide is, in effect, an extreme form of what we now term ethnic cleansing. Ethnic cleansing that stops short of genocide is terrorism since it is undertaken with a target audience in mind. There have also been claims of cultural genocide made where the educated members of a minority group are eliminated to deprive the group of effective leadership. Such processes, when they are attempts to suppress a culture may be more realistically referred to as "ethnocide" since they seek to eliminate an identity rather than the group.[24] The removal of the leaders or the elite is designed to accelerate the assimilation of other group members into the general population. Forced assimilation, however, is not terrorism since individuals can avoid "punishment" by adopting the required language, religion, or other official attributes. Cultural genocide, assimilation, and ethnic cleansing are more likely to involve the state as an actor or as a tacit supporter given the need for resources, but these activities can qualify as terrorism.

Causes

The causes of terrorism have both long-term and short-term components. Dissidents may be triggered to launch violent attacks when troops fire on demonstrators, when a country loses a war, or when the economy collapses. There are usually more long-term general causes that explain many of the occurrences of terrorism in the world. They could be consistent over time and region or the causes might vary over time and space. Given the prevalence of terrorism and the vast amount of recent writing on the subject, it is surprising that there is not more work that is devoted to identifying causes in any systematic fashion. It has even been suggested, however, that finding the cause of terrorism is not really possible because they vary too much.[25] It may not be possible to identify a single cause if there are multiple causes of the political violence, especially because in an increasingly complex world the motives of terrorists are becoming more complex.[26] Perhaps more importantly, it must be remembered that terrorism is a technique that can be used by different groups, in different circumstances, and for different ends. Different groups can copy terrorism, and the appearance of terrorism in one context could lead to imitators. There have been just enough perceived successes by terrorists groups to fuel the adoption of the methods by other dissidents (or governments).[27] Success for the dissidents need not be defined as total victory. While violent dissident groups obviously seek to attain some ultimate political goals, they may also seek shorter term or tactical objectives. When all is said and done, the effectiveness of any act of terrorism can be judged by the intentions of the perpetrators and what they hoped to accomplish.[28] Since terrorism is a technique that can be used with communal, ideological, and instrumental goals, it would not be a response to just one cause, and there could be a larger number of potential factors associated with outbreaks of such violence.[29]

Many analysts look to the political objectives of the groups as a means of determining the causes of terrorism. The causes thus correspond to various types of terrorism—religious communal, national communal, and ideological. Governmental use of terror against its own citizens is often considered separately because the underlying cause of that violence can be an inability of the government to control its own population, but it need not be since government violence may be based on communal, instrumental, or ideological considerations. In terms of general causality terrorism can result from many of the same factors that lead to other kinds of political violence. Causes for rebellions, riots, terrorism, coups, and civil war include social and economic inequalities, the lack of opportunities for participation, economic problems, relative deprivations, and government repression among others.[30] The dissident groups resort to terrorism because they perceive that the government is not responding appropriately to their needs, although the terrorists get to define what constitutes a failure to respond. Differing definitions of causes and responses may help to explain why terrorism does not always end even when the causes are dealt with.[31] The dissidents determine those responses that are not adequate enough and therefore "cause" terrorism. The perception, the analyses, the religious or ideological convictions, or the theories of the terrorists do not have to be correct—they simply have to believe them to be correct. They often hope to mobilize the population with the violence by demonstrating that rebellion is possible or that the government has been misleading the public in some fashion. Whether a rebellion is possible or the government is manipulating the people in the eyes of the dissidents need not be in accord with more objective assessments. The dissidents may see economic inequality when gaps between the rich and poor are actually declining. They may desire to go back to some golden age of morality or vision of small town harmony that never existed. They may blame the political system for the decline of interest in their religion when that decline has nothing to do with national policies. Thus, there is always the possibility that the goals of the terrorists—ideological, communal, or instrumental—are not based on facts, but they are relevant nevertheless. It is also possible that the governments may not be responding to legitimate demands of the dissident groups or large segments of the population, and governments may indeed be repressive and manipulative. Governments in closed political systems may indeed be failing to respond to popular demands unless violence or the threat of violence changes their policies. In other cases, acceding to the demands of one violent group may generate violent responses by other groups in the society.[32] In other circumstances, governments may not be able to meet the demands of the dissidents except by imposing unwelcome politics on the majority of the population. Incorporating the religious views of a minority into state law, accepting the racism of extreme nationalists, or implementing extreme ideological views are just not possible in most countries. In these cases a resort to terrorism and violence by the dissidents is the only option that remains if they want to achieve their goals.

One factor that has clearly contributed to the appearance of groups using terrorism has been the absence of a strong state structure. Domestic terrorism was almost totally absent from totalitarian societies such as Hitler's Germany, Stalin's Soviet Union, or Saddam Hussein's Iraq. Totalitarian regimes and many firmly entrenched authoritarian regimes have similar advantages when they have to deal with terrorists or potential terrorists.[33] The security forces present in such countries dealt with suspected terrorists quickly and effectively. In totalitarian states torture was regularly utilized to extract intelligence from any captured member of groups. If the dissidents were operating abroad, their families became hostages or targets for assassination teams sent out against them. Weaker authoritarian systems and democracies, however, provide greater opportunities for terrorist groups to act.[34] Walter Laqueur, in what comes close to a general theory of the causes of terrorism, suggests that this type of political violence had to wait to appear in modern times (except for a few ancient exceptions) because it had to wait for nationalism and democracy to appear in the world.[35] Nationalism provides the spark and the fuel for mobilizing populations and democracy creates political systems where citizens expect results. Democracies can also be more vulnerable. Respect for the rule of law and the need for evidence for convictions in trials combined with weaker security forces can all provide an advantage to dissidents willing to use violence to achieve political objectives. In other cases weak governments of whatever kind may provide terrorist groups with a relatively safe haven, even if unintentionally. When a government cannot control its own territory, other political groups can take advantage. They may not attack the local government (for practical reasons), but they can use the territory as a base for attacks elsewhere. While today governments may normally control their own territory, from a historical perspective many governments frequently have not done so. The presence of a weak state structure is not specifically a cause of terrorism, but it can clearly become a contributing factor that has facilitated and will facilitate such activities. While state weaknesses of various kinds were probably more likely in the past than in the present, democracy is more prevalent today.

States in transition from one form of government to another, even from one form of authoritarianism to another may also be more vulnerable to terrorism since government capabilities are usually more limited during such periods.[36] Governments for which demands exceed capabilities find it difficult to maintain internal control, and the resulting political decay can lead to various kinds of violence.[37] New governments usually need to build legitimacy and may face significant problems in meeting the needs of citizens. The security and police forces may also be disrupted during the transition as well, providing dissidents with more opportunities to resort to violence with less fear of detection or arrest. Even governments changing from one form of authoritarianism to another could face enhanced terrorist activities since the new leaders are unlikely to be able to totally rely on the old military, security, and police apparatus. Political systems moving from authoritarianism to democracy may face the greatest outbursts of terrorism since control mechanisms are weakened and vulnerable during the transition and the new democratic system will face the same limitations in dealing with terrorism as the existing established democracies.

Another potential cause that plays a role in the appearance of terrorism is the breakup of empires or multiethnic states.[38] When such states dissolve, there invariably are boundary disputes and problems resulting from admixtures of populations. Much of the violence associated with the demise of empires may involve conventional warfare, but there is a possibility of resorts to terrorism as well. Further, many of the successor states will be weak states or states in transition and thus especially vulnerable to groups that are likely to use violence. The troubles that afflict countries in these circumstances can be communal or ideological since ideological dissidents may see the times of trouble as an opportunity to assume power and implement their own particular brand of politics and policies.

One final potential general cause of terrorism remains to be discussed. Globalization and modernization can place societies and political systems under great stress. With these processes new ideas, institutions, products, and forms of organization encroach on local societies. Modernization can undermine the existing political institutions in states and lead to political decay and weakness.[39] The social, cultural, and religious values of any society can be challenged by outside ideas. Also with globalization come changes in economic structures, which of course are related to the social and political structures of most societies. It has been suggested that global economic forces undercut local economies when they come into contact. Market-based systems destroy traditional economic relationships and create insecurity for many groups that suffer economic loss when they are unable to compete.[40] Economic globalization of the local economies has been a cause of increased inequality in many states while limiting the ability of states to deal with the resulting inequalities.[41] Further, the rampant consumerism that has come with recent globalization can be seen as one factor that undermines the basic values of a society.[42] In the developing world any manifestation of modernity, especially industrial facilities, can become legitimate targets for attack by dissidents opposed to the negative consequences of their new world situation.[43]

Some of the conflictual effects of modernization have been captured in Samuel Huntington's ideas about the clash of cultures or clash of civilizations.[44] His views incorporate ideas about complex interactions among social, economic, and political factors that will change the nature of conflict in the modern world. In an increasingly smaller world there has been much more contact among different cultures and civilizations, and with this contact has come the prospect of greater violence. The cultures in question are in part religiously defined and separated into Western Christianity, Eastern Orthodoxy, the Islamic World, the Confucian/Taoist tradition, and Hinduism. The intersections of the boundaries of these cultural areas can become zones of conflict, and Huntington suggests that the conflicts of the future may occur on these fault lines between the various cultures, perhaps most particularly along the borders between Islam and other civilizations and within Islam.[45] There has been some evidence that conflicts are actually more likely to occur along these fault lines.[46] Others, however, have found fault with the general theory and have suggested that future conflicts are likely to follow other lines rather than follow the path suggested by Huntington and empirical studies have found mixed support for his views.[47] Huntington's views have generated a great deal of interest and controversy, and they do indicate that in general the politics of identity rather than economic inequality have become more important in the world.[48]

Modernization can also affect the prevalence and types of terrorism as a consequence of its relationship with technology and weapons availability. The world had to progress industrially for there to be the current concern over weapons of mass destruction. New inventions have resulted in weapons that might favor either the government or the dissidents. Steel swords initially favored the organized state that could manufacture them, but rebel groups then could easily arm themselves on an equivalent level. Dynamite gave dissidents an increased potential for using bombs effectively.[49] Modern electronics provided remote control detonations, instantaneous communications, guided surface-to-air missiles, and a mass of other potentials that favor dissidents, and have provided the potential for launching increasingly lethal attacks.[50] Security forces often have access to advanced technology surveillance, extensive computer banks, and impressive tracking devices. The overall imbalance of lethal resources may affect the likelihood of dissidents resorting to terrorism. If arms are simple and readily available to the opposition, the violence may be more akin to war since the options available to the dissidents are rebellion and set-piece battles or guerrilla warfare. If government arms are greatly superior (armored knights versus peasants with scythes or helicopter gunships versus revolutionaries with handguns and shotguns), terrorism may indeed become a more viable option for dissidents. Rebellion is not possible, hence greater reliance on a weapon of the weak.

Summary

In the following chapters, incidences of terrorism will be analyzed. Attention will be paid to a number of actors involved with these terrorist movements, including the type—communal, ideological, or instrumental, whether there were efforts to impose mass casualties, and how successful the various movements have been. The experiences of the most important groups discussed will be summarized in tabular form under five headings: Group, Type, Objectives, Casualties, Success. This form of summarizing the material should help to answer some key questions. Have some periods of time been more prone to particular types of terrorist organizations? Has terrorism been more frequent in some time periods than others, and if so, why? Has terrorism in certain periods been associated with mass casualties or has the violence been more controlled and selective? Has the violence of the different periods been characterized as ethnic cleansing with the associated terror or genocide with the associated horror? How often have governments relied on the use of terrorism against their own citizens as part of efforts to remain in power? These distinctions and the possible answers to these questions must be an integral part of any analysis of terrorism.

CHAPTER THREE

Terrorism in the Ancient World

While terrorism is not normally thought of as a phenomenon that was prevalent in the ancient world, there are at least some examples of it from early periods of history. There were secret societies in ancient China that worked against early dynasties, but their revolts involved conventional warfare, and there is no indication that anti-government activities involved the use of any terrorist techniques.[1] The clearest indications of early uses of terrorism in ancient times came from the internal politics of Rome during some periods of the Republic, Jewish revolts in the Eastern Mediterranean first against the Seleucid Greeks and then against its incorporation into the Roman Empire, and battles between different factions in the Eastern Roman/Byzantine Empire. In these cases there is little doubt that organized groups were using violence directed toward target audiences beyond the immediate victims in order to achieve political objectives. In these cases the violence was frequently organized and widespread enough to meet the criteria for terrorism.

Terrorism in the Graeco-Roman World

In ancient Greece there is very little direct evidence for the use of terrorist violence to achieve political objectives. There was, however, violence and civil conflict in many Greek cities, including conflict between the rich and the poor, between oligarchs and democrats, intra-elite struggles, and disagreements over foreign alliances.[2] These fights among the various factions may have included some use of terror, as did similar struggles in ancient Egypt.[3] These political confrontations provide some indirect indication that factions within various city-states were willing to use violence against each other. There were also many changes in government and factional struggles in cities throughout the Greek world. While the outcomes of the struggles are known, the methods used are not. Terrorism was unlikely to be a common weapon in the Greek city-states. The population of active citizens in most of the cities was generally too small to make terrorism an effective option. The terrorists would not be able to maintain their anonymity. During the long Peloponnesian Wars, there were many references to either Sparta or Athens assisting factions currently out of power. The Spartans favored aristocratic groups, while Athens supported more democratic groups. While there is a possibility that terrorism might have been practiced in at least some circumstances, there is no clear evidence of particular groups that undertook such actions.

The Roman Republic and the later Empire underwent a number of periods of political conflict. There were two significant periods of turmoil in the Republic. The first occurred during the Early Republic and involved the competition for power between the Patricians and the Plebeians, a struggle that took two centuries to resolve. The second was in the Late Republic, and it involved conflicts among different factions within the city-state. The Civil War involving Sulla, the Social War between Rome and its Italian allies, and the maneuverings first of Pompey and Caesar and then Anthony and Octavian were all part of this internal conflict. The violence was a symptom of political failure, and it was one cause among many behind the fall of the Republic and its replacement by the Empire. Interestingly enough, the period of the Middle Republic was one of relative tranquillity. In this era there were no disturbances of normal political activity, and no Roman is known to have been killed or even injured in political violence.[4]

The struggle between the Patricians and the Plebeians involved the higher nobility and the lower nobility in the fifth and fourth centuries BCE. The Plebeians were seeking a greater share of political power. While lower in status than the Patricians, they were hardly representatives of the lower classes of Roman society. They were seeking to create opportunities for greater upward mobility. The losses suffered by the Patricians in the many battles of Rome had always necessitated the advancement of selected Plebeian families into the upper ranks of the nobility. The Plebeians, however, were now seeking a more comprehensive change in the status quo, and in the fifth century BCE the struggle over participation and power led to violent social conflict.[5] There were riots in which Patricians were threatened with bodily harm or assaulted.[6] There were even cases of Patricians being formally tried in court and sentenced to death to cover the fact that they had been killed by an angry mob.[7] The struggle between the two groups does not appear to have been marked by consistent violence or prolonged campaigns that threatened the Patricians. While the violent actions undoubtedly played a role in the ultimate decision of the Patricians to incorporate the Plebeians into the ruling class peacefully, many of these violent actions appear to have been spontaneous in nature—that is, mob action.

In the period of the Late Republic violence became virtually endemic in the political system. From 133 BCE to the end of the modest democracy that was Rome, political factions increasingly utilized violence to achieve their ends. The leaders of the different factions, the *Optimates* and the *Populares*, used crowds of supporters to dominate the assembly proceedings and to intimidate their opponents. Organized violence and the threat of violence were being regularly used to achieve political ends.[8] Increasingly, the clients and the supporters of the factions appeared in the streets with arms to achieve their political objectives. Prominent leaders in Rome eventually came to need ad hoc armed bodyguards to go to the assemblies.[9] The tactics of intimidation resulted in brawls between the armed groups from each side, sometimes resulting in injuries and death.[10] Clearly, decisions in the Senate and other assemblies reached the point that intimidation was responsible for the votes that were cast. This reliance on violence and intimidation had come to be an integral part of Roman politics.

As the violence became more pronounced in Rome, leaders of the different faction became targets. In 133 BCE Tiberius Gracchus, a leader of the *Populare* faction was killed for pushing reforms that threatened the power structure, and in 121 BCE his brother Gaius was killed for many of the same reasons.[11] The *Optimate* faction resorted to force in a systematic crackdown on Gaius and his followers. Gaius and thousands of his supporters were killed "to intimidate and deter the people."[12] In later years a number of leaders from different factions were killed either in spontaneous outbreaks of fighting or as more calculated actions.[13] The well-known assassination of Julius Caesar in the waning days of the Republic is probably the best example of an assassination that was designed to remove a leader whose political ideas or goals had become too dangerous for his opponents and even some of his friends.

Both the Greeks and the Romans had trouble maintaining their control in the former kingdoms of Israel and Judea. When Alexander the Great's Empire dissolved after his death, Israel and Judea generally were part of the domains of the Seleucid successor state centered in Syria. Initially the Jews accepted the replacement of Persian authority with that of the Greeks. In the second century BCE, however, relations between Jews and Greeks soured as Hellenic culture and religious ideas were becoming more prevalent in the Jewish lands. The Maccabees eventually raised the banner of revolt for the Jews. They began with guerrilla strikes and were eventually able to meet the Greek armies on the battlefield. The Maccabees after many battles, defeats as well as victories, finally succeeded in driving the Greeks out and reestablishing an independent Jewish state. During the struggle the dissidents attempted to terrorize those Jews who had adopted Greek culture or attitudes.[14] This terrorism was designed to unify the Jewish community behind the rebels in their efforts to attain independence.[15] It was reasonably effective in reducing collaboration with the Greeks and eliminating dissension among the Jewish population.

Eventually the independent Jewish state became another province in the Roman Empire. In the second half of the first century CE, tensions between Jews and Romans appeared. A number of groups opposed to the continued Roman rule appeared. Collectively known as the Zealots, there were actually a number of different groups that often fought with each as much as with the Romans. Many of these rebels sought to emulate the Maccabees and to once again reestablish an independent state that would be free from the external cultural contaminants that undermined Jewish religion. The first step in their efforts to free their land was to neutralize the support that Rome had among the Jewish population. To this end, they attacked prominent citizens who practiced or advocated cooperation and coexistence with the Romans.[16] Assassins armed with daggers assaulted the collaborators openly on city streets. The attacks not only eliminated leaders among the pro-Roman forces but also intimidated others, who might be supportive of the status quo. The rebels also used surprisingly modern tactics in their struggle. They kidnapped prominent individuals, including a son of the high priest, to exchange for captured members of the group.[17] Over time these attacks were successful in silencing opposition within the Jewish community to the idea of revolt. As a contemporary observer on the scene noted, "More terrible than the crimes themselves was the fear they aroused."[18] The revolt itself lasted from 66 CE to 70 CE. The Roman legions after initial setbacks captured Jerusalem and all the rebel strongholds. The revolt of 66 CE was not the last one; it inspired two later revolts. From 115 CE to 117 CE there was a revolt in Cyrene by the Jewish population, directed against non-Jews, and this violence spread to Egypt and even to Cyprus and Mesopotamia.[19] In 132 CE there was a final revolt that was led by Bar Kokhba. The rebels gained control of Judea and the violence spilled into neighboring provinces. The Romans were able to put down this revolt only with difficulty and after significant losses.[20] While both these revolts were serious, there is little direct evidence that the participants used terror to coerce the cooperation of those who favored cooperation with Rome.

The early violence in the Republic of Rome was replicated in the Eastern Roman Empire. Political violence appeared in the Byzantine Empire from 400 CE to 600 CE. There were political factions that were organized as partisan groups for the games in the circus in Constantinople. The two most important factions of the time were the Blues and the Greens. The Blues tended to favor aristocratic interests, especially the older landowning elite, and orthodox religious beliefs. The Greens were less aristocratic, associated with functionaries at the court who were often drawn from the commercial class, and had links with the Monophyistic beliefs (the view that Christ had only a single, divine nature as opposed to both human and divine natures).[21] These factions engaged in riots and demonstrations as a means of influencing the emperor to make policy changes. Officials were attacked and general intimidation was frequent with the factions. The factions were initially important in the capital, but eventually the two factions were represented in every city and province.[22] The violence of these groups contributed to the instability of the Empire and exacerbated its weaknesses.

Objectives, Causes, and Results

In Greece the conflicts that appeared, especially during the Peloponnesian Wars, involved efforts to coerce or intimidate political opponents. To some extent, the goals had ideological elements (popular rule or noble rule) as well as instrumental elements when a faction allied with Sparta or Athens in order to seize power for its own sake. The efforts of the various factions seeking changes in Rome at first glance would appear to be ideological since in both the early and later Republic periods the activities were directed toward expanding the ruling elite. Such indeed was the goal for the Plebeians, and they were somewhat successful in this regard. The ruling group was expanded as intended, and there was a larger elite. The newly enfranchised Plebes, however, were absorbed into the ruling group, and they generally deferred to the older established families.[23] Not all the Plebeian families were incorporated into the ruling aristocracy. Thus, the change toward a more inclusive and open political system was somewhat limited, but since it was more open than before, the gains in membership were real for at least some families.

At first glance, the struggle between the *Populares* and the *Optimates* would appear to be ideological since the leaders of the *Populares* such as Tiberius and Gaius Gracchus were attempting to change the laws for the benefit of the people. There are real indications, however, that the political goals of both factions were more instrumental than ideological. The *Populare* faction relied on the people as a resource to be used in an intra-elite struggle for power.[24] The greatest fear for the *Optimates* was not that the common people would gain power but that an opposing faction would come to dominate the political system and reap the social, economic, and political rewards that came with that domination. As a consequence, the primary objectives of both factions were largely instrumental and not ideological. The uprisings and violence of the circus factions in the Byzantine Empire were a reflection of the loss of control by the government. Early emperors had prevented the creation of any organization that could lead to civil disruption or threaten the political system, but the later emperors failed to maintain this policy.[25]

The various revolts of the Jews versus both the Greek Seleucid and the Romans are much easier to classify as communal. In this particular era, community was largely defined in religious terms. For example, the Samaritans were considered distinct from Jews because of religious differences, not because they descended from persons outside the original Twelve Tribes. In the various revolts, the major enemies were those associated with the pantheistic Greek and Roman cultures that threatened to overwhelm the Jewish religion. Even in the revolts against the Roman Empire, the intruding cultural influence was Greek. During the revolt of 66 CE, the rebels not only attacked Roman troops and Jewish collaborators but also the Greek inhabitants of the cities they controlled.[26] The later revolts in Cyrene and Egypt were directed against Greek populations in places such as Cyrene, Alexandria, and Cyprus. The heaviest fighting in Africa was between the Greeks and the Jews, with the attacks being directed against Greek temples and holy places, providing additional evidence of opposition to Greek cultural activities, and when Jewish rebels captured Salamis in Cyprus, they slaughtered the Greek inhabitants of that city.[27] There is little evidence that they attacked the other indigenous peoples in the areas of revolt. The Jewish rebellions and attendant violence was clearly a reaction to integration in a wider world. The Graeco-Macedonian armies of Alexander the Great brought new ideas, institutions, and influences into the Fertile Crescent. The outside influences came with foreign practices and contaminants that threatened the more insular religious society that was present. The replacement of the Seleucids by the Romans simply reinforced this danger since Greek culture expanded with the Roman armies.

The political violence and terrorism of the Late Republic was in its own way a consequence of the process of globalization and modernization that was going on in the Mediterranean world in this period. By the time of the late Republic, Rome had begun to acquire an empire. The defeat of Carthage meant that the provinces of the former enemy became sources of great wealth for the state. The defeat of Macedonian armies in Greece also began to give Rome access to the wealth of the East. Suddenly, control of the government in the Republic became more important because the government controlled more wealth. For the *Optimates* and *Populares* the wealth from the Empire was valuable in its own right as a means of enriching the leaders of the factions, but it was also important for winning elections (frequently through bribery which was rampant in Rome) and maintaining the social dignity of leading families.[28] The wealth was both an end and a means to an end. Ultimately, control of the government was critical to continued political success, and it could not be left in the hands of the opponents.

These various examples also demonstrated the vulnerability of certain kinds of states to terrorist violence. The Roman Republic was at best a weak authoritarian state or a quasi-democracy. The state lacked a repressive security apparatus. One of the things that permitted violence to get out of hand so quickly was the absence of a police force.[29] Armed retinues were so effective at intimidating opponents because there was no police apparatus to attempt to preserve order, and military troops were not permitted in the city. (When they were eventually permitted into the city, the system became much more authoritarian!) Officials had to rely on the legitimacy of their office in gaining compliance.[30] If such popular support was not forthcoming, the officials were powerless unless some noble supplied forces from his followers or retinue. While the riots and demonstrations in the Byzantine Empire had ideological or religious differences behind them to some extent, much of the violence seems to have been directed toward gaining power or policy changes in order to benefit from the control of the government. In this sense, it was instrumental for the persons involved. The violence probably continued in part because at least some of the time it was successful in bringing about the changes desired by the rioters and their organizations. In the case of Judea, the imperial presence was also fairly weak. The Greeks needed troops elsewhere, as did the Romans. Both empires tried to rule as indirectly as possible and to limit the costs of maintaining order. The Zealots were able to murder opponents as easily as they did because there was no local police force and because there were only a handful of Roman troops. It required the transfer of significant resources from outside the province to defeat the revolts in 66 CE and 135 CE.

One final point in regard to these examples is the evaluation of their success in achieving political goals. The case of the Plebeians is the most marginal in the sense that it involved limited violence and the violence may not have been part of a broader organized strategy. The Plebeians, however, were the most successful in achieving their basic objective of an expanded political elite that included at least some members of their group. The terrorist violence of the Late Republic was less successful. The intimidation of the nobles and the assemblies worked at times, but eventually the factions that attempted to use popular forces to gain in the intra-elite struggles lost the political battle. The established aristocracy largely maintained control of the political system up to the establishment of the Emperorship. The use of terror in the various anti-imperial Jewish uprisings resulted in both successes and failures. The Maccabees were successful in the use of terror, guerrilla warfare, and regular battles in eliminating pro-Greek support in the Jewish population and in winning independence. Their ultimate success was in part due to the fact that there were dynastic disputes and civil wars that weakened the Seleucids. The Seleucids also had to face threats from Persia in the east and Rome in the West.[31] The presence of these threats from the outside meant that the Maccabees did have some external support, albeit of an indirect kind. In the case of the Jewish revolt in 66 CE, terror was extremely effective in silencing domestic opposition to the rebellion, but the rebellion took place in an era when there were insufficient foreign distractions for the Romans. In 113 CE there were few distractions to the Roman efforts to regain control in Egypt, Cyrene, and Cyprus. In the last revolt in 134 CE, Hadrian had to campaign to pacify the frontier in the East, but the success of Roman arms meant that this revolt too was crushed.

Summary

There are only a few clear cases of the use of terrorism that can be extracted from events in the ancient world. The use of terror and intimidation in Rome involved efforts to win political power and control elections. The later violence in the Byzantine Empire was similar in many regards in terms of the objectives of the groups. The uprisings of the Jews against the Greeks and the Romans constitute the earliest examples of national liberation struggles. Many of the key targets of the acts of terror were not the foreign occupiers but the collaborators or potential collaborators among the population. These insurrections also displayed very clear antagonism toward outside cultural influences and the negative aspects of the globalization occurring in this era.

Group	Type	Objectives	Casualties	Success
Plebeians (possible example) 500–300 BCE	Ideological	Expand the elite to include new group	Relatively few deaths	Yes—elite in Rome eventually expanded to include the Plebeians
Factions in Late Republic in Rome	Largely instrumental but elements of ideology	Control of political system with concomitant reward	Relatively few casualties due to terrorism	Use of violence by one side balanced by similar use on the other with no long-term advantages gained
Circus factions in Byzantine Empire	Largely instrumental with some ideological and religions issues	Control of political system, policy changes in some cases	Deaths from terrorist actions limited, but heavy casualties with the larger outbreaks of violence	Sometimes successful in changing policies or placing different leaders in power
Maccabees in Judea	Communal (religious and national)	Independence and elimination of alien influences	Apparently moderate due to terrorism	Terrorism and other types of warfare effective in achieving independence
Jewish Revolt in 66 CE	Communal (religious and national)	Independence and elimination of alien influences	Fairly heavy due to terrorist attacks	Very successful in eliminating opposition to rebellion, but rebellion failed
Later Jewish revolts in 115 and 134 CE	Communal (religious and national)	Independence and elimination of alien influences	Unclear since level of terrorism unclear	Rebellions failed to gain independence at great cost

CHAPTER FOUR

The Middle Ages to the Renaissance

From the fall of the Roman Empire in the West to the Renaissance and the Reformation, there are relatively few clear-cut examples of active terrorist groups for which we have information. Warfare in China, India, and the empires of the Americas also appear to have been conventional ones. The arms available to the rebels and dissidents were similar to those in the hands of governments (although the governments frequently had the advantage of better organization and organized military units). There are a few examples of systematic terrorist violence in this period. The activity of the Assassins in the Levant and Persia from the eleventh to the thirteenth centuries was in many ways the best chronicled. In addition, the city-states in Italy were often in turmoil in the Middle Ages. There were different types of political violence that occurred, including some activities involving attempts to intimidate and instill fear in opposing groups. A third case involves the appearance of some similar kinds of political violence in the great peasant uprisings in Europe. The last of these traditional peasant uprisings, and in some respects the greatest, occurred in Germany and the surrounding areas in the early sixteenth century—the German Peasant War of 1525.

Assassins, City-States, and Peasant Revolts

The Nizari, generally known as the Assassins, were an offshoot of the Shia branch of Islam. The Shia group broke off from the mainstream Sunni group early in the history of Islam, and the Nizari sect, related to the Ismaili group, was itself a minority within the Shia community. The dominant Sunni often persecuted the Shia adherents, including the

Nizaris, especially when such groups were successful in attracting new adherents away from the mainstream.[1] The group was able to establish itself in mountain strongholds and castles in the Levant and Persia. The safe refuges were necessary since in both areas the adherents faced persecution from the dominant Sunni states that surrounded them, including the states established by the Sejluk Turks in Persia and Arabs in Syria. The sect sought to protect itself by sending out assassins to kill the rulers or high officials of the neighboring states that threatened the group. The victims were killed in knife attacks, usually in public places such as mosques or royal courts. The choice of public places not only demonstrated the power of the group but also guaranteed that news of the event would spread.[2] The actual assassins normally made no attempt to escape, and they were often killed on the spot.

While the Assassins were responsible for killing the Crusader King of Jerusalem, they were much more active against the orthodox Sunni leaders of the surrounding states. Early in their existence, they had developed a following in the Syrian city of Aleppo. The leadership in the city was Sunni, but for a period they tolerated the Nizari presence. Eventually, however, the leaders turned against the Nizaris, and many members were killed by soldiers or Sunni mobs. The leaders responsible for the attacks went to great lengths to protect themselves from retaliation, but the Assassins were successful in killing them.[3] The killing of these leaders, however, was not just retaliation for the massacres; they also served as warnings to any other leader who would be tempted to persecute the sect. In other cases, Sunni rulers or officials were given warnings in an effort to gain favorable changes in policy for the Nizaris. If the changes did not occur, their death would follow. The successful attacks that did occur made it possible for the threats alone to become effective as leaders changed policies or avoided persecuting the Nizaris out of fear of attacks—a special form of deterrence in this period. In keeping with the long-range goals of expanding the religious community, the sect would even infiltrate followers into households of prominent individuals in case they needed to be available for an assassination in the future.[4] The ultimate goal of the Assassins was to survive and to bring about policy changes in the surrounding state by inspiring terror in rulers. Every successful attack sent warnings to other rulers who might be tempted to attack the sanctuaries of the sect or its followers. It is also important to note that the message of the Assassins spread to the necessary audiences in an era with pre-modern communications system, indicating that terrorism does not require the modern media to be successful.[5] Ultimately, the Assassin strongholds were overrun and destroyed by the invading

Mongols. Like the more orthodox Sunni states around them, they fell to an outside invader.

The Italian city-states from the beginning of the thirteenth to the end of the fourteenth centuries were especially volatile politically. There were many changes in the forms of government in these periods, with frequent alternations between republican forms and more aristocratic forms of government. None of the cities were true republics since the great families always had more power. When the governments of the cities were more open politically, there were frequent conflicts among the great families or the guilds for control or for the occupation of major offices. During this relatively volatile period, there were many outbreaks of violence. There were at least some efforts to use force and violence to terrorize and intimidate opponents. In some cases the violence reflected power struggles among the great families for control of the political structure of the state or for access to the more lucrative posts in the government. The families maintained large groups of clients and armed retainers for use against opponents. Street clashes between rival family factions were all too common. The crowds in Italian city-states could be volatile—"bloodshed and street-fighting were every-day matters."[6] The street battles were often straightforward, quasi-military efforts to defeat one's opponents. In other cases, rivals resorted to assassinations to remove their enemies.[7] Partisan mobs raging through the streets, the deaths of supporters, and attacks on property were often part of organized campaigns to achieve political power.[8] When Shakespeare sets the stage for *Romeo and Juliet* within the context of competition between the Capulets and the Montagues, he captured the tenor of these times extremely well. In other cases, the violence that occurred was between the general population and either the great families or the princes. In these cases the struggles involved disagreements over the forms of government. Dukes and counts could be driven into exile.[9] At other times, they would be returned to power by popular demand. The great families would seize power from the prince or the people. Some transfers required only a show of force while others involved actual fighting. When popular governments came into power, they were often short-lived. The wealth, influence, and organization of the great families provided major resources that could be used to swing government control back to the oligarchy.[10] Thus, it is not surprising that the population sometimes preferred a prince to the aristocratic or more oligarchic forms of government.

While internal strife was rampant in many Italian cities, not all of the city-states reflected these patterns of violence. Venice was usually quite stable under the rule of its great families, and other cities had long periods of stability. Florence, like many other cities, however, underwent numerous changes in either the form of government or the leadership. Contention among leading families in Genoa was quite frequent. There were over fifty coups, revolts, and civil wars between 1257 and 1528, and fifteen changes in the government or leaders due to the activities of foreign powers.[11] Rome and the cities in the papal state were particularly unstable. Competition among the leading families itself became so fractious that popes frequently were forced out of Rome to reside in other towns near the seat of the papacy.[12] Eventually, the pope abandoned the city for a period, seeking the relative security of the papal territory in Avignon in France.[13] While there were other reasons for the move to Avignon, the insecurity that always threatened the streets of Rome was one important factor.

Throughout the Middle Ages in other areas of Europe there were peasant revolts. The German Peasant Revolt of 1525 was one of the last of these traditional revolts, and it is one for which we have more historical information. This series of peasant uprisings was actually ideologically conservative in nature since the peasants were attempting to regain traditional rights and privileges that had been usurped by the nobility, the towns, and especially by church officials.[14] Any gains that the peasants made through their revolts were invariably temporary since the military forces of the nobility or the state were more than capable of defeating peasant armies. Even when agreements on the restoration of rights were made, they were eroded over time. During these uprisings, there were some indications that some of the violence might have been terroristic in nature. Attacks against nobles, their families, and supporters were selective and discriminating, at least at times.[15] Since only those who violated peasant norms were attacked, the violence at times sent a relatively clear, if perhaps unintended, message to other landholders and officials.

Objectives, Causes, and Results

The Nizaris were a group, of course, that had a strong religious communal identity. The sect was able to acquire its strongholds and maintain its position against local political leaders during a time when the local states were relatively weak. The intrusion of the Crusader states into the area probably enhanced the ability of the Assassins to continue their policies since the Sunni states were further weakened as a consequence of defeats at the hands of the Christian armies. The continuing goal of the Assassins was to protect their community from persecution. The Assassins were remarkably successful in their efforts to protect the group. Soldiers, sultans, and ministers were terrified into complying with the wishes of the sect.[16] The group survived for two centuries as an outnumbered minority surrounded by other, potentially antagonistic, stronger, religious groups. It has been suggested that the efforts by the sect to defend its religious autonomy were fruitless.[17] The key is not that the Nizari statelet was eventually overwhelmed but that it lasted as long as it did. The group was also ultimately successful since adherents of the sect still survive today!

The peasant revolts as typified by the revolt in Germany and elsewhere in 1525 were much less successful. These revolts had a general, even if vague, ideological motivation. There was, of course, an implicit class base to the struggles—peasants against the elite landowners. While the revolt in 1525 was influenced by the beginnings of Protestant teachings in the Reformation, it was not grounded in communal religious differences or theological views. Even though there was a class element, the peasant goals were conservative in orientation since they sought to regain old rights rather than to create a new political or economic system. The political violence in the Italian city-states, including the use of terrorism, was most often of instrumental variety, although there were some ideological elements involved at times. There was a general lack of any communal element since the protagonists were of the same religion and identified with the same communities. The groups in the struggles actually often had primary loyalty to a smaller group—the family bloc, a class, a guild, or a faction.[18] The contending factions were usually seeking political control of the state machinery in order to exercise power and/or to enrich themselves.[19] One noble faction was much the same as another in terms of how they intended to rule. They changed their orientations when convenient. Policy differences were "the most transparent cloak for personal ambitions and immediate advancement."[20] Ideological rather than instrumental issues did appear in some of the political conflicts in the Italian city-states. The great families were often opposed to the popular factor, reflecting the differing views of the two groups over how the political system should be structured and who should participate. There were clearly elements of a struggle between two distinctive classes.[21] The governments in power were never able to develop effective techniques for staying in power. The nobility in Florence attempted to create a secret police to reduce threats from the popular classes, but this early effort at organized repression and political control ultimately failed.[22] Thus, the victories attributable to violence, whether in the form of terrorism or in other forms, were temporary.

The peasant revolts, the turmoil in Italy, and the activities of the Assassins all occurred within fragmented state systems. The lack of stronger governments invited violence. The Italian governments in the cities were weak, and the very weakness invited struggles for control.[23] The peasant revolts occurred in fragmented political systems where local power was insufficient to deal with the uprisings. The Assassins survived in a fragmented system as well. It is perhaps appropriate to note that it was a strong state in the form of the Mongols that was able to eliminate the power base of the Assassins. While weak state structures helped the groups, it is difficult to see the activities in any of these three cases as a response to any clash of cultures since the conflicts occurred *within* cultural areas. It is possible, however, that more general elements of wider economic activities and changes were triggers for some of the violence. The peasants seeking to maintain their existing privileges were reacting to the slowly increasing levels of economic integration present in Europe that had encouraged the landholders to seek a greater surplus from the land for sale in more distant markets. The Assassins also appeared in parts of the Middle East that were involved in greater trade. The sect, like other Shia groups, did attract the poor and the dispossessed, underprivileged groups.[24] These disadvantaged groups, of course, could have included many of those who suffered from the ongoing economic changes. In the case of the Italian cities, there were major external economic interactions for the larger ones. The great banking families were Italian, and many cities had major trade partners and commercial relations with other regions. Changes in markets, the presence of new competitors, the closure of trade routes, the failures of the great family banks because of defaults abroad, and similar economic events sparked unrest and increased turmoil in the cities.[25] The greater involvement of the Italian cities in international trade in this period may explain why the trading cities in Germany and the Low Countries were more stable.

Summary

There were only a few reasonably clear examples of the use of terrorism from this rather lengthy time period. The Assassins were the only group that primarily relied upon terrorism. In the case of the peasant revolts and the internal struggles in the Italian cities, terrorism was simply an adjunct of other kinds of violence and apparently never a major weapon.

The Assassins were eminently successful with their campaigns of political murder as a means of protecting their religious community from the more orthodox Sunni groups. The peasant revolts, on the other hand, were not successful in the end. The ideological and instrumental violence in the Italian city-states had mixed patterns of success and failure. There were enough successful rebellions, coups, and takeovers with the corresponding benefits for the users of the attacks and intimidation for other groups to persist in such efforts. Probably the most consistent areas of success were the instrumental efforts that led to the occupation or control of key offices with the concomitant access to greater wealth and power.

Group	Type	Objectives	Casualties	Success
Assassins	Communal	Survival of group and extension of religious beliefs	Relatively few	Successful for two centuries in preserving the sect and neutralizing other states
Peasant revolts	Instrumental with an element of ideological	Regain old privileges being lost to land owners	Relatively few from terrorist actions	No long-term success
City-States of Italy	Largely instrumental but some ideological elements	Power for personal gain or power for group	Endemic violence resulted in casualties, and terrorist acts contributed	Terrorism as an adjunct led to changes in leadership and policies at times

CHAPTER FIVE
===

Terrorism in the Age of Revolutions

The Reformation was the forerunner to what is often called the Age of Revolutions that lasted from the mid-seventeenth century to the end of the eighteenth century. The Reformation highlighted communal identities in the form of the religious persecution that went hand in hand with the religious diversity that appeared in this period. Kings and princes often saw minority religious groups as potentially disloyal to the crown. The resulting religious persecutions, however, usually qualify as repression rather than state terrorism. Individuals knew they would be arrested if they were caught practicing an unacceptable religion. There were attacks by indigenous Muslims in South and Southeast Asia against the European colonizers. There are no examples of terrorism in the Puritan Revolution and the Glorious Revolution in England, but there were terrorist incidents connected with the outbreak of the American Revolution, the uprising in Haiti, a series of rebellions in the Andes in Spanish America, and, of course, the French Revolution—including the period of the Reign of Terror.

Years of Change

Religious conflicts in Europe led to both ambiguous and more clear-cut cases of the use of terrorism. The Inquisition, for example, sought to gain converts, not to kill the members of unacceptable groups. The basic tool of the Inquisition was creating fear in the potential heretics in order to force compliance. The Inquisition was not exactly a state agency, but it operated with the approval of the prince or government. Its actions, however, were not part of government edicts. As a consequence, it is an ambiguous case of state repression and an equally ambiguous case of non-state action. The massacres of French Huguenots on St. Bartholomew's Day started when the king had the Protestant leader killed. The news of his death sparked riots where local Catholics attacked Protestants in Paris and then other cities in France.[1] The violence was not centrally directed and was contrary to royal commands; thus, it reflected popular feeling against the Huguenots. The battle between the monarchy and the Puritans that led to the Puritan Revolution had primarily political motivations with religious overtones. While the civil war in England did not involve terrorism (even though government repression was present), the reconquest of Ireland by Puritan armies under Oliver Cromwell was quite bloody. The aftermath of the conflict, however, did lead to one of the first clear efforts to practice ethnic cleansing. Cromwell, as Lord Protector, declared that the Irish Catholics could either convert to Protestantism or move to the western part of the island to the old Kingdom of Connaught and County Clare. The activities to expel the Irish Catholics involved nongovernment groups in many cases. Some Catholics were actually forced to migrate, and the empty lands were intended as rewards for veterans of the Protestant army, and the local Protestants at times took advantage of the opportunity to drive out the local Irish. These efforts were most successful in Ulster in the north. Most of the Irish, however, managed to avoid being forced to try to survive confined to a quarter of the island. Local officials often found the efforts at expulsion to be beyond their resources; landholders wanted to preserve their labor supply; other Protestants wanted no part of a process that would have resulted in the deaths of many of the Irish.[2]

The battles of the American Revolution were conducted as a conventional war complemented by extensive guerrilla actions and campaigns by irregulars, especially in the southern colonies. Atrocities and massacres did occur as part of the war. These actions were complements (sometimes undertaken in an intentional fashion) to active military campaigns and thus not terrorism. The period leading up to the actual fighting in the American Revolution did witness a campaign of political terrorism. Supporters of the crown were often subjected to attacks by groups of patriots (the Sons of Liberty or others). Their homes and businesses were wrecked, and some were even hanged in effigy.[3] Loyalists were tarred and feathered by angry dissidents with some frequency as well.[4] All of these actions indicated that there were real costs involved in supporting the existing system, and the attacks undercut support for the English government. It is not surprising that officials were affected by the threats. They sometimes chose not to enforce the law, others resigned their positions, and some refused to accept such positions.⁵ The attacks on property and person not only punished the immediate victims but also sent warnings to a broader audience, best indicated by the difficulty that the Crown had in filling some official positions. The Boston Tea Party and similar actions elsewhere (the Tea Party was not the only attack resulting in the destruction of tea, it was simply the most famous) were in a way the culmination to this campaign of assault and property terrorism.⁶ The dumping of the tea in Boston Harbor was symbolic, but it also indicated that the property of Crown supporters was not safe anywhere in the colonies.

A second anti-colonial rebellion—actually a group of rebellions—in the Spanish colonies in South America occurred in the highlands of the Andes, in what is now Peru and Bolivia, in 1780. Dissatisfaction with Spanish rule led to a series of interconnected uprisings in the region that were reacting to the same problems. The most significant was the rebellion led by Jose Gabriel. He was in the direct line of descent from the Inca kings, and he styled himself as Tupac Amaru II (Tupac Amaru was the last Inca king who was executed in 1572 for leading a rebellion against the Spanish). There were groups in other areas that also rebelled on their own at this time, such as Tomas Kutari in what is now Bolivia. The rebels found their key sources of support in some of the Indian communities and, to some extent, the mestizo population of the colonies. The Peninsular Spanish (Peninsulares), who were at the top of the political, economic, and social hierarchy, were the clear enemies in all the rebellions since only they were allowed to hold the top positions. Most but not all of the creoles (Europeans born in the colonies) eventually sided with the colonial authorities, although they had their own grievances with the privileged position of the Peninsulares.⁷ Many mestizos and Indian communities actually remained loyal to the Spanish as well. Unlike the rebellions in the Thirteen Colonies, these rebellions in South America were defeated.

As was the case with the American Revolution, there were no clear instances of terrorism being used during the rebellions themselves, although there were massacres of Spanish (Peninsular and creole) and reprisals by forces loyal to the crown. There were similarities to the American Revolution during the prelude to the actual rebellion. There were attacks on property and individuals to protest taxes, tribute levels, levies for labor, and the general corruption of local officials sent from Spain. The Spanish had set up the *repartimiento* system, which required the local communities to purchase commodities at official prices, similar to the monopoly on tea of the East India Company, that were frequently at higher than market prices.[8] The local authorities also abused the labor requirement that the Indian communities supply workers for the silver mines, keeping workers longer than allowed. The lengthened labor tours contributed to the relatively high levels of fatalities among the workers.[9] In the period before the actual outbreak of hostilities, tax officials were assaulted, and many individuals refused to accept such appointments because of the fear of popular retaliation.[10] Local riots even forced the recession of some tax increases.[11] The protesters remained loyal to the monarch until their protests and attacks failed to end the practices of the officials.

The French Revolution (discussed later) had impacts in its colonial possessions including Haiti. The political changes occurring in Paris led to disruption and violence, and some terrorist actions, between different groups in Haiti. Initially, the large landowners, the less wealthy whites (the sans-culottes of the colony), and the free blacks and mulattos were ranged against each other, with the relatively wealthy mulattos often siding with the wealthy whites.[12] The mulattos because of their wealth became special targets for lynchings and intimidation by the less prosperous whites in the early days of the revolution in the colony.[13] The unrest in the colony eventually contributed to a very violent slave uprising in 1791. While it was not the first such rebellion in a colony with an extremely repressive system of slavery, it was to be the most successful. The initial attacks by the slaves were against the European population. The slave armies then became involved in the power struggles in the colonies involving the other groups. The casualties in the colonies mounted due to battles and massacres and efforts by some locals to exterminate members of other ethnic groups. The almost continuous wars and violence between 1791 and 1804 led to the deaths of more than 350,000 people—whites, mulattos, and blacks.[14] One of the final chapters in the struggle to establish an independent state in Haiti came in 1804. Dessalines, the founder of the Republic of Haiti, feared that the whites were conspiring to reinstitute slavery; therefore, he ordered the death of almost the entire white population of the island to prevent any possibility of a white elite ever returning to power. Approximately 5,000 men, women, and children were killed, and the surviving whites fled the island in this early example of ethnic cleansing.[15]

Another form of anticolonial protest appeared in the Muslim communities in India and Southeast Asia. It was a somewhat unique form of terrorism in that it largely involved efforts by individuals in the periods after the Europeans had defeated local armies. Conventional military campaigns and even guerrilla warfare had failed to prevent the continuing

European encroachment and conquest. Along with colonialism came efforts by Christian missionaries to convert the local populations. In reaction to these events, individual Muslims would then practice a form of suicidal attack, *pagsabil* (*juramentado* in the Philippines). An individual would arm himself and attack any European or their local Christian allies that they found, fighting until he was killed. In a few cases two or three individuals would attack as a group in this suicidal venture. These attacks occurred in Malabar on the Indian coast—against the Portuguese, then the Dutch, and then the British—Aceh in the Dutch East Indies, and in the southern Philippines against the Spanish.[16] These attacks sought to defend the integrity of the local community and intimidate the target audiences. The resulting fear that they inspired in colonial authorities and in other Europeans often did lead to better treatment of local Muslims and kept the colonial powers from interfering in local Islamic communities.[17] The same techniques were later also used by individual Muslim peasants in the Malabar Coast to gain better treatment for Muslim tenants from Hindu landlords.[18] The one element partially lacking from the definition of terrorism in the case of *pagsabil* was organization. Local religious authorities or other leaders often blessed these attacks, but there was no terrorist network behind them. The suicide attacks were launched in a cultural context that recognized that this kind of resistance was a defense of the community against the outsiders, and the attackers were considered heroes and martyrs by the local populations. The attacks were, in effect, an early form of leaderless resistance; thus, the separate attacks bore a close resemblance to a terrorism campaign, and the series of individual attacks were a fundamentally equivalent process.

The major revolution in this era that was not colonial in nature was the French Revolution that resulted in the overthrow of the monarchy and included the Reign of Terror. Violence, including terrorism, was a part and parcel of this revolution. Terror was used by the political groups competing for power and then by the state itself. The lines of people awaiting the guillotine were more of an example of state repression by the government or by a series of governments. There was still an element of terror, however, because citizens could not avoid death by obeying the law since so many executions lacked justification or cause. Further, not all the violence that occurred in the early days of the revolution was undertaken by the government or even with the complicity of members of the government. Much of the violence was designed as a part of larger efforts to try to gain control of the government, and different political groups sought to intimidate and terrorize their opponents or to influence or change government policies.

The violence that surrounded the revolution had many sources, including the political struggles for the control of the National Assembly, the Convention, and other government bodies. The executions that occurred during the Reign of Terror actually became a form of political combat between competing factions in the revolutionary government.[19] One early struggle, with many permutations, was between the radical Montagnards and the moderate, but much less well organized, Girondins—a struggle that the radicals eventually won. The Montagnards were very effective in organizing the lower middle classes, the sans-culottes. The sans-culottes took to the streets when it was necessary to support the radicals in their struggles for political control. Street riots were often used to pressure the different legislative bodies or their committees, as well as government ministries throughout the period of the early revolution. Employees in the ministries were sometimes lucky to lose only their jobs and not their lives.[20] The street violence was one important factor that eventually helped the radicals to expel the more moderate Girondins from the legislature in 1793.[21] Once the moderates had lost control of the Convention and Robespierre came into power, the Reign of Terror followed. Not all of the violence that occurred in the early days of the Revolution was linked to the leaders or different political factions in the government. Local groups stormed jails and executed those that they assumed were enemies of the Revolution. Mob actions occurred spontaneously or at the hands of local political leaders attempting to create or influence policy. When the Girondins were in power they were afraid of a counterrevolution, but they were even more afraid of the masses in Paris.[22] The storming of the Tuileries Palace and the massacre of the Swiss Guard that led to the imprisonment of the king, was undertaken by the sans-culottes in Paris despite efforts of some of the political leaders to prevent it.[23]

Causes, Objectives, and Results

All three basic types of terrorism appeared in this era. The activities preceding the American Revolution and the Andean uprisings as well as the violence in Haiti were largely communal in nature. The communal base was largely racial in Haiti. In what was to become the United States, the objectives were national while in the Andean Highlands, in Spanish America, the communal base was regional with elements of ethnicity involved since there were divisions between Europeans and Indians. Tupac Amaru initially attempted to expel only the Peninsulares from the region and to unite all local Peruvians in a new political system.[24] Eventually, in some areas the conflict took on a racial tone, even to the point of being genocidal. The rebels sought to eliminate Peninsulares, creoles, mestizos and any that supported them.[25] The Inquisition had a purely religious communal basis for its quasi-state activities, as did the attacks against the French Huguenots. The attacks by the Muslims against the Europeans in the Dutch East Indies, the Philippines, and the Malabar Coast combined religious and ethnic communalism. The early efforts at ethnic cleansing by Cromwell in Ireland also involved ethnic and religious factors. For the Puritans the repression was justified because the bulk of the Irish suffered from the stigma of being Catholic. Thus, the repressive measures were greater and private violence was often tolerated. Throughout this period, however, there was a trend toward an increasing importance of communal identity based on ethnicity, or language (Haiti, the Andes to some extent), or place (the American colonies, the Andes) rather than religion, especially since the ethnic communal examples generally occurred later in the era.

The violence of the French Revolution was largely based in ideology. The radicals were seeking to impose their version of an ideal political system on the country. Part of the ideological battles included conflicts between the secularism of the radicals and the religiosity of other elements of society. The clergy were as much the favorite targets of the radicals as were the nobility.[26] Radical ideology also explains some of the initial conflicts in Haiti between the rich white and mulatto colonists and the less wealthy white colonials. The egalitarian ideas of the Revolution carried over to the island colony and provided encouragement for the lower class whites in the colony to attack the plantation owners.[27] The other cases discussed in this chapter did not involve major ideological components. The colonial elites in the Thirteen Colonies clearly were ideological in their demands for the rights of Englishmen and limits on the monarch and parliament. There were similar views on greater equality and fairness in Spanish America. These ideological views reinforced local feelings of identification, but the ensuing rebellions were aimed at separatism rather than reform of the systems. The Inquisition and the Muslims in Asia seemed to lack any ideological basis for their attacks.

All of the activities involved some elements of instrumental terrorism. There were small elements involved in the preludes to the American Revolution and the uprisings in the Andes since the objectives included the reduction of taxes, corruption, and other impositions on the citizens. The French Revolution, however, provides the clearest example of cases of instrumental terrorism. At least some of the intrigues and violence, including marshaling the support of mobs in the street involved efforts by individuals or groups to obtain political advantages and power for its own sake. There were not always major policy differences involved. The efforts of the radicals to drive out the moderates did not end the violence and terror; the radicals then turned upon each other.

Globalization and the interface of different civilizations and cultures explain some of the terrorist violence that occurred. The Inquisition and the Muslim suicide attacks in Southeast Asia were reactions to the encroachment of new ideas. In the case of Muslim Southeast Asia, it was the ideas that came with the arrival of the Europeans, first as explorers and traders and then as conquerors, that led to a violent reaction. The suicide attacks were a by-product of the confrontation between the Western powers—Portuguese, Dutch, English, and Spanish—and the local Asian Muslim communities.[28] The interaction was a violent one, and is an example of a clash of civilizations. The arrival of the Europeans was also related to an expanding global economy. The need for assured supplies of spices and the other goods led to involvement with local rulers and the beginnings of the colonial empires with bureaucrats and clergy quickly following. Economic changes and transformations associated with globalization did have effects elsewhere in this period. There were also efforts at economic mercantilism that spurred increasing violence, including property terrorism. The American colonists and the dissidents in the Andes were reacting in part to restrictive mercantilist practices that limited economic gain. The *repartimiento* was eminently mercantilist in its efforts to ensure profitable returns for local producers, and the British Navigation Acts limited trading opportunities in many ways. Various French governments up to and including that of Napoleon sought to control Haiti because of the importance of sugar production on the island—production that was reliant on plantations and forced labor or slavery. The National Assembly maintained the French mercantilist policies that continued to force Haiti to export its products to France.[29] None of the other cases, however, can be categorized principally as reactions to globalization.

Some of the outbreaks of terrorist activities identified in this chapter were not always a consequence of the presence of weak state structures. The failure of the Inquisition and other forms of religious persecution, such as Cromwell's efforts in Ireland, were examples of the inability of the state to triumph in terms of achieving its stated goals. The Inquisition was not strong enough, not even with the active support of some monarchs, to defeat heresy or prevent the continued practice of Judaism or Islam in Spain. In the case of the British colonies in America, the state could not control the Sons of Liberty and associated groups, but the strength of the English state was demonstrated by its ability to achieve a stalemate with the rebels. It was the entrance of France, Spain, and others on the side of the American colonies that turned the tide in the war. The violence in the early years of the French Revolution clearly resulted from the weak structures of the early revolutionary governments. This state weakness also carried over to Haiti and contributed to the violence there since political direction from France was inconsistent and contradictory and material support was absent. In the case of the Muslims in Southeast Asia, it was the strength of the European states and their colonial creations, not their weakness, that led to the *pagsabil* attacks. The preliminaries to the fighting in the Andes occurred in a political system that was in transition in a different way than was the case for France or Haiti. The Bourbon monarchy was actively seeking to reform the colonial system and to provide greater protection for the colonial subjects. Unfortunately, for the system and for the residents of the Andean territories, the reform efforts were not strong enough to triumph. They were strong enough, however, to disrupt the old relationships and patterns of rule.[30] The Bourbon attempts at reform, instead, led to disaffection in the colonies, especially those elements of society that were actively engaged in trade.[31] The fact that the colonial system was in transition probably did contribute to the turmoil and unrest in the Andes.

The relative successes of the various groups that utilized terrorism were mixed. The Inquisition and similar religious persecution often failed in establishing religious conformity within any national church. Cromwell's efforts in Ireland failed in its overall goals since the local leaders often failed to apply his measures in many areas. The attacks by the Catholics in France failed to eliminate the Protestant population in that country or convince the survivors to convert. The Muslims in South and Southeast Asia were relatively successful in achieving their goals. The response by the local authorities was often fairer treatment of local Muslims and the modification of objectionable policies. These early examples of leaderless resistance were perhaps as successful as they were because the colonialists were so few in number, increasing their vulnerability to individual attacks. Of course, since there was turnover among colonial bureaucrats, merchants, and other representatives of the European colonial society, periodic outbreaks of *pagsabil* were necessary.

Terrorism in conjunction with rebellions in Haiti, the Andes, and the Thirteen Colonies had varying degrees of success. The ethnic cleansing that was sought by some of the former slaves was successful as whites and some mulattos fled. When Haiti at last obtained its independence there was only a tiny white population (probably less than 1 percent) and a very small mulatto group (no more than 5 percent).[32] The terrorism against property and officials that preceded the rebellions in North America and South America were quite successful in many ways. Support for the authorities and the colonial systems were weakened, loyalists were intimidated in both cases, and dissidents were encouraged and attracted to what was to become the rebel side. The colonial authorities or groups in the metropole were also provoked. In the Andean region local elites, who were benefiting from the corruption in the system, attempted to strike back and regain control. Control was necessary for them to gain the financial rewards they had come to expect. They lacked sufficient strength to reestablish themselves, and their efforts drove more of the population toward the rebel cause. In the Thirteen Colonies the leaders of the colonial dissidents actually were quite careful to avoid fatalities. Property attacks and assaults were effective in intimidating opponents, but they were not too violent since they did not drive the population to side with the crown.[33] The Boston Tea Party is a classic success story for the local dissidents. The British were placed on the horns of a dilemma. If the Crown failed to respond, it would appear weak and face the prospect of losing support of the local loyalists. If the Crown attempted to punish the perpetrators, it would risk alienating the local population. Ultimately, the British decided to close Boston Harbor in retaliation and public opinion throughout the colonies rallied to the dissident cause. In both the Andes and the Thirteen Colonies the attacks on property and the personal assaults helped to set the stage for upcoming rebellions.

It is more difficult to specify how successful the political violence and terrorism were in France during the early years of the Revolution. Clearly, the Montagnards benefited from the terror and intimidation. Robespierre's ability to destroy the Girondins paralyzed any opposition that might have appeared in the Convention and left him with a free hand.[34] This uncontrolled violence in the streets and the reliance on violence by competing factions probably led to the official adoption of terror by the government as a means of providing some control over the process.[35] The violence, however, led to the eventual overthrow of the radicals. In a very broad sense the radicals did triumph because France (and eventually much of Europe) was transformed in the direction that the Montagnards and other radicals sought.

Summary

Examples of terrorism were present in the Age of Revolutions. The property terrorism in the British colonies and attacks against officials in the Andes were effective in the limited sense of rallying support and provoking imperial responses. Once the fighting started, however, conventional arms determined the outcomes. Terrorism in France and Haiti was successful in propelling groups into power for instrumental, ideological, or ethnic reasons, but the very success of the actions made the actual governance of the countries more difficult. The suicide attacks in Southeast Asia were also reasonably successful in preventing abuses and forcing the colonial authorities to consider local feelings. This period also reflects another change that was occurring in the relationship between governments and potential dissidents. The weapons available to government forces were becoming difficult for dissidents to acquire. The rebels in the British colonies were able to match the weapons of the British army. The Haitian rebels were much less well-armed than their opponents, but they benefited from the hostile terrain and the deadly effects that yellow fever had on European troops. Tupac Amaru's troops lacked the superior weaponry available to the royalist forces. The Asian Muslims had learned that they could not hope to defeat European forces. They were "incapable of succeeding against the Europeans, and attempted merely to terrorize European troops or settlements."[36] These groups had adopted a weapon of the weak in the face of overwhelming conventional military superiority. In this era the growing imbalance between dissidents and government forces may have begun to encourage more reliance on terrorist activities by those groups opposed to the status quo.

Group	Type	Objectives	Casualties	Success
Inquisition	Communal (religious)	Prevent heresy	Limited	Failed to maintain Catholic dominance in all cases, but some countries remained faithful
St. Bartholomew's Day Massacre	Communal (religious)	Eliminate minority religious practice	Heavy	Protestantism survived but was weakened
Cromwell's expulsion policy in Ireland	Communal (ethnic and religious)/ elements of ethnic cleansing	Clear lands for Protestants and reward loyal troops	Fairly high from both direct and indirect actions	Largely failed since Irish Catholics remained in most parts of Ireland

Continued

Continued

Group	Type	Objectives	Casualties	Success
Pre-American Revolution	Communal (national)	Provoke the British, protest, rally support	Property damage and assaults, few deaths	Successful in rallying support, provoking the government, intimidating loyalists
Pre-Tupac Amaru II and others	Communal (national and ethnic)	Protest policies, remove local corrupt officials, rally support	Very limited casualties and property damage	Provoked a negative response and rallied support, intimidated some officials
Haiti	Communal (ethnic)	Terror used in efforts to control local government	High from war and ethnic cleansing, moderate or low from terror	Played a role in the ultimate success of nationalist struggle
Pagsabil in Muslim Asia	Communal (religious)	Protest against colonial status and European policies	Limited casualties	Successful in getting local authorities to change policies
French Revolution	Ideological with some instrumental and government use of terror	Change and control the governmental system in France	Fairly high from local activities and the Reign of Terror	Old regime destroyed in France and terror helped different factions gain power

CHAPTER SIX

The End of the Napoleonic Wars to World War I

The rise of Napoleon, and his eventual defeat, ushered in a new era in both national and international politics. Mass mobilization of states and civilian armies had become more prevalent, as had nationalism. France mobilized millions based on both ideology and nationalism, and the coalitions organized against Napoleon relied on national feeling as well. The remainder of the nineteenth century witnessed a number of conflicts, including some that involved reliance on terrorism. The examples include the continuation of *pagabsil* in parts of Asia, the Boxer Rebellion, activities of Chinese secret societies in other settings, the anarchists, and the Serbian Black Hand. There was the persecution of the Mormons before the Civil War, terrorist violence surrounding the debate over slavery in the Kansas Territory, and the actions of the Ku Klux Klan after that conflict. The first use of terror tactics by Irish nationalists against Great Britain occurred during this time, and there was terrorist activity in Bengal in British India. Terrorism also played a role in the efforts of various Christian nationalities to break free of the rule of the Ottoman Empire. This period saw the beginning of governmental use of terrorism against citizens of the state by the Black Hundred in Russia and the attacks against the Armenians in the Ottoman Empire that ended with a genocidal campaign during World War I. State governments in the United States were involved in forcing out Indian populations by supporting groups that were terrorizing the Indians. In this period there were also instances of foreign governments supporting terrorist organizations in other countries.

Terrorism Around the World

The suicide attacks by Muslims in parts of Southeast Asia, described in the previous chapter, continued into this period. While such *pagabsil* attacks gradually disappeared elsewhere, they continued in the Philippines. The attacks only ended when the United States took over political control of the islands and the Muslim inhabitants realized that efforts to force their conversion to Christianity had ended.[1] Elsewhere in Asia, the Boxer Rebellion broke out at the end of the century. The Boxers (the Society of the Righteous Harmonious Fists) began as a typical secret society, but as they grew their objectives expanded. The Boxers became intent on driving all foreign influences out of China. They were able to draw upon the increasing discontent with the foreign presence in China. There had been riots in 1891 that were directed against foreigners and that seem to have had official, if clandestine, support since the simultaneous outbreak of the riots was unlikely to have been coincidental.[2] In 1898, there were additional anti-foreign riots that seemed to be more spontaneous in origin.[3] The Boxers built upon and drew strength from these earlier incidents and attacked foreigners and all kinds of foreign influences in the country, including Chinese Christians and eventually even foreign diplomats in the capital of Peking.[4] They were eventually defeated, but not before they gained the military support of the Manchu dynasty and many local officials. The intervention of a multinational military force from the European countries, Japan, and the United States defeated the Boxers and the Chinese military units that were fighting with them. The court's decision to support the Boxers was the wrong one for the dynasty, since the defeat in this confrontation sped up the process that led to the overthrow of the monarchy by Sun Yat-sen in 1911.

There were numerous other secret societies that originated in China. These societies or triads spread to other parts of Asia with Chinese migrants. The societies flourished with the migrants in places such as Malaya and the Dutch East Indies where they frequently became concerns for the colonial authorities. The different secret societies frequently used violence against each other, and for the Chinese communities in Malaya and the Dutch East Indies they became a state within a state. Their own members were victims of their violence as the societies sought to maintain group cohesion, and infrequently, officials were also targets for the violence. Much of the violence in Malaya and the Dutch territories occurred within the context of a frontier society.[5] Chinese tin miners had pushed into the interior of the Malay Peninsula where there was no government or very weak government authority under Malay chieftains or the British. There were battles between different secret societies for control of tin mines, trade routes, or control of various kinds of criminal activities.[6] Once the British established a more effective presence in the interior or in Singapore for that matter, the societies engaged more and more in a variety of criminal endeavors. In the 1850s the societies did mount attacks against the Christian Chinese in Singapore since Christianity threatened the hold that the societies had on the Chinese population. It is estimated that over 500 converts were killed.[7] These attacks had multiple motivations, but clearly maintenance of group cohesion (or control) was one important part of the reason for the attacks.

The United States saw a variety of terrorist activities in this era, more so than is usually acknowledged. The Mormons, founded by Joseph Smith in New York, had unorthodox religious beliefs that made them unpopular with local communities. They left New York and attempted to establish themselves in Illinois, Iowa, and Missouri. The local citizens reacted negatively to their presence and attacked their communities and individual Mormons as well. In Missouri and Illinois, the Mormons established communities in such numbers that they threatened to gain local political control through the ballot box.[8] Their political threats combined with their unusual religion led non-Mormons to rely on violence to expel them. The Mormon communities in Missouri were the first to suffer from property attacks, assaults, and deaths. A virtual civil war threatened to erupt between the Mormons and non-Mormons. The state militia intervened, but under the direction of the governor they sided with the non-Mormons. At this time the Mormon communities in Iowa were also dealing with threats and attacks.[9] The settlements in Illinois also suffered from persecution. As the Mormon population grew, including the refugees from Missouri, tensions increased. Assaults and property attacks by both sides began, and the violence escalated and began to result in deaths.[10] Joseph Smith and his brother became victims. They were arrested in connection with some violence, and while they were being held in jail, a mob stormed the jail, with the connivance of those supposedly guarding them, and killed them.[11] Faced with the death of Smith and the increasing violence in Illinois, the Mormons agreed to migrate to the west. The Mormons eventually migrated to Utah where they were safe from the religious persecution of the majority groups in the United States. Once they had agreed to leave, most of the non-Mormons ceased their attacks.[12] Die-hard anti-Mormons continued their attacks against the small number of Mormons who remained behind—often for financial reasons, and eventually militia companies and mobs were successful in forcing even these to leave.[13]

The issue of slavery also generated tension and violent feelings in various parts of the United States. Terrorism became an integral part in the struggles for political control of the territorial government in Kansas. Pro-slavery groups in Missouri frequently crossed over into Kansas to lend support to the settlers in the territory who favored slavery. The Missourians stuffed ballot boxes in local elections and intimidated the settlers who wanted to keep slaves out of the territory.[14] The battles for control became more and more violent with attacks on antislavery settlers by pro-slavery groups and attacks on pro-slavery settlers by those who wanted to make Kansas a Free Soil state.[15] Both sides were successful in intimidating members of the other side, and settlers from both groups fled the territory in fear.[16] At the height of the power of the pro-slavery groups in the state, territorial officials and their supporters occupied Lawrence, one of the centers of free soil feeling. The town was attacked, printing presses that published antislavery views were destroyed, and buildings were burned.[17] Groups in the Northern states, in turn, raised funds to send additional free soil settlers to the territory, and they bought guns and ammunition for the new settlers and for those already there.[18] One of the most famous—or infamous—attacks was by John Brown and his followers when they murdered five southern settlers in 1856 (the Pottawatomie Creek Massacre). The death toll from all the violence totaled at least 200 persons, one of the reasons that the territory came to be known as Bleeding Kansas.[19] The territorial governments in Kansas sided with one side or the other at various times, and there were even competing legislatures in the territory at one point in time. The settlers favoring slavery initially dominated the legislature. The tide eventually turned in favor of the groups opposed to the extension of slavery. They were able to gain control of the territorial legislature, and the national government provided troops to help control the violence from both sides and support the territorial government. John Brown had left the territory to seek support in the Northern states, although he did return to launch raids against pro-slavery groups in Kansas and Missouri and to free slaves (that he later transported to safety in Canada).[20] Once it became obvious that the territory would not be open to slavery, John Brown left Kansas, ultimately to launch his failed raid on the government arsenal at Harpers Ferry in an effort to start a slave insurrection in the South.

The Civil War settled the slavery issues in the United States, but it created a new opportunity for terrorism to appear in the former Confederate states during Reconstruction. The KKK (and similar organizations under a variety of names) appeared and sought to intimidate and terrorize freed slaves as well as whites who were participating in the new power structure. The main objective of the KKK was to return to the prewar situation in terms of the political system and those that would be in control of the state governments. The struggle was often a violent one. Battles between black militias and the Confederate veterans were not unusual. Both the groups in this struggle used terror tactics, although the freed slaves suffered the most.[21] The KKK used violence against Republicans to keep them from voting when social and economic pressures were ineffective in keeping them from the polls.[22] The first state governments in the former Confederacy sided with the freed blacks, so this struggle by the KKK involved attacks on government officials. Eventually, Reconstruction was ended, in part because of compromises made in the disputed presidential election of 1876.

The British rule in Ireland had long been contested by armed uprisings and rebellions. By the last half of the nineteenth century, Irish nationalists had begun to resort to the use of terrorism in their efforts to get the British to leave the island. In 1867 there were dynamite bombs set off in London. Then, in 1882, the Chief Secretary for Ireland and his deputy were assassinated by the nationalists in Dublin.[23] By the end of the nineteenth century the British also had to deal with outbreaks of terrorism in India, especially in Bengal. Between 1897 and 1908 there were a series of attacks by Indians seeking greater rights for Indians and even independence.[24] There were groups of Indian nationalists that adopted the techniques of the anarchists and began assassination campaigns.[25] Some of the nationalist leaders did not think that terrorism would win independence for the country, but they felt that it could set the stage for an armed insurrection that would then be aided by a mutiny of the Indian army.[26] The British authorities broke up the organization of students responsible for most of the attacks before World War I.

The Balkans witnessed a great deal of violence in this period. There were periodic uprisings directed against the Ottoman Empire by Christian groups in the region, and a number of wars that drew in the European powers. Most of the violence was in the form of guerrilla warfare by the Christians in the empire or conventional battles if they could mobilize enough forces. Among the groups that appeared in the waning years of the Ottoman Empire was the Internal Macedonian Revolutionary Organization (IMRO or VRMO)—as opposed to an external group in Bulgaria. IMRO participated in the struggles that led to the end of Ottoman control over Macedonia, and the group continued to be important after World War I. The targets for the terrorist attacks included

Turkish officials and inhabitants in Christian areas. Other attacks were launched against European installations and targets to gain greater publicity for the cause of the Balkan Christians. At Salonika IMRO sank a French ship in the harbor that had delivered munitions for the Turkish army, threw bombs at the Constnatinople Express, cut the city's gas supply and bombed cafes, the post office and a bank.[27] Some of the targets were chosen to include installations identified with the foreign supporters of the Ottoman state. At the end of the nineteenth century, Bulgarian dissidents bombed the German Bank and the German School in Salonika because Germany was a strong supporter of the Turkish state.[28] The armed uprisings by the Christian populations frequently failed when there was no outside support. The Christian populations then faced severe reprisals by the Turkish officials, military, or irregular troops. The massacres of the Christians inevitably inflamed public opinion elsewhere in Europe and led governments to intervene on behalf of the Christians. Reforms usually led to autonomy for the Christian areas, and autonomy then led to independence. Leaders of the dissident movements used the insurrections and terrorist attacks to incite Ottoman reprisals that would then trigger the external interventions.[29] The Ottomans were progressively pushed back until the First and Second Balkan Wars left them with only a small area of Europe under their control.

The new states formed from the breakup of the Ottoman Empire in Europe contributed to terrorism. In Serbia, there were groups that sought to form a Greater Serbian state that would unite Serbia with the other Serbs and Slavs, especially those in the Austro-Hungarian Empire. The Black Hand was a group formed in Serbia (with the support of the Serbian government and Tsarist Russia) to pursue this objective by using terrorist attacks in efforts to weaken Austrian and Hungarian rule over Slavic territories. The Black Hand even intervened in Serbian politics to have the state pursue a Greater Serbia. The elimination of one ruling dynasty in 1903 and its replacement with another more effective dynasty involved the Black Hand.[30] There was a campaign of assassinations, culminating in the assassination of Archduke Franz Ferdinand in Sarajevo in 1914 that triggered the outbreak of World War I.[31]

The Ottoman Empire also faced problems from the Armenian population in the Empire. The Armenians were Christians in the Islamic state, and had their own history as well. Armenian dissidents attempted to adopt the methods of other groups, including the Christians in the Balkans and the Russian anarchists (discussed later). The dissidents hoped to radicalize the Armenian population in the empire and to provoke a

Turkish reaction that would bring about Western intervention on behalf of this Christian minority.[32] Partially as a consequence of these attacks and partially as part of a broader plan, the Armenian nationalists acted by seizing the National Bank in Constantinople in 1896. The attack sparked three days of massacres of Armenians in the capital and elsewhere in the country. The Turks were provoked into retaliation, and the European countries did protest, but the protests were not effective enough to accomplish a halt to the killings.[33] There was also no attempt to force reforms that would have led to Armenian autonomy.

The anarchists undertook one of the more sustained campaigns to change governments in Europe in the later part of the nineteenth century. The anarchists initially attempted to convince the populations of the European countries of the correctness of their ideas through education—propaganda of the word. They were seeking greater equality for the working classes in the European countries and more popular input into governments. When they failed to bring about the necessary changes by propaganda of the word, some members of the movement decided to adopt propaganda of the deed—violent attacks on the government. They thought that violent actions would inspire the masses directly to overthrow their governments in spontaneous revolutions or lead the governments to become more repressive, thereby alienating their populations. A cycle of attacks and increasing repression would lead to the revolution and overthrow of the system.[34] The anarchists moved to bring about this chain of events by attempting to assassinate state leaders or key government officials. The attacks on leaders and royalty lead to the deaths of President Carnot of France in 1894, Spanish Prime Minister Canova del Castillo in 1897, Empress Elizabeth of Austria-Hungary in 1898, King Umberto of Italy in 1900, and President McKinley of the United States in 1901. There were also unsuccessful attempts against Queen Victoria of the United Kingdom, King Louis Philippe of France, and Kaiser Wilhelm I of Germany.[35] Many of these assassinations were part of organized campaigns, but some of the attacks were undertaken by individuals who were inspired by the theories or the examples of the anarchists.[36] The actions of the anarchists provide another early example of a series of leaderless resistance attacks that can be similar to more organized campaigns.

One of the most active anarchist groups was the People's Will (*Narodnaya Volya*) in Russia. These anarchists built on the more or less spontaneous outbreak of assassinations that began in the 1870s.[37] They targeted government officials, with Tsar Alexander II being the ultimate target of their efforts. They killed a number of high-ranking members of the Russian government, and after many attempts on the Tsar, they finally succeeded in killing him in 1881.[38] Notwithstanding the successes of the group, the Russian security forces were able to contain the threat that they posed. It is noteworthy that one of the victims of the government crackdown was Lenin's older brother who was arrested and executed for plotting to assassinate Tsar Alexander III, the successor of Alexander II.[39] There were also extensive anarchist organizations in Spain. In addition to assassinations, the Spanish anarchists also launched broader bombing campaigns designed to weaken the government.[40] For the most part the European anarchists had faded from the scene before or shortly after World War I, but in Spain they remained a political force until the end of the Spanish Civil War.

The anarchists were not the only group to use campaigns of terror in Tsarist Russia. The Socialist Revolutionary Party adopted the tactic in the early 1900s. The Social Revolutionaries also used industrial strikes and property attacks, especially against landowners in the rural areas, to supplement a campaign of assassinations.[41] The party formed a special group for the assassinations, which became the most important weapon for attacking the government, and it was successful in killing a number of high officials, including the Tsar's uncle and the governor-generals of Finland and the Caucasus while local groups of the party undertook assassinations of police, detectives, and informers.[42] Even with the intelligence provided by well-placed double agents, the government had to rely on a high level of repression to battle the challenge presented by the Social Revolutionaries. More than 1,000 death sentences were given out to members of the party who were tried in the courts.[43] The combination of intelligence work and repression was effective in defeating the Social Revolutionaries in their attempt to overthrow the government.

There were also instances in which governments supported groups that were attacking citizens within the state. The slavery and antislavery forces in Kansas received some support from the territorial officials at different times. Local government officials and state officials sided with local populations in driving the Mormons westward. In Illinois, the murder of Joseph Smith was one of the most obvious examples, but hardly the only one. Those charged with the murder of Smith were later acquitted after a lackluster prosecution.[44] The Russian government formed and supported the Black Hundred in the late 1800s. The group was religiously conservative and supportive of the Orthodox Church and was formed to defend the government against those groups that were threatening it and which were attempting to bring about social and political change. Liberal democrats and Jewish leaders were the special targets for assassination by this group.[45] During this same time period, the government at times facilitated the periodic anti-Jewish pogroms by the general population that reflected the frustrations of the people as well as religious intolerance. While the government did not usually organize these attacks, it often permitted them since the Jewish minority provided a convenient scapegoat to divert popular attention away from the problems that would otherwise be blamed on the government.

There were other examples of the involvement of governments in the United States with terror against various Indian tribes. The Indian population in North America was often decimated by European diseases, and the Indians were pushed westward by war, first with colonialists and then by the new United States. The movement of the Five Civilized Tribes into the Indian Territory (Oklahoma) represented a more conscious effort by a variety of government and nongovernmental efforts to relocate Indians from their lands in the eastern United States. The Creeks and Seminoles, as well as tribes elsewhere, were relocated to the west as a consequence of the defeat in wars—wars often undertaken in defense of their lands. The Choctaws in Mississippi and the Chickasaws in Mississippi, Alabama, and Tennessee realized the futility of attempting to remain on their lands more or less voluntarily agreed to be relocated, making the best of a bad situation.[46] Other tribes in the East came to similar conclusions and agreed to relocation. The fifth civilized tribe, the Cherokee, was ousted from their lands through a combination of pressures that involved government support of terrorism efforts by white settlers. The government support included both direct action and studied inactivity.

The Cherokee lands were located in Georgia, and the state government intentionally sought to force the Cherokees to relinquish their land. The government passed a number of laws designed to make their continued presence more difficult. Indians were made non-persons in state courts, thus limiting their contractual rights and opportunities for them to defend themselves and their properties from white settlers.[47] When gold was discovered in northern Georgia in 1829 where the Cherokees resided, additional laws were passed denying the Indians the right to prospect for gold or to mine it in order to deprive the Indians of the financial resources that would come with the gold discoveries.[48] When violence between Indians and whites did occur, the state authorized a private militia, the Georgia Guard, to provide "police services" in the area. The Guard used its position as a police force to side with the white inhabitants (as it was expected to), and to bully the Cherokees.[49] Faced with the hostility of the state government and violent attacks by individual whites, the Cherokees filed suit with the U.S. Supreme Court to protect rights that had been guaranteed to them by treaties with the United States. The Supreme Court twice ruled in favor of the Cherokees, but four Georgia governors in succession enforced legislative discrimination against the Indians and ignored the rulings of the Supreme Court and the provisions of the treaties, and President Andrew Jackson and President Martin Van Buren refused to take any action to support the Supreme Court rulings or do anything else to help the Cherokees.[50] The Cherokees eventually gave up the unequal struggle with the white inhabitants and migrated to the Indian Territory.

A final case of government involvement in violence against a group of citizens involves the Armenians in the Ottoman Empire. The failures of the 1890s and early 1900s led to reprisals, as noted. When the Ottoman Empire joined Germany in World War I against Britain, France, and Russia, the Ottoman Turks doubted the loyalty of the Armenian population in Eastern Anatolia. They especially feared that the Armenians would support the Russian armies in the region, and the government launched a policy of ethnic cleansing that then became genocide against the Armenians. Local Turkish and Kurdish villagers were armed and encouraged to attack the Armenians. Additional deaths were a consequence of expulsion. Armenians, including the elderly and children, were forced to march across arid terrain and deserts with inadequate food and water under the guise of relocation away from the war zone.[51] The genocidal intent of the authorities was obvious since the refugees were misled into believing that they were being moved. The government attempted to disguise the fact that most of the deported people were dying.[52] The government was not attempting to instill terror into Armenian population; it was attempting to prevent the outbreak of terror that would make the deportations and deaths more difficult. It is estimated that the attacks, and the deportations, and massacres led to the deaths of almost two million Armenians.[53] Only about 20 percent of the original Armenian population of the Ottoman Empire survived the war, and many of them died during the fighting surrounding the creation of the Turkish Republic after the war.[54]

Objectives and Causes

The majority of the cases discussed earlier had communal roots. The groups practicing terrorism were disturbed by what they saw as discrimination or threats from other communal groups; consequently, their goals were largely communal in nature as well. The secret societies in Asia, the Boxers in China, and the continuing suicide attacks by Muslims in Southeast Asia were a response to threats to their communities. The communal nature of the Boxers was obvious from their targeting both foreigners and Chinese Christians. The Christians were not targeted because of their religious differences but because the Boxers saw them—correctly—as an opening for foreign influences to enter Chinese society.[55] The earlier disturbances of 1891 also involved similar negative reactions to increasing Western penetration of the Chinese interior.[56] The nationalists in India had a clear communal objective. The use of terrorism by the Christian dissidents in the Balkans and the Armenians elsewhere in the Ottoman Empire were also communal in nature with religion and nationality or ethnic identification reinforcing each other. The activities of the Serbian Black Hand were a continuation of these efforts, although in this case the basis for the terrorism was ethnic/national. The beginnings of terrorism in Ireland that appeared in this era were similar in their communal background, although the communalism had less of a religious cast than in the next century since both Catholics and Protestants were active in the dissident groups.

In the United States communal terrorism also dominated. The activities of the KKK were obviously communal in nature as the Klan sought to limit the rights of the freed slaves and to reestablish the dominant position of the white population. The attacks against the Mormons were also communal in nature rooted in religious differences and were an example of communal "religious cleansing" that was successful since the local authorities were either unable or unwilling to protect the unpopular minority. The forced relocation of the civilized Indian tribes and other tribes was also rooted in communalism. The majority group regarded the Indians as inferior and as an obstacle to progress and civilization. Elsewhere, the Jewish pogroms in Russia were based in religious communalism on the part of the participants (although the reasons for government support were different). The Armenian genocide and earlier efforts at ethnic cleansing in the Ottoman Empire were clearly communally based as well, combining ethnicity and religion, again with a significant element of government involvement.

While communal identity lay behind much of the terrorism in this period, ideologically based terrorism also appeared. The anarchists and Socialist Revolutionaries in Russia were clearly ideologically motivated. What is often overlooked is the ideological background to the violence that occurred earlier in Kansas. The differences on the slavery issue were rooted in differing ideological views. Most of the free state settlers in

Kansas were opposed to slavery in the territory, but many of them were not actually abolitionists. The northerners who were supporting the free soil settlers, however, were more often abolitionists on religious and ideological grounds. The supporters of slavery also had an ideological base. While some southerners supported slavery as such, others did not believe in slavery but still felt that it was a political issue that needed to be dealt with at the state level (even though they recognized that their states would be very slow to move toward emancipation). Both sides in the conflict feared a loss of broader political rights if they should lose the struggle over slavery and political control in Kansas.[57]

There were some examples of instrumental terrorism in this era. The efforts to push the Indians out of their lands reflected the greed of the white population for land and other resources in addition to communal antagonisms. The support of the Russian government for local groups and the Black Hundred that attacked the Jews in the pogroms was largely instrumental in purpose. The pogroms were a means of refocusing discontent from the government to an unpopular religious minority, making the continuation of the Czarist regime more likely. The Black Hundred was similar in many respects to the later right-wing ideological groups that appeared in Europe.[58] They were suspicious of foreigners and were isolationists. The opposition to capitalism and liberalism that characterized the organizations was in part a consequence of its opposition to the foreign origins of the ideas.[59] The activities of the Chinese secret societies outside of China would appear to have been largely instrumental in terms of controlling resources and members.

While communal concerns, ideology, and practical considerations were causes of terrorism in this period, other factors were in play as well. The effects of globalization and modernization were obviously present in some cases. The suicide attacks in Southeast Asia continued to be a reaction to the intrusion of outside influences. The Boxer Rebellion clearly represented a clash of cultures or civilizations. "The Boxer uprising was the first spontaneous uprising of the Chinese people to the growing Western presence in China."[60] The involvement of court officials and elements of the military later on reflected their "last desperate attempt to preserve the integrity of Chinese civilization," at least as they saw it.[61] The Boxers also had strong support from the Chinese who had been displaced by modern technology that came with the increasing role of foreigners.[62] In Russia, the government was facing the prospect of losing ground to the more industrialized West. Further, the effects of global recessions could be felt in the country at a greater level than before. The economic system was in flux because of urbanization and industrialization.[63]

The Jewish population was often seen as agents for these unwanted changes.

Weak state structures contributed to some of the terrorist incidents. The Boxers benefited from the lack of any real centralized control by the government. The absence of an effective territorial government in Kansas contributed to the violence there. The local militias that were available to the territorial authorities were ideologically biased on the slavery issue. The United States initially had very few troops available to help control the violence. One reason for the relatively weak initial response from the national government was political. A number of Northern Congressmen were unwilling to vote to provide funds for U.S. troops to support the pro-slavery territorial authorities.[64] Later, the state governments in the South after the Civil War were clearly not capable of consistently controlling the KKK. The local governments frequently jailed Klansmen for long periods of time because local juries would acquit defendants if they were brought to trial.[65] In time the KKK was able to operate with little fear of retaliation or prosecution.[66] The persecution of the Mormons was possible because of the limited capabilities of state governments and local officials. Effective government in Illinois had broken down, and both sides in the conflict lost confidence in the system. With the failure of government, violence became more legitimate, especially for the majority population.[67] In the United States before the Civil War there was no possible appeal by the minority against a democratic majority.[68] Elsewhere, the ruling Czarist regime in Russia was an example of an incompetent authoritarian state that found terrorist prevention to be difficult.[69] The Chinese secret societies in Malaya and the Dutch East Indies developed and flourished in areas that lacked any kind of effective state struggle, permitting them to develop the organization and garner the resources that made them effective when normal colonial government reached areas where they were entrenched. The establishment of effective government then limited terrorism where it had previously existed.

Successes and Failures

Some of the terrorist efforts in this period were successful in obtaining at least some of their goals. The Muslim suicide attacks continued to have some of the effects that they desired. The activities of the various national groups in the Balkans helped to set the stage for the eventually successful wars of liberation, but they do not seem to have made a major contribution to the final victories. Perhaps, even more important was the ability of the groups to use terrorism to generate additional publicity about the situation of the Christians in the empire.[70] Public opinion in the Great Powers of Europe was one of the more important factors in the ultimate successes of the dissidents. The activities of the KKK in the southern United States played a role in the transfer of power back into the hands of the former, white leadership.[71] The violence against the Mormons was quite successful. The Chinese societies in Malaya used violence to effectively maintain group solidarity within the migrant communities and to defend themselves against outsiders. Given the fact that both sides in Kansas used terrorist violence against the other, it is somewhat inevitable that the tactics would have been used by the winning side, although the losing slavery forces also used them. The attacks by John Brown were among the more effective in intimidating pro-slavery groups. It has been suggested that Brown intentionally used the Pottawatomie Creek deaths to spread terror among the pro-slavery groups, and that the attacks raised the morale of the free state side in the conflict.[72] His return to Kansas for a second campaign of raids instilled both anger and fear among pro-slavery settlers.[73] When Brown escorted slaves that he had liberated through the Midwest, none of the police officials dared to attempt to recover them due to public hostility to returning fugitive slaves to their owners. In Cleveland federal marshals did not dare to arrest him even though there was a reward for his capture.[74]

The successes of John Brown and the Black Hand went beyond their immediate activities, and at some level they both gained their ultimate objectives. The assassination of Archduke Franz Ferdinand and his wife triggered the start of World War I. While war was likely to have broken out eventually, one of the outcomes of the war was the breakup of the Austro-Hungarian Empire and the creation of Yugoslavia under the Serbian royal family. John Brown had goals that went beyond keeping Kansas a free territory. He apparently hoped to start a battle between the two sides that would spill over into the rest of the nation.[75] When the Kansas conflict was resolved, Brown went on to attack the federal arsenal at Harpers Ferry. He was aware that a civil war might result from the raid, but he saw such a conflict as essential to ensure the abolition of slavery.[76] His activities and his execution inflamed opinion in the North and South (differently of course) so that compromise became less likely and the war that he thought was necessary did become more likely. Brown's activities led to a chain of events that climaxed in a major war that led to the achievement of total abolition.

It is not surprising that the cases where governments assisted groups in their use of terror were many of the successful examples in this chapter. The Russian government's support for the Black Hundred and at times for the anti-Semitic pogroms did displace public antagonism or remove threatening political opponents. The Cherokees and other tribes realized the futility of struggling to keep their lands. They were coerced into voluntary relocation. The inaction of the national government sealed the fate of the Cherokees despite the legal victories before the U.S. Supreme Court. There was at least local support by government officials in the efforts to drive out the Mormons in Illinois, Iowa, and Missouri. The ethnic cleansing and genocidal activities of the Ottoman Turks also were successful in achieving its goals against the Armenians, although similar efforts against the Christians in the Balkans led to European interventions that inevitably led to a loss of territory by the empire. While it is not surprising that instances of state support were also examples of successful terrorism, the cases also illustrate an element of weaknesses in the state structure since governments have to use less direct means or inaction to attain the goals that were desired.

There were also terrorist efforts by groups that were failures. The Boxers failed to drive out the foreign influences that they feared. In fact, the attempt to do so brought down the Manchu dynasty and provided openings for political movements that were more open to foreign influences. The efforts by the Armenian nationalists failed. The scattered activities of the Irish nationalists failed to seriously challenge British rule in the island, although the occasional assaults did keep alive the idea of an independent Ireland. The efforts of the Bengali groups failed to achieve independence for India or Bengal. Their efforts, however, were not necessarily a total failure. In 1909, the British reformed the local councils. Many in Calcutta saw the reforms as a direct result of the terrorist campaigns since the British authorities were now more willing to compromise with moderate Indian nationalists because of the attacks of the violent nationalists.[77] The anarchists failed to directly bring about any noticeable change in countries where they attempted assassinations. None of the policy changes they sought were put into place. The People's Will in Russia did achieve a limited form of success beyond the individual assassinations. They began a confrontation between the Russian society and the government, and the confrontation made reform by the state virtually impossible since reform would be seen as weakness. As a consequence, the Russian state was kept from adapting to current events and making changes that might have preserved the system.[78] The

Social Revolutionaries continued the assault against the state, but they were not successful either. One indirect consequence of the assaults against the state was Vladmir Lenin's conversion to the cause. He played a key role in bringing down the system in Russia, even though the mass dissatisfaction with the hardships caused by World War I was much more important.

Summary

The period before World War I was an increase in campaigns of terrorism, or at least of incidents of identifiable terrorism. The largest group of cases was communal in nature, and national identity rather than region was becoming the basis of the communalism. In other cases, the communalism was either ethnic or a mixture of ethnic and religious factors (the Balkans, the Armenians, the Irish). Ideological terror appeared as well with the abolitionists and pro-slavery groups in Kansas. The activities of the anarchists and the Social Revolutionaries in Russia were clearly rooted in ideological beliefs. Instrumental or practical terrorism was also present. The Chinese secret societies, especially in Malaya, were the most obvious. The Black Hundred and government support for pogroms in Russia also had elements of instrumental terrorism since continuation of the regime was a key objective. State support for terrorism against its own citizens, often for such instrumental reasons, also appeared to be on the rise.

No one cause explains these campaigns. Globalization continued to be important in the violence in Muslim Southeast Asia and with the Boxer Rebellion. Modernization played a role in stirring up nationalism in various parts of the world. Increasing nationalism and opposition to foreign elements was present in Ireland, the Balkans, Armenia, and also among the members and supporters of the Black Hand and the KKK. Weak state structures were sometimes important in permitting terrorism, but they were not always present. There were relatively few instances of external state support for terrorist groups in other countries. The Black Hand is the major exception in this regard. For the most part, however, governments avoided supporting groups in other countries. The Irish diaspora in the United States provided very important financial support for the Irish Republican Brotherhood (forerunner of the Irish Republican Army) in the latter part of the 1800s.[79] Perhaps, the greatest weakness that was obvious in this period was the inability of established government structures to deal with pressing political issues.

European governments failed to deal with the rise of the working classes. Successive administrations in the United States failed to deal with settler–Indian conflicts, the Mormon persecutions, the slavery issue, and the reintegration of the former Confederate states into the country with rights for victors and losers. The Tsarist regime in Russia failed to adapt to modernity. The Ottoman Empire could not meet the demands of national groups overlain with a heavy dose of religious communalism. A politically developed state is one that is capable of meeting the demands placed upon it.[80] If the demands are increasing, then the political institutions of the state need to adapt as well in order to govern effectively. In this period, such an adaptation was not happening and terrorism was the consequence.

Group	Type	Objectives	Casualties	Success
Chinese secret societies	Practical/communal (ethnic)	Freedom of action and group cohesion	Relatively few	Mixed, but some successes in establishing themselves and achieving freedom of action
Boxers	Communal (ethnic)	Drive foreign influences out of China	High among Chinese Christians, moderate among foreigners	Rebellion suppressed and traditionalists in Chinese court discredited
Cherokees (and other Indian removals)	Communal (ethnic)	Force Indians to relocate to the West (with state support or inaction)	Few direct deaths, but many Indians died in the process of relocation	Generally successful in forcing the Indians to relocate
Bleeding Kansas	Ideological	Establish political hegemony for free-soil or slavery groups	Moderately high with casualties in both camps	Successful in achieving some goals and terrorizing opponents although terrorism on one side helped to offset terrorism on the other
Mormon persecutions	Communal (religious)	Drive out Mormons (with state support or inaction)	Relatively few	Successful

Continued

Continued

Group	Type	Objectives	Casualties	Success
Ku Klux Klan (first appearance)	Communal (ethnic)	Terrorize freed slaves and return political control to whites	Variable, but probably high overall	Generally successful, especially when state governments returned to local control
Christians in Ottoman Empire	Communal (ethnic and religious)	National liberation struggle	Few deaths from terrorism, many in other types of conflict	Independence attained, but terrorism played only a small role
Armenians in Ottoman Empire	Communal (ethnic and religious)	National liberation struggle	Few deaths in the attacks, very heavy in reprisals	Independence not obtained and situation of Armenians worsened
Genocide against Armenians	Communal (ethnic and religious)	Ethnic cleansing and then extermination	Extremely high	Successful, Armenian population of the empire decimated
Black Hand	Communal (ethnic)	Join southern Slavs to Serbia	Relatively few direct casualties	Terrorism helped to precipitate World War I which led to establishment of Yugoslavia
Irish nationalists and Irish Republican Brotherhood	Communal (largely ethnic but some religious elements)	National liberation struggle	Relatively few	No immediate success, but kept idea of resistance alive for the future
Indian/Bengali nationalists	Communal (ethnic with religious support)	Greater autonomy for India and even independence	Relatively few	Minimal, but the British may have decided to court moderate opinion with concessions as a consequence
Anarchists/Socialist revolutionaries	Ideological (leftist)	More open government system with redistribution of wealth	Moderate over all years and countries	No direct changes occur due to campaigns of terror

Continued

Continued

Group	Type	Objectives	Casualties	Success
Black Hundred	Ideological and instrumental	Eliminate leftist domestic opposition to government	Low to moderate over time	Opponents eliminated but government system fails
Pogroms in Russia	Communal (religious on part of rioters) and instrumental on part of government when involved	Locals attempt to drive out religious minority while government seeks to displace popular anger	Moderate to high (higher when government tacitly supports the violence)	Religious minority survives and government survives a number of crises but ultimately falls

CHAPTER SEVEN

Terrorist Groups between the Wars

The end of World War I brought many changes in borders, and new states appeared in Eastern and Central Europe. It is not surprising that there were significant disputes over the borders in these new states, and many countries underwent crises where large numbers of citizens identified with other nations or with nations that they hoped to establish. There were outbreaks of fighting both within and between states—including the Civil War in Russia and the Russo-Polish war. Government structures in the new states were especially fragile since they had had no time to become rooted in their societies. The presence of fragile political systems and uncertain borders combined with economic dislocations to set the stage for violence by dissident groups. The economic difficulties were hardly resolved when the Great Depression occurred. These major economic difficulties led to the creation of right-wing and left-wing parties that were willing to use violence and terror to attain their political objectives. The first stirrings of anticolonial violence that had been present before the war also continued, and the period witnessed major efforts at ethnic cleansing and even genocide.

National Liberation Movements, Communists, and Fascists

National liberation struggles were more important after World War I. Fighting between different groups occurred in many places, and in many cases foreign governments supported related ethnic groups in neighboring states and other opposition groups. There was terrorism associated with conflicts in the Balkans. The IMRO sought to attach parts of what was now Yugoslavian Macedonia to Bulgaria. The majority of the Macedonians spoke a language closer to Bulgarian than to Serbian and most of the inhabitants also belonged to the Bulgarian branch of the Orthodox Church.[1] They had few direct links to the old Serbian state or the new state of Yugoslavia, and the idea of union with Bulgaria found many supporters in the area. IMRO conducted guerrilla and terrorist operations in the 1920s and the early 1930s, attempting to disrupt the establishment of an effective Yugoslav government authority in the area. The group was responsible for killing nearly 200 Yugoslav officials and wounding many more. IMRO also launched attacks against Serbian settlers in an effort to force the migrants out of the region and weaken Yugoslav control.[2] IMRO enjoyed the covert support of the Bulgarian government for much of this period. It had base camps in Bulgaria and its power and influence extended into Bulgarian politics. Eventually in the mid-1930s the government began to see IMRO as a threat to the Bulgarian political system, or at least to the security of the current leadership. Troops attacked the IMRO bases and support areas and reestablished control for the central government.

The Macedonian dissatisfaction with incorporation into Yugoslavia was heightened by the policies of the government. Ethnic Serbs filled most of the key political and military positions in the Kingdom of Serbs, Croats, and Slovenes (later to be officially named Yugoslavia). The government often used harsh methods when imposing centralized control in areas of the new state that were not populated by Serbs. In Macedonia, the Serbian army and police were given orders to kill local leaders who cooperated with the Bulgarians, while campaigns against Muslims in Bosnia and Herzegovina and Albanian communities in Kosovo were undertaken.[3] As a consequence, many groups in Yugoslavia challenged the validity of their incorporation into the new state.[4] There were many Croats in the new state who opposed the overrepresentation of the Serbs in the leadership positions.[5] They had hoped for a more equal role in the new country but were disappointed. One of the dissident Croat groups willing to use violence was headed by Ante Pavelic. He combined Croatian nationalism with a right-wing fascist ideology in the Utashe party. The Utashe, as well as some others, used terrorism in their efforts to create an independent Croatia. Pavelich, the Albanians, and the Macedonians all received aid from Italy and Hungary.[6] Hungary and Italy, in addition to Bulgaria, had claims on Yugoslav territory. The Italians and the Hungarians provided funding and arms for the Croat Utashe and operated training camps for members of the movement. The Hungarian and Italian intelligence services also passed along information to the Croat nationalists.[7] The most spectacular terrorist action by the Croat dissidents was the assassination of King Alexander of Yugoslavia in Marseilles in 1933 while he was on a state visit to France. The Yugoslav political system survived this attack, but the opposition to the central government dominated by Serbs remained extensive. When the Germans and Italians invaded the country in 1941, resistance in many areas was limited. The Axis partners dismembered the country creating an independent Croatia while Germany, Italy, Hungary, and Bulgaria all acquired Yugoslav territory for their own.

The IRA launched a campaign to drive the British from the island, building on the failed Easter Rising in Dublin. The tactics included both rural and urban guerrilla activities and a campaign of terrorism. British administrators and police became targets for terrorist attacks. Those Irish who were willing to work with the British became special targets, and the local Irish police suffered much more heavily than the British military soldiers.[8] The Irish attacks and British retaliation finally led to a situation in which a political solution to the continuing violence became preferable for both sides. According to the treaty between the two sides, the island was partitioned. The Irish Free State consisting of most of the island was created with Dominion status, but it was still part of the British Commonwealth, even though it had almost total control over its own domestic policies and foreign affairs. Six counties in the north (i.e., Northern Ireland) remained as an integral part of the United Kingdom. The treaty did not meet with the approval of the Irish nationalists who opposed partition and wanted to sever all links with Britain. A civil war between the new government and the maximalists opposed to the treaty resulted. The maximalists kept the name IRA and used guerrilla raids and terrorism in their efforts to defeat the Free State forces.[9] Ultimately the IRA failed to win control and gave up the armed struggle. After this Time of Troubles, the Irish Free State was relatively peaceful. The IRA did launch a few attacks in an attempt to liberate Northern Ireland in 1938 and 1939. There were a few attacks in the north, and over a hundred bombs were planted in a number of English cities, although there were only a few casualties.[10] The campaign drew little support and did not mobilize the population of Northern Ireland or strike a responsive chord in the south. The British police and security forces easily dealt with the threat and the attacks stopped.

Nationalist agitation reappeared in India after the end of World War I, and there was a new round of terrorist attacks. For the Indian nationalists, the success of the IRA provided them with a model of how terrorism could be used to obtain independence from the British.[11] Bengal and northern India saw periodic outbursts of terrorist violence with militant Hindus at the center of the activities. The targets were not only the British colonial authorities but Muslims as well.[12] The efforts by the nationalist groups to create an uprising were not successful, and the British were able to deal with the dissidents without much difficulty. The British also had to deal with terrorist violence in their Mandate in Palestine. The tense situation between Jewish settlers and the Arab native population led to outbreaks of fighting between the two groups. The Arabs hoped that their attacks would dissuade additional Jewish settlers from migrating to Palestine or coerce existing settlers to leave. They also wanted to force the British to restrict additional Jewish immigration to the Mandate so that Palestine would retain a clear Arab majority. Jewish groups began attacking the Arabs, convinced that the British were failing to protect the Jewish settlers. The Irgun, one of the more militant groups, was especially active in targeting the Arab population in general.[13] The Jewish terrorists sought to drive Arab populations out of at least selected areas in addition to protecting their settlements. The more extreme groups such as the Irgun and the Stern Gang attacked British officials in an effort to influence British policies in ways that would be favorable to the Jewish population of Palestine, including allowing increased Jewish immigration. The violence resulted in significant casualties at times when fighting was heavy, as in the years immediately before World War II. At one point of time there were 77 British, 250 Jews, and over 3,500 Arabs fatalities.[14] British authorities in Palestine and London wavered between the two groups, attempting to limit Jewish immigration for some periods and easing restrictions in others. In both the Jewish and Arab communities there was a significant popular base for the violence in this period. The Arab population generally supported the efforts to limit Jewish emigration, and the Jewish terrorists that operated before and during the war became heroes to the groups supporting the violence.[15] Most of the Jewish groups decided to end attacks against the British and to support the Allied war effort when World War II started. The Arab nationalists in Palestine awaited the outcome of the war as well, with many Arabs no doubt hoping for German or Italian victories that would lead to a world situation more favorable to them. Not all the groups ceased their terrorist activities. The Stern Gang assassinated Lord Moyne, the British resident minister for the Middle East, in Cairo in 1944.[16]

The KKK resurfaced in the United States in 1915 when it was refounded in Georgia. The original organizations had faded into insignificance when Reconstruction returned power to the white Southerners. The new Klan now embraced both Christian fundamentalism and patriotism. As the organization spread in the 1920s, it extended the scope of its intolerance beyond Black Americans to include Orientals, Jews, Catholics, and recent immigrants (many of whom were, of course, Catholic or Jewish). Catholics and Jews were the main target because these groups constituted a greater menace to the American system.[17] There were numerous attacks and lynchings resulting in the deaths of thousands of Black Americans and others.[18] Because of its focus on minority groups, the KKK was often able to enjoy the tacit support of state and local officials. Seldom was anyone prosecuted and if prosecutions did occur, convictions by all-white juries were unlikely. The group probably achieved its greatest power in Indiana where the local Klan leader was able to make and break local political leaders because of the voting strength of the members. The power of the Indiana chapter collapsed only when the leader was compromised because of a personal scandal. In other areas of the country support had begun to fade by the time World War II began.

Terrorist violence appeared elsewhere in conjunction with elections and political activities. In Nicaragua in the 1920s, both the Liberal and Conservative parties relied on local paramilitary gangs in many areas of the country. The task of the gangs was to intimidate and terrorize peasants so that they would support the appropriate party in the periodic elections. Peasants and opposition politicians were tortured, mutilated, and killed as warnings to others.[19] There were a series of murders and assassinations between 1920 and 1923 in the Weimar Republic by German nationalists who felt that the politicians had sacrificed or were sacrificing the interest of Germany to serve foreign powers. In the Rhineland, the nationalists also assassinated members of separatist organizations, who were willing to detach the area from Germany.[20] There were a series of similar assassinations in Japan by young military officers and cadets who felt that the Japanese leaders were ignoring the true national needs of the country. These officers assassinated or attempted to assassinate prime ministers, high-ranking military officers, or other government ministers or officials, who were seen as being pro-foreign and not nationalistic enough.[21] The assassinations destroyed the developing system of parliamentary democracy, and Japan almost became a political system with policies determined by assassination.[22] The series of murders did permit the pursuit of extreme nationalist policies and did serve to quiet the potential opposition by other groups in society.

Many of the political struggles and violence in Europe were between Fascists and conservative groups on the right and the social democrats and communists on the left. Italy was one of the first countries to see such street violence on a large scale. Shortly after World War I ended, the Socialists had begun to occupy factories and land and challenge the political system, the capitalists, and the state. The Fascist Party, formed by Benito Mussolini was mobilized to oppose the leftist groups. The party formed action squads that went out into the streets to protect against attacks by the socialists, and they carried the battle to the other side by attacking party offices, newspapers, and rallies of the socialist party.[23] The street violence in a country, where not everyone was literate, provided a means of practical communication of propaganda that did not rely on the media.[24] The election campaigns were literally being fought in the streets, and the Fascists ultimately emerged victorious in these encounters. The struggles were deadly for both sides. In August 1922 alone, the Fascists were reported to have killed 3,000 people and to have lost 300 of their own in the street battles.[25] The Fascist use of violence on such a large scale by a party to achieve political objectives was an innovation for this time period.[26] The victories in the streets and the fear that the fighting had created in the upper and middle classes ultimately permitted Mussolini to successfully undertake his march on Rome in 1922 that elevated him to power.

Later in the period, the Nazi Party in Germany adopted similar tactics. The most important Nazi group that participated in the street battles was the Sturmabteilunger (SA) or storm troopers. One of the initial purposes of the SA was to protect Nazi party meetings and rallies from disruption by forces of the left. While other groups in Weimar Germany were involved in the street battles that occurred, the Communists and the SA were responsible for most of the fighting, and they suffered most of the casualties.[27] Both the left and the right became adept at provoking street battles, and such brawls became the order of the day in many cities.[28] As Mussolini had done in Italy, the Nazis used the violence to present themselves as the party best able to defend the country against the dangers from the left.[29] This violence, in addition, had symbolic importance. Since the left used street demonstrations to publicize their views. The German right began to contest the control of the street as part of a process of confronting the leftists on their own grounds. The Nazis and the SA carried this confrontation to its logical conclusion.[30] The Nazis were able to use the street violence to help them to become the dominant party on the right and to incorporate other nationalist forces. Further, the violence weakened the political parties in the center of the system, leaving the Nazis as the alternative to the Communists. The SA quickly proved to be of declining value to the Nazi regime once it was in power. Hitler moved to eliminate a variety of enemies and potential threats to his leadership in 1934. In the Night of the Long Knives somewhere between 400 and 1,000 individuals were killed. Among the victims were many prominent leaders of the SA.[31]

Street violence among parties of the left and the right was not restricted to Italy and Germany. Finland had faced a civil war similar to that of the Soviet Union after World War I, in which the Whites triumphed over the Reds in bloody fighting. A local Fascist party, the Lapua movement, appeared drawing upon the anticommunist feeling in the country. The Lapua members assaulted socialists, attacked newspapers, and broke up meetings. They developed the technique of kidnapping leftists and dumping them across the border in the Soviet Union. In many cases the Soviet security forces in a period of high paranoia regarded them as potential spies. Some disappeared into the Soviet penal system, and those that returned were warned about continuing leftist political activities.[32] These local Fascists tried to seize power, but the Finnish army stood by the government and the effort failed.[33] In Austria some of the initial street violence originated with leftist groups in protest of government actions. These demonstrations and counter-demonstrations from the right led to inevitable street violence and battles.[34] The Heimwehr was a conservative, nationalist organization with fascist elements formed around veterans of World War I. Although not as radical as the SA in Germany, it took to the streets to support conservative groups against the left. It was able to beat the socialist forces in the street battles. Eventually the violence led to the creation of a conservative authoritarian regime more friendly to the right than to the left.[35] Street battles between Fascists and the left elsewhere in Europe had similar results. The Fascists did not win control of the governments as in Italy, but they created enough turmoil that the existing leaders imposed authoritarian governments to control the violence. Some of the right-wing groups suffered under these governments, but they had been successful in defeating the left and undermining the idea of parliamentary democracy.

In Rumania, the local fascist party not only sought to defeat forces of the left, but it directly challenged the government. Corneliu Codreanu was one of the founders of the Legion of the Archangel Michael, which was the militant arm of the fascist Iron Guard. The Legion and Iron Guard attacked the leftist parties and used street violence much as the Italian Fascists and the Nazis had done. It was highly nationalistic and sought to remove foreigners from Rumania and favored the complete segregation of the Jewish minority in the country.[36] The members of the Iron Guard, especially those in the Legion, like the anarchists before them became advocates of the propaganda of the deed.[37] They felt that the masses could be inspired into action by their deeds. The Legion went further than most of the other groups involved in street violence. It formed death squads whose goal was to take revenge "at all costs" for attacks on the movement.[38] The members of the squads would carry out their missions regardless of the consequences in terms of their deaths or capture. The costs were often high. Between 1924 and 1937 nearly a dozen important political personalities were assassinated, but over 500 Legionnaires were killed in the same period, usually by the police.[39] Codreanu's movement was gaining strength and was in a position to actually assume power. The Iron Guard was prevented from taking advantage of its increasing strength by a royal coup. Codreanu and more than 1,000 Legionnaires were imprisoned, and many, including Codreanu, were killed while in prison. The king did not remain in power for long. The Iron Guard forced his abdication but the king made a comeback as the head of a conservative authoritarian government without the Iron Guard.[40]

Governments also used Fascist groups to deal with dissidents while supplying the government with a convenient cover to avoid responsibility for attacking its own citizens. The Italian government accepted an offer of Fascist support for dealing with the crisis from food riots and a general strike in 1919.[41] Shortly after Hitler came to power, members of the SA and the Nazi Party attacked Jewish business in Germany after a German diplomat had been killed in Paris by a Jewish dissident protesting the Nazi anti-Semitic policies. The police authorities did not intervene to prevent these attacks, which were presented as a spontaneous outburst of anger by the German people.[42] The German government was able to avoid taking official responsibility for the actions of the attackers, even though the party and the government managed the whole event.

Governments facilitated terrorism in other ways in this era. Judges and police in Weimar Germany sometimes looked the other way when right-wing nationalist groups attacked leftists. Even when nationalists were brought into court, they frequently received very light sentences for serious crimes, or if given harsh sentences they later had them commuted.[43] Hitler's short sentence for the attempted beer Hall Putsch in 1923 is a classic case in point. Communists were often punished more severely for their part in the street violence than the Nazis.[44] The Nazis very consciously avoided direct confrontations with the state authorities or assaults on the government.[45] Hitler's strategy of avoiding confrontations with the state provided immediate rewards for the party and supporters who might be arrested. In other countries, some opponents could rely on government forbearance in police activity, prosecution, or sentencing. In Nicaragua, Conservative gangs were never prosecuted for their activities to gain votes for the ruling party since the judiciary was controlled by the Conservative Party.[46] In Italy there was clear bias on the part of the police and the courts to favor the Fascists in many areas although in some regions Fascists were arrested in numbers corresponding to their activities.[47] In Austria the police disproportionately arrested leftists involved in the street fighting in that country.[48] In the United States, the KKK frequently operated with relative impunity. The decentralized nature of the U.S. political system meant that patterns varied from state to state, but local governments were frequently part of the problem.

This period also saw significant violence by governments against their own citizens without the reliance on intermediary groups. The activities of Stalin's NKVD in the Soviet Union were not hidden from the public. Generally, the arrests, imprisonments, and executions were publicized to create fear. The secret police in the USSR came in the middle of the night to arrest people not because they wanted to hide their actions but to make the event more terrifying and to increase the fear of the average citizen.[49] "Manipulation of various forms of terror and the threat of terror became the dominant characteristic of the Soviet art of government."[50] The efforts in Nazi Germany in regard to a Jewish "Final Solution" were not intended to engender terror. The goal of the Holocaust was to eliminate Jews, the Gypsies, and other groups as well.[51] The Nazis built upon the anti-Semitism already present in parts of Europe and gained collaborators in many countries. The best indication that the Nazis and their collaborators were intent on genocide is that, much as was the case for the Armenians in Turkey, there were efforts to deceive the victims in order to make them more compliant. When the Jews were ordered to the train stations, they were told that they were being relocated to the East or to worksites or factories. Given this deception, there was obviously no effort to generate terror in any target audience. The most extensive collaboration with the Holocaust occurred in the puppet state of Croatia set up under Ante Pavelic and the Utashe after the Axis invasion in 1941. The regime in Croatia either killed Jews and Gypsies in its territory or sent them to the death camps. Virtually no member of either group survived.[52] In Croatia, including most of what is now Bosnia and Herzegovina, the Utashe targeted local Orthodox Serbs for a campaign of terror. Hundreds of thousands of Serbs were killed and hundreds of thousands were driven out of the new Croatian state in a campaign of ethnic cleansing. Other Serbs were forced to convert to Catholicism in order to avoid death or expulsion.[53] The attacks on the Serbs were not true genocide but rather ethnic cleansing since the ultimate goal of the Utashe was not extinction but a homogenous Croat population.

There was also somewhat more external support for some terrorist organizations. The Bulgarian government aided IMRO for most of its existence. The aid was sometimes very active, but at the very least IMRO was allowed to operate by Bulgarian authorities. The Croat groups received aid from both Italy and Hungary and they hoped to gain territory if Yugoslavia collapsed. Italy also provided aid to the Austrian Heimwehr as well.[54] The Nazis in Germany supported the Austrian NDSAP in its activities in Austria, as well as the German nationalists in the Sudetenland in Czechoslovakia. Austrian regimes, including the conservative authoritarian regime that came to power in 1934, faced thousands of terrorist actions in the streets mounted by the Austrian Nazis. The creation of the authoritarian regime, in fact, in part was a response to the Nazi attacks.[55] The Communists who were in power in the USSR supplied assistance to other Communist groups, including those that used violence and terrorism. The Comintern was explicitly designed to aid Communist parties in various countries. The Irish in the diaspora, especially in the United States, remained an important source of funding and support for the IRA, and Jewish settlers in Palestine also had important outside funding, some of which no doubt aided in the terrorist operations.

Causes and Objectives

Communal and ideological terrorism dominated this period, and sometimes the two were intermingled for the groups involved. The battles of the Irish, the Indians in Bengal, and both the Arabs and Jews in Palestine were communal, national liberation struggles. The Jewish settlers in Palestine were largely secular in their orientations; they were defined as Jewish culturally (and therefore nationally) rather than religiously. Religious differences did reinforce the national differences for the Irish, Indians, and Arabs. IMRO was also a national liberation struggle that lacked any religious distinction since Serbs, Bulgarians, and Macedonians were largely Greek Orthodox. The Croatians, both as terrorists fighting Yugoslavia and the rulers of a state, represented a special blend of ethnicity and religion. Serbs and Croats speak a related language and are not obviously from different ethnic groups; thus, religion was the dividing factor. The religious nature of the communalism was obvious in the opportunity given to Serbs to survive by converting to Catholicism after Pavelic came to power. Communalism in the form of racism was also obvious in the persecution of the Jews (and Gypsies) by the Germans and their collaborators. Finally, communalism was present in the obvious racism of the KKK, and there was religious bias in the opposition to Jews and Catholics. There was also an element of national communalism since the immigrant communities were targeted for being new and culturally different from the Anglo-Saxon society considered to be the norm in the United States.

The ideological basis for terrorism was most obvious in the clashes between the left and the right in Italy, Germany, and elsewhere in Europe. For the Marxists, the motivation was overwhelmingly ideological with virtually no other elements. The Fascists, Nazis, and other right-wing groups often had nationalism incorporated into the ideology. The assassinations that occurred in Japan were undertaken in pursuit of an ideology with a major component of nationalism. The earliest assassinations in Weimar Germany also have the hallmarks of an ideology with a large element of nationalism incorporated into it. The early German violence and the actions of the Japanese officers were intended to change government policy in order to avoid "national betrayal."[56] The terrorist attacks against the new government of the Irish Free State were rooted in ideological differences with elements of nationalism. The antigovernment forces were more extreme in their nationalism than the group that accepted the treaty with the United Kingdom. In Rumania the communalism involved more of an element of religious identity given the significance of religious feelings for the Legion of the Archangel Michael.

Instrumental terrorism was relatively rare in this period. The major exception was the violence by the gangs in Nicaragua in the 1920s. The Gestapo and the NKVD were used to entrench the existing governments in power; therefore, there was a strong element of instrumental terror being used to complement ideological and other factors. Among Stalin's targets for the purges and terror were potential opponents. They were chosen not for ideological differences but to keep them from challenging for power. The street violence of the Fascists and the Nazis also served some instrumental purposes since the attacks against the left were quite successful in attracting more recruits to the party and the combat squads. The successful actions also attracted additional, even essential, funding.[57] In the final analysis, while the terrorism did have some instrumental purposes, the goal of most of the terrorist violence was to attain power in order to implement ideological or communal policies and to bring about change in the political system.

While nationalism and ideology drove the organizations that used terror, other factors were present in fueling terrorism. Clearly the crises, unrest, and changes resulting from World War I were often a factor. World War I disrupted political systems and challenged old ideas.[58] It is probably no coincidence that Fascism was weakest in exactly those states that remained neutral during the war.[59] It is difficult to conceive of Fascism gaining support in Italy had there not been the events of the World War.[60] The dissension by groups within the new state of Yugoslavia reflected dissatisfaction with the peace settlements and boundaries. The social and economic disruption of the war provided a background for the left and the right to recruit followers. In other countries, defeat in war fueled increased nationalism. Boundary changes meant that new territories and populations had to be integrated into existing states (Rumania, Italy, Serbia in effect) or entirely new states had to develop within their new boundaries (Poland, the Baltic States). The large number of boundary rectifications meant that foreign governments were more likely to support terrorist groups in other countries as part of an effort to weaken a neighbor in order to reclaim lost territory or otherwise gain territorial advantages.

There were a number of countries with weak political structures, a situation aggravated by the war. The violence in Nicaragua in the 1920s was in a country with "a weak state, indirect or caudillo rule, [and] the fragmentation of political authority."[61] The various dissident groups in the new state of Yugoslavia were able to take advantage of the weaknesses of the new state with its fragile institutions. Weak governments elsewhere in Eastern Europe provided opportunities for groups like the Legion of the Archangel Michael and others. Italy, after the war, was having difficulties with demobilized soldiers and the unrest that came with the economic dislocation after the war. The Weimar Republic was an exceedingly weak governmental system in its first years, and like many other governments it was weaker in the aftermath of the Great Depression. In other cases, however, weakness of governmental structures cannot explain the appearance of terrorism. The struggles of the IRA succeeded after the war not because the British state was weak, but because the public and the government were increasingly uncomfortable with the amount of force being used in counterterrorism efforts and with the casualties involved.[62] The government of the new Irish Free State, however, was especially vulnerable to attack by the dissidents who disagreed with the achievement of only partial victory. The Indian violence in Bengal did not arise because of any weakness of the colonial regime. The British authorities in Palestine were also not governing within a weak colonial system, although both the Jewish settlers and Arab inhabitants were able to take advantage of the presence of limited British resources to deal with the communal attacks. The government under assault by nationalists in Japan was not especially weak. The terrorism of the KKK is an intermediate case. The state governments in many parts of the country were not weak, but they were supportive of the terrorist activities that were occurring. In other cases, government officials and politicians were intimidated. The national government at this point in U.S. history lacked the necessary laws to intervene in state affairs in order to counteract the activities of the KKK—even if it had desired to take action.

Globalization and modernization were factors in the outbreak of some of the terrorist violence in this era. The anti-colonial struggles in Ireland, India, Palestine, and Macedonia were not anti-modern or reactions to globalization in any major way. The leftist parties using violence in electoral struggles in Europe were, of course, motivated by their ideological views of the role of capitalism in the world, but their battles were with domestic capitalism in their own countries. The local economies had not yet been internationalized enough in most cases for communists, socialists, and social democrats to concentrate their activities to be concerned about international capitalism. The rise of fascist movements and other right-wing parties, however, does reflect a violent response to increasing globalization. The extreme nationalist parties sought to establish authoritarian rule in their countries that would serve socially conservative ideals.[63] These ideals were at least in part a reaction to the changes that had come with modernity. Fascism was a response to the new forms of labor organization and class conflicts that came with relatively rapid modernization, and terrorism proved to be a very effective mechanism for the fascists to express their opposition to socialism, liberalism, democracy, and Communism.[64] The fascist movements in Eastern Europe, perhaps best typified by the Legion of the Archangel Michael in Rumania, sought to reincorporate religion into their societies.[65] The attempts to reinvigorate religious influences also involved efforts to root out foreign or alien influences—exactly those influences that would come with increasing globalization. The anti-Communism of so many of these groups was also in part an effort to drive out alien ideologies. These fascist groups, including those in Western Europe, also drew heavily upon groups that had been disadvantaged by the modern economic society. The Iron Guard, for example, gained its strength among students in a time when there was a shortage of positions in society, especially for students just leaving school.[66] Indeed, it is possible to argue that fascism, as a generic phenomenon movement with a variety of national forms was basically a defensive response to a changing world and the intrusion of outside ideas. The penetration of societies throughout Europe and the world by new ideas and international connections raised the specter of "contamination" by outside ideas and influences. The actions of the KKK with its antipathy to all persons who were different and outside the mainstream culture are another example of the same general phenomenon. The extreme nationalists, who were often not fascist, were also often reacting against a changing world.

Successes and Failures

The anti-colonial struggles had a mixed record in this era. The Irish nationalists were successful in achieving self-governance for most of the island. It is clear that the terrorism and guerrilla attacks were quite important in convincing the British to negotiate. The attempts of the hardliners to prolong the struggle, however, were a distinct failure. The efforts of the Hindu nationalists were not successful at this time, although the British authorities may have made more concessions to the moderates than they otherwise would have. The terror campaigns of the Croats and IMRO were not successful at first glance. The Croats briefly achieved an independent state as an Axis satellite, but it did not survive World War II. IMRO initially was successful in fighting against the central government of Yugoslavia. The Macedonian dissidents were successful in generating violent Yugoslavian (Serb) responses to the attacks. There were reprisals, where all the males in a village were killed as well as other excesses carried out by irregulars that were supported by the government.[67] These attacks helped to generate more support, rather than less, for IMRO. Both the Croats and IMRO, however, did prevent the consolidation of the Yugoslav state, which quickly collapsed when the Germans and the Italians invaded. Tito and the Yugoslav League of Communists were able to rebuild the state, but they could not create a true sense of national unity. Interestingly enough, today there is an independent Croatia and Macedonia. It is just possible that the struggles of the 1920s and 1930s kept alive the nationalist feelings of the local populations. Without the early attacks Yugoslavia might actually have survived into the twenty-first century.

The terrorist attacks by Arabs and Jewish settlers in Palestine were not successful at this time. Neither group could threaten the British position or drive the other group out. They were successful in that both groups survived and they remained to challenge the British after the war. There were other limited successes attributable to the violence since the British at various times tried to appease both groups with concessions. For example, by 1939 the British had promised the Arabs that Palestine would be independent in ten years, and they placed a limit on allowable Jewish immigration.[68] The proposal would have ensured a Palestinian majority in the federated or confederated state that the British envisioned. Thus, the violence had apparently served the interests of the Arab community. The extremist Jewish groups, such as the Irgun, concluded that violence was an effective method for changing British politics; therefore, the Irgun decided to increase the attacks against the British.[69] Further, both the Arab and Jewish terrorists were generally able to use violence to maintain some level of group solidarity and to keep up the hopes of their respective communities.

Elsewhere successes were more obvious. The Japanese nationalist and early German nationalists were successful in having some of their policies adopted by the government. For a long period the KKK was able to intimidate groups that it feared although its position eventually did weaken. The election gangs in Nicaragua were also able to provide the votes for their parties in many areas of the country. The electoral violence and street fighting in Europe were failures for the Communists and other leftist parties. For the Fascists and others the terrorism was largely successful as a weapon in struggles to gain power.[70] Violence by the Lapua Movement led to the national parliament passing a law outlawing the Communist Party.[71] Even when the fascists did not achieve power themselves or directly gain policy changes, they were partially successful in battling the forces of the left, and even the idea of democracy. Their actions led to the establishment of conservative authoritarian regimes that were a reaction to the violence in the street. In Portugal terrorism and street violence by the left and the right undermined the government of the Republic and resulted in the conservative authoritarian regime that eventually came to power in 1926.[72] Lastly, the genocidal activities undertaken by the Nazis and their allies and the purges ordered by Stalin were also successful in many ways. Both Hitler and Stalin successfully terrorized their populations and largely avoided domestic threats to their continued rule. The Holocaust was also all too successful in eliminating the targets of the actions.

Summary

It has been suggested that the interwar period was characterized by a "predominance of state terrorism or terrorism 'from the top' (the Stalin period and fascism)."[73] Only in the case of Nicaragua with the Conservative Party, Hitler, and Stalin was the terror directed by the state. In other circumstances the state permitted violent groups to operate, but in actual fact much of the terrorism was from below. Many of the terrorist activities for this period were also based in communalism. In the case of the Fascists, Nazis, and nationalists, the communalism was intertwined with ideology, a deadly combination for the enemies and other victims of these extremists. The only groups driven almost exclusively by ideology in the period were the Communists. The Nicaraguan gangs were the one example of terrorist activities that were largely instrumental. The other fairly obvious conclusion is that not only were there many terrorist groups operating in the period between the wars, but also most of them achieved at least some successes in terms of their objectives. It is true that many of the gains were temporary or that successes led to eventual defeat, but terrorist actions were part of effective strategies for achieving political objectives. The Indians, Croats, and Macedonians failed, at least at this stage of their struggles, but the efforts did not disappear with the failures. Sometimes for dissidents "not losing is winning" and survival holds out the hope for victory or concessions in the future.[74] On the whole, many groups succeeded, at least in part with the use of terror.

Group	Type	Objectives	Casualties	Success
IRA versus British I	Communal (ethnic)	Independence	Moderate, including many civilians in intense struggle	Irish Free State created with few limits on independence
IRA versus Irish Free State II	Ideological with nationalist overtones	Elimination of remaining restrictions on Irish independence	Moderate to severe	Failed
Indians in Bengal versus British	Communal (ethnic with some religious overtones)	Independence for Hindu state	Few	No perceptible success except to keep idea of independence alive

Continued

Continued

Group	Type	Objectives	Casualties	Success
IMRO	Communal (ethnic)	Independence for Macedonia or union with Bulgaria	Moderate from terrorism	Failure, although eventually an independent Macedonia appears
Arabs in Palestine	Communal (ethnic)	Independent Arab Palestine	Heavy for Arab population, moderate for Jewish settlers, light for British	Some concessions from British at times on levels of Jewish immigration
Jewish settlers in Palestine I	Communal (ethnic based on religious culture)	Independent Jewish state in part of Palestine	Heavy for Arab population, moderate for Jewish settlers, light for British	Idea of independent state kept active for Jewish population
Croat Utashe I	Communal (ethnic with religious overtones)	Independent Croatia	Very few	Failed until Axis established independent Croatia; eventually independent Croatia reappears
Croat Utashe II	Ethnic cleansing	A Croatia free of minorities	Very heavy among Jews, Gypsies, and Serbs	All Jews and Gypsies killed or flee, Serb population reduced substantially
Nationalist Japanese officers	Ideological nationalism	More "active" foreign policy by government	Very few	Japan pursues empire building in Asia
Nationalist in Weimar Germany	Ideological nationalism	Fight foreign influence in Germany and leftists	Very few	Some success in influencing government policies
Political gangs in Nicaragua	Instrumental	Control voters and elections	Moderate to heavy	Effective in controlling elections and terrorizing opponents
KKK	Communal (ethnic with religious)	Control Blacks, Jews, Catholics, and immigrants	Heavy over the course of years	White power structure in southern states survives

Continued

Continued

Group	Type	Objectives	Casualties	Success
Fascists in Italy	Ideological	Defeat left and gain power in Italy	Heavy for left and Fascists	Left suppressed and Mussolini gains power
Iron Guard in Rumania	Ideological with religious overtones	Defeat left and gain power in Rumania	Moderate, Iron Guard members undertake virtual suicide attacks	Left eliminated from Rumanian politics and Iron Guard briefly comes to power
Fascist parties in other countries	Ideological	Defeat left and govern country	Varies from light to heavy	No party comes to power, but many conservative dictatorships created in response to violence and terror
Nazis and SA in Germany	Ideological with ethnic overtones	Defeat left and gain power in Germany	Many injured with a few killed	Left eliminated and Nazis come to power
Stalin in USSR	Instrumental	Prevent challenges to Stalin	Very heavy in purges of individuals and groups	Stalin remains in power and population terrorized
Hitler in Germany	Instrumental with communal overtones	Prevent challenges to Hitler, genocide	Heavy among opponents, very great in Holocaust	Hitler remains in power, millions of Jews and others murdered

CHAPTER EIGHT

The End of Empires and Terrorism

From the end of World War II to the late 1960s the great European empires were in the process of breaking up, leading to the formation of many new independent states. The defeat of European armies in North Africa and Southeast Asia in World War II raised doubts in the minds of local populations about the superiority of the European colonialists.[1] The British, French, Dutch, and Belgians had to recover from the ravages of war; consequently, they had fewer resources available to maintain the empires than would otherwise have been the case. While most of the terrorism that appeared in this period was linked with the national liberation movements in those colonies where the Europeans had hoped to remain, there were some groups practicing terrorism that had no connections with national liberation movements.

The Effects of Crumbling Empires and a Cold War

Colonial groups seeking independence from European powers often used terrorism in their national liberation struggles. Some of the violent struggles were based in guerrilla campaigns against the colonial power. The Cold War between the United States and the Soviet Union that began in this period was a background for many of the terrorists groups that operated. From 1946 to 1958, in Colombia, there was a period of violence between the Liberal and Conservative parties that left as many as 200,000 people dead.[2] The fighting involved in *La Violencia* was conventional or hit-and-run raids; it did not involve terrorism in any major way. It did, however, set the stage for terrorist violence that afflicted Colombia in later years. The efforts of the IRA to unify Northern

Ireland with the Republic continued in its intermittent fashion in this period. The IRA undertook occasional attacks after World War II to protest the continued affiliation of Northern Ireland with the United Kingdom. The brief campaigns in 1956 and 1962 did not accomplish very much, seriously threaten the British position, or last very long.[3] These attacks were apparently not primarily designed as part of an effort to force the British to relinquish their position in the north. They seem to have been more for the consumption by the members of the IRA. Maintaining the morale of the organization or at least the hope of eventual reunification was the underlying reason for the attacks.[4] Of course, there was probably at least the faint hope that the actions would force a British withdrawal and permit the reunification of the island.

The continuing problems that the British faced in Palestine after the war were much more severe than the isolated attacks in Northern Ireland. A Jewish group resumed attacks on the Arabs and the British colonial officials and soldiers. The leadership of the Jewish community in Palestine wanted to prevent limitations on Jewish immigration and wanted to demonstrate that the British could not rule Palestine without Jewish cooperation.[5] The Stern Gang and Irgun, which was now led by Menachem Begin, planned to weaken British rule by striking at the symbols of British authority.[6] The Irgun attacked a variety of economic targets in the Mandate, and it kidnapped British soldiers and killed them in reprisal for the execution of captured Irgun terrorists.[7] The most spectacular attack by the Jewish dissidents was a bomb that was planted in the King David Hotel in Jerusalem, which served as a headquarters for the British administration. Over 90 people—British, Jewish, and Arab—were killed in the blast.[8] The boldness and effectiveness of the attack was exactly the kind of blow that the dissidents needed to undermine the British position and to attract international attention. The British progressively deployed more and more troops, but they were unable to defeat the terrorists. Eventually the British became unwilling to devote the resources—financial and military—to maintain their position in the Mandate. Unable to broker a partition plan the British turned the problem over to the United Nations and announced their imminent departure. The UN partition plan was rejected, and in the ensuing war between the Arab Palestinians and the Jewish settlers, the Jewish inhabitants gained control over most of Palestine, setting the stage for later conflicts. They then held their ground against the armies of the neighboring Arab countries.

British colonial rule was also challenged in Malaya and Singapore. The World War II resistance movement in occupied Malaya relied heavily upon the local communists. After the end of the war the Malayan Communist Party (MCP) hoped to gain political control of the colony. When strikes, demonstrations, and other means proved to be ineffective, the communists returned to the violent tactics.[9] British policies in Malaya favored the indigenous Malay population over the Chinese inhabitants, and the MCP relied principally upon the Chinese population in the colony.[10] The British were able to contain the guerrilla attacks early on in the conflict, and the MCP began to rely more on terrorism in their efforts to undermine the colonial administration. They particularly targeted the rubber plantations in Malaya in an effort to undermine the economic value of the colony.[11] The attacks increasingly targeted British civilians, and civilian casualties were higher than the losses suffered by the security forces.[12] The dissidents also targeted anyone in the Chinese or Malay communities that cooperated with the British administration.[13] The British were able to deal with the terrorism, and the remaining guerrilla threat in the countryside was largely contained by the early 1950s.[14]

The British also faced a liberation struggle in Cyprus that began in 1955. The Greek majority on the island was seeking an end to British rule and wanted to bring about a union between the island and Greece. The Greek nationalists, the National Organization of Cypriot Fighters (EOKA) launched a guerrilla and terrorist campaign to gain independence and union. The dissidents sought to focus international attention to the situation in Cyprus with these actions. The EOKA leadership chose to limit its reliance on guerrilla activities since activities in the countryside would have less publicity value than an urban campaign of terrorism supported by selected rural guerrilla activities.[15] In addition to attacking British administrators and personnel, the EOKA targeted Greek Cypriot police and investigators who cooperated with the British.[16] As was the case in Palestine, the British mobilized a considerable number of troops to deal with the violence, and they managed to contain it, but they were unable to defeat the dissidents. The British government eventually opted to grant independence to Cyprus, but it did not allow the desired union with Greece.

In addition to the problems in Cyprus, Palestine, and Malaya, the British faced a rebellion in Kenya, which involved a significant number of terrorist attacks. The Mau Mau Rebellion arose among the Kikuyu and related peoples who were located around the capital of Nairobi. Land pressure in this area was quite severe, in part because the white settler population had appropriated much of the best land, which was, in fact, one of the key factors in the outbreak of the violence that began in

1952.[17] The first attacks were on European property and cattle.[18] The attacks quickly escalated to include a few assaults on white settlers, but most attacks were directed against African Kenyans who had remained loyal to the colonial government.[19] After a slow start in containing the rebellion, the British were successful. The support network for the Mau Mau in Nairobi was quickly eliminated, leaving a variety of isolated groups in the countryside that were eventually defeated one at a time. Fewer than a 100 Europeans died, including members of the military and security forces, while approximately 2,000 Kenyans loyal to the colonial government died. The dissidents suffered around 12,000 casualties.[20] By 1959 the last remnants of the dissidents had been eliminated by the British troops and their African auxiliaries.

The French faced a national liberation struggle in Algeria that involved a significant amount of terrorist actions on the part of the Muslim Algerians. French options were complicated by the presence of more than a million French settlers (*colons*), who elected members of the French Parliament in Paris, assuring themselves of a significant friendly political voice in the government. The National Liberation Front (FLN) had been involved in sporadic guerrilla fighting in the countryside since 1954, but in 1956 the Algerian dissidents decided to strike at the civilian population in the European sectors of Algiers and other cities. Bombings and other attacks led to significant casualties among the *colon* population, which included women and children.[21] The *colon* population often responded with attacks on Algerian Muslims, and the military adopted severely repressive measures as well. The cycle of attacks on civilians and the escalating responses from the French was in accord with the plans of the FLN to eliminate any possibility of compromise between the two sides and to enlist the mass of the Algerian population on the side of the FLN.[22] The battle for control of the cities lasted for a year until the reinforced French military was able to destroy the urban terrorist networks through the liberal use of torture of captured suspects.[23] The FLN also targeted Muslims, who had remained loyal to France, even conducting massacres in some villages of those who had failed to side with the nationalists.[24] The guerrilla conflict continued in the countryside after the end of the urban campaign. Although the FLN still conducted sporadic terrorist activities in the cities, they never mounted a campaign like the one that was undertaken in 1956. In 1962, the French government entered negotiations with the FLN that ended with the creation of an independent Algeria.

The *colons* and many military officers reacted negatively to the prospect of the negotiations leading to independence and sought to prevent them. When political pressure and even the threat of a military coup failed to end the negotiations, the officers and others went underground and formed the Secret Army Organization (OAS) to continue the struggle by unconventional means. There were attacks on French authorities and even a number of attempts to assassinate President Charles DeGaulle for his willingness to consider independence for Algeria. In addition to the several assassination attempts against DeGaulle, the OAS launched more than a thousand other attacks in Algeria and mainland France.[25] Notwithstanding some spectacular attacks and support from many segments of French society, the French eventually defeated the OAS. The leaders were either captured or went into exile and ceased the struggle. When Algeria gained its independence, most of the *colons* fled to France, and there was no longer any basis for a dissident movement determined to keep Algeria French.

The end of empires also resulted in a different kind of terrorist violence. In India in 1947–48, Nigeria in 1966, and Indonesia in 1965 there were outbreaks of communal violence that resulted in very real ethnic cleansing by the majority communities. In India, the division of the old British colony into Hindu and Muslim areas exacerbated tensions between the two communities and violent confrontations broke out. A member of the militantly Hindu Rashtriya Swayamsevak Sangh (RSS) assassinated Mahatma Gandhi while he was attempting to help bring an end to the communal violence.[26] The death of Gandhi removed a powerful voice for moderation and reason in the country. The intensification of the communal violence then led to almost all of the Hindus in Pakistan leaving for India. Most of the Muslims who could flee India for Pakistan did so, although millions remained behind. News of the massacres on one side of the border led to retaliation on the other in a viscous cycle of communal attacks. Local police and military forces prevented many atrocities, but they could not stop them all.[27] At the end of these forced migrations there were more than half a million dead.[28] In Nigeria, there were two military coups in 1966 that led to outbreaks of communal violence in the north of the country. In the first coup in January, junior officers killed many of the leading politicians and some high-ranking officers as well.[29] Most of the political leaders from the east of the country where the Ibo (or Igbo) people were the most numerous survived, and the general who assumed power after the coup was also an Ibo. Many northerners thus saw the coup as an Ibo plot to dominate the country. These ethnic differences were compounded by the fact that the northerners were largely Muslim while the Ibos were largely Christian. The Ibos had also benefited economically from colonialism. They were well represented among the civil servants and the merchants in the north because their region of Nigeria had been colonized first. In May, northern mobs began attacking Ibos in their region.[30] Soon thereafter there was a second coup in July in which the Ibo influence in the government diminished. In late September more severe attacks against the Ibos in the north broke out. Some soldiers joined the mobs, and a number of the local political leaders encouraged the violence. At least 10,000 easterners, and perhaps as many as 30,000, died in the massacres. Another million people became refugees.[31] The treatment of the Ibos in the north was one of the factors that led to the attempt of the east to secede from Nigeria as the nation of Biafra and the resulting civil war. Indonesia also faced an outbreak of communal terrorism. An attempted coup in Indonesia in 1965, supported by the Communist Party of Indonesia (PKI), failed, but the attempt did lead to greater involvement of the military in the government and the eventual creation of a military regime. In the immediate aftermath of the coup attempt, there were attacks on PKI members and the resident Chinese, who were perceived to be sympathetic to the coup and the communists. Hundreds of thousands of party members and the Chinese (200,000–500,000 according to the best estimates), died in the violence, while other Chinese fled the country.[32]

There were other groups that used terrorism in this period that had no connection with the national liberation struggles. The KKK in the United States continued its effort to terrorize southern blacks and their northern supporters. The KKK, however, was unable to stop the civil rights movements, and the 1964 Civil Rights Act and the 1965 Voting Rights Act, and the actions of the Department of Justice; and the FBI decimated the group. In Italy, there were a variety of neo-Fascist movements present in the 1950s and 1960s. They glorified Mussolini's role in Italian history and wanted to reestablish the Fascist state. Different groups undertook a handful of terrorist operations, but no one group lasted very long as the Italian security services were able to consistently arrest key members. New groups would appear but none could maintain much continuity. These groups feared that Italian democracy was too weak to deal with threats from the left, and they saw the Italian Communist Party (PCI) as a Trojan Horse that would make Italy a satellite of the Soviet Union. These groups launched "false flag" attacks that looked as if they had been undertaken by the left. The neo-Fascists wanted to force the Italian government to implement stronger security measures against the communists.[33] In effect, they were hoping to help create a conservative authoritarian regime much as had been done in Europe before World War II.

There was also a significant terrorist campaign in Venezuela. A variety of dissident leftist groups appeared that were willing to use terror against the government in the 1950s, first the Movement of the Revolutionary Left (MIR) and then the Armed Forces for National Liberation (FALN). The triumph of Fidel Castro, in Cuba, encouraged these groups to seek to undermine the reasonably democratic govnerment in Venezuela. Many of the members of these groups were university students and youth leaders who broke with the established political parties when they became disillusioned with the democratic process.[34] These young leftists in their first resort to violence tried a rural guerrilla campaign, but when this effort failed, they resorted to an urban terrorism campaign.[35] The leftists focused many of their attacks on the oil industry in the country and attacks launched against industrial facilities concentrated on property owned by U.S. firms.[36] The Venezuelan government was eventually able to meet the threat from the dissidents and to triumph. By the mid-1960s, the leftist groups had given up the violent struggle and returned to peaceful politics.

There was little direct state use of terror in this period. In the Soviet Union, Stalin's repressive tactics from the period before the war continued until his death. There were also a series of purges of local communists in the East European satellite regimes that were formed. The military in Indonesia in 1965, however, did encourage some of the attacks on the Chinese and PKI members.[37] The elimination of the local supporters of the civilian Sukarno regime made it easier for the officers to assume more and more power. Similarly, the local police and leaders in the northern part of Nigeria also stood on the sidelines or joined the attacks on the Ibos in many cases. Haiti in the Western Hemisphere did evolve into an example of state terrorism in this period. Haiti had suffered under a series of dictatorial governments throughout its history. Francois Duvalier won the election in 1956 with army backing and through the use of intimidation.[38] Once in power, he began to institutionalize the repression that had always been present in the country, creating a system that relied on terror to rule.[39] Duvalier increasingly took more and more control and relied on the secret police—the tonton-macoute—and a militia to terrorize opponents, potential opponents, and the population in general. Neither age nor gender nor position in society protected individuals. Families and whole villages were killed for the transgressions of one person.[40] When President-for-Life Duvalier died in 1971, terrorism had become endemic in Haiti. In theory the regime passed into the hands of his son, but Jean-Claude Duvalier lacked the government abilities to maintain the institutions of terror, and he was persuaded to resign and leave the country.

Governments did aid terrorist organizations in other countries in this period. The Cold War meant that the United States and the Soviet Union, and their respective allies, aided dissidents in countries friendly to the other side. The KGB and CIA engaged in contests and confrontations in a global setting.[41] The leftists in Venezuela received aid from Cuba once Castro had become established. The neo-Fascists in Italy received some support from the intelligence services of conservative (and authoritarian) regimes in Spain, Portugal, Greece, and a number of Latin American countries. The various groups also had links with other right-wing groups elsewhere—the so-called Black International.[42] The new state of Israel developed an effective secret service as well, which engaged in operations against its Arab counterparts and sought to defend against their actions. Israel even attempted somewhat more complex activities. In the Lavon Affair (named after the minister of defense at the time), Israeli agents in Egypt attacked American targets in a false flag operation. The goal was to have the United States believe that attacks had been undertaken by Egyptian extremists in order to disrupt relations between the United States and Nasser's Egypt that were improving at this time.[43]

Causes and Objectives

The bulk of the terrorist organizations that operated in this time period were communal in some form in an era of obvious national liberation struggles. The IRA efforts actually had more of an instrumental goal since the attacks were designed to keep the hopes of the organization alive rather than to achieve the immediate union of Ulster with the south. The Malayan insurgency had more ideological elements, but it did have some communal elements since the support for the dissidents was largely contained within the Chinese community. The more spontaneous outbreaks of violence in India, Indonesia, and Nigeria were also communal. In Indonesia and Nigeria, it was a combination of ethnic and religious communalism. In India, the basis for the conflict was essentially religious, especially in the east where Hindu and Muslim Bengalis attacked each other solely on the basis of religious differences. The KKK was also communal in nature.

The OAS in Algeria is harder to classify. In some ways it was obviously communal since it was an attempt to protect the European *colons* from being overwhelmed by the Muslim Algerians. In other respects the OAS was interested in retaining at least parts of the Empire for France. It did not solely rely on the support of the *colons*; it also had substantial support among the population of mainland France.[44] It shared characteristics with some of the extreme right groups since it was seeking to help a military government to come to power, at least in Algeria if not in France, an action that is typical of right-wing groups seeking to create more authoritarian systems.[45] Ideology also served as the basis for the Italian neo-Fascists as they sought to create a stronger central state. Finally, the FALN in Venezuela was clearly an ideologically based group. The violence associated with the Duvalier regime in Haiti appears to have been largely instrumental and to have lacked any ideological base.

While the ideal of nationalism and independence was spreading in this period, there were few indications that such views were reactions to globalization. Many of the populations seeking independence sought to model their governments on the former colonial power, hardly a sign of negative reactions to global processes in the societies in question. Malaya and Venezuela provide the first signs of leftists protesting the effects of global capitalism on different societies. The Communist leaders in Malaya could see capitalist Great Britain in the background and the MIR and FALN could see the multinational oil companies and the United States as major supports for the government that they sought to overthrow. The KKK's activities were a continued reaction to modernization and the idea of racial equality. The neo-Fascist groups in Italy and the OAS in Algeria were fighting against changing trends as well.

To some extent all these communal examples could reflect a clash of cultures, but colonial situations by their very nature often involve unequal hierarchical relationships between different areas that lead to uprisings, rebellions, and terrorism (although there was no great cultural divide between Britain and Ireland). The communal violence in India, Indonesia, and Nigeria was a more basic communalism with less overt nationalism, and reflected more of a clash of cultures. The fault line in India was between Hindus (and Sikhs) on the one side and Muslims on the other. In Nigeria, the division was between Christian east and Muslim north, while in Indonesia the line was between the largely Muslim Indonesian population and the non-Muslim Chinese, who were not part of the local culture. The differences in cultures appear most important since the Indonesian form of Islam has often been syncretic and accepting of local beliefs and other religions.[46] The Chinese in Indonesia and the Ibo in Nigeria were not only religiously but also ethnically different from their persecutors. They were members of groups that were better off economically; thus the different levels of modernization exacerbated communal tensions.[47]

Weak states clearly facilitated the violence of this period. The European colonial powers involved in World War II (France, Great Britain, Belgium, the Netherlands, and Italy) were weakened by the conflict and saw the ends of their empires except for some small possessions. The new states of India and Pakistan were also too weak initially to deal with the massive communal violence they faced. The bureaucracies and the militaries of the two separate states had come from the old unified Indian army and the Indian Civil Service, and they were unprepared or unable to deal with all the outbreaks of fighting that occurred. In 1965, in Indonesia the government in power after the coup attempts was in transition. Initially, it was probably unable to stop all the violence against the Chinese community. As the violence continued, however, there was support for the continuation of the attacks by the military. In Nigeria, the military regime that came to power in January 1966 was also too weak to effectively deal with the violence. In fact, the military officers that eventually took charge were unprepared to govern the country. The pogroms against the Ibos in the north could not be stopped by the national government with its limited resources and even more limited legitimacy. The second military government was also initially weak. Haiti faced a different problem. Although Haiti had long been independent, there was neither a leadership with a national sense of purpose nor effective political institutions; thus, it was always verging on the brink of state failure.[48] Disjunction between the political and civil society facilitated the violence in that country that peaked under Duvalier.[49] The KKK did not face weak states in the same fashion as it did before World War II, and, consequently, it was increasingly marginalized by a national government capable of and willing to take action. The OAS may have seen the French government as weak, but it was strong enough to deal with the OAS. Similarly, the government in Venezuela had its weaknesses, but it was able to defeat the campaigns of the MIR and FALN.

Successes and Failures

The use of terrorism by dissident groups between 1945 and 1968 had noteworthy successes and failures. The efforts in Kenya and Malaya failed. One factor they had in common was the absence of any nearby country to provide safe havens or a supply base for the dissidents. In Malaya, the failure of the Communist dissidents to attract any support from the Malay community was one additional great weaknesses of the dissidents.[50] In the national liberation struggles of Algeria, Cyprus, and

Israel there was some external support from either the neighboring countries (Tunisia, Morocco, or Greece) or sympathetic populations (the Jewish communities in the United States and elsewhere). In the case of Palestine, the British opted to leave without establishing an effective government in its wake. For the Jewish terrorists, the goal was to weaken British resolve. The Irgun "did not have to defeat Britain militarily; they only had to avoid losing."[51] This approach was central for many national liberation terrorist campaigns since most of them could not hope to win an outright military victory. What made it an effective strategy in these cases was that the colonialists had someplace to return to when they gave up the battle for control. In Algeria, the French had not been defeated militarily. They had gained the upper hand in their battles with the guerrillas in the countryside and the terrorists in the cities; they had effectively won the military campaign against the FLN. The continued control of the territory, however, had become too costly.[52] The dissidents had lost the battles, but they had managed to win the war. The FLN was quite successful in polarizing relations between the Muslim and *colon* communities. In Cyprus, the colonial power also gave up, but the EOKA set the stage by provoking the British to overreact to the attacks, which led the majority of the Greek inhabitants of the island to side with the dissidents.[53] The loss of public support, of course, was one factor that led to the British decision to withdraw. In these cases the colonial power withdrawal was an immediate reaction to the violence. Even the failure of the Mau Mau in Kenya may have sped up the decision of Great Britain to grant Kenya its independence.[54] The communal violence in India, Indonesia, and Nigeria was also largely successful for the groups that were involved. Pakistan lost almost all its Hindu citizens and the Muslim population of India became much smaller than it otherwise would have been. Similarly, the attacks in Indonesia resulted in the decline of the Chinese population in the country through death and migration. In Nigeria, the northern mobs were successful in forcing the Ibos out of the region.

The OAS, of course, failed in its terrorist campaign. For DeGaulle and others in the French government, the threat from the OAS was ultimately less threatening than the potential for continued violence from the Muslim majority in Algeria. Further, once the *colon* population had fled Algeria for France, there was no purpose behind a continuation of the activity. The OAS case is one of the few examples where circumstances have conspired to remove the basis for the terrorism. The regime based on terror in a poor country such as Haiti could be successful for only so long. Similarly, the KKK was increasingly unable to maintain its position in the southern United States. The neo-Fascists in Italy, the IRA, and the left in Venezuela also failed, although the IRA did preserve the organization for potential operations in the future. There was some evidence that there were groups in the government, especially in the military and the security forces that actually sympathized with the goals of the neo-Fascists and were considering intervening to strengthen the repressive capabilities of the state.[55] These plans were discovered and many officials were retired or otherwise relegated to the sidelines of the Italian political system.

Summary

The years after World War II were characterized by the breakup of long-established colonial empires, accelerated by World War II. It is probably significant that Portugal and Spain, neutrals in the war, held on to their colonial territories longer than the European states involved in the war. The violence in the Indian subcontinent reflected the fact that British India was a collection of groups only unified by a colonial power. This colonial India did not survive the departure of the Europeans, reflecting another aspect of the demise of empires. The British had united rather disparate groups together in Nigeria as well, and the violence after independence was a reflection of this colonial creation. Indonesia was a colonial amalgam as well, but since the Chinese were scattered throughout the country, they did not present a threat to state integrity unlike the situation in India and Nigeria.

Another facet of terrorism in the period was greater reliance on communicating the goals of the organization to the outside world. The Jewish groups in Palestine and the Greek Cypriots were particularly anxious to get their case to the outside world. The dissidents even planned some of their operations in ways that would maximize the publicity value of the actions. This type of planning indicates that the groups were very much aware of the different target audiences and the role of the media in reaching at least some of them. In national liberation struggles, it is essential that the populations back in the mother country realize the costs of continuing colonialism. During the 1950s and the 1960s the appeals to world opinion also had some effect in terms of bringing pressure to bear on democratic governments in Europe. Guerrilla actions were often costly as the losses sustained by the FLN in Algeria, the communists in Malaya, and the Mau Mau in Kenya demonstrated. Dissident terrorism was often necessary because of the military weakness of the national liberation struggles or the other groups. In this period the established state governments continued to outclass the dissidents in terms of armaments and military weaponry. Terrorism by clandestine groups rather than violence in the streets had thus become the norm. The neo-Fascists in Italy could not mobilize groups for street battles in the same fashion as after World War I; thus, they had to resort to bombs and other kinds of attacks. The communal ethnic cleansing operations in India, Nigeria, and Indonesia (at least initially) had popular bases and could proceed with little reference to the military forces available to the governments. The ethnic terrorists were armed as well as or better than their targets. Notwithstanding the military advantages of the governments in power, there were a number of successful uses of terrorism in this period, just as there were in earlier periods that were analyzed. It has been noted that anti-colonial struggles reflect special circumstances that will not be repeated in the future.[56] Successful applications of terrorism, however, were not limited to the anti-colonial struggles even in this period.

The national liberation struggles and communal violence highlight the importance that communal differences had for the period as a whole. The activities of the KKK and OAS also had communal elements. Ideology was important for the OAS, the neo-Fascists, and the FALN, and it was quite important in Malaya. What is really missing from the cases in this era is any real evidence of instrumental terrorism except for the very limited activities of the IRA and the Duvalier regime in Haiti. There were instrumental objectives at times for the other groups; probably the most frequent type of instrumental tactic was the targeting of collaborators by the national liberation groups. Ultimately, even this targeting had as much communal reasons as instrumental ones. The period after the war did not match the period before the war when ideological terrorism, at least from the right, was much more successful. These results would suggest that some periods of time and circumstances were more conducive to particular kinds of terrorist groups.

Group	Type	Objectives	Casualties	Success
Jewish settlers in Palestine II	Communal (ethnic and religious)	Create independent Israeli state	Moderate	British withdrawal permits Israel to win war of independence
EOKA in Cyprus	Communal (ethnic)	Create independent state and union with Greece	Moderate	British grant independence to Cyprus but prevent union with Greece

Continued

Continued

Group	Type	Objectives	Casualties	Success
Communists in Malaya	Ideological with large communal component	Independence from Britain under communist regime	Moderate from terrorism, heavier with casualties from associated guerrilla warfare	Effort fails and Malaya and Singapore become independent as scheduled under noncommunists
Mau Mau in Kenya	Communal (ethnic)	Independence	Low from terrorist actions, heavy with guerrilla actions	Effort fails, although outbreak might have sped up British decision to grant Kenya independence
IRA III	Communal (ethnic and religious)	Union of Ulster with Ireland	Few	No effect on British presence in north but may have helped to maintain IRA organization
FLN in Algeria	Communal (ethnic)	Independence	Heavy in terrorist phase, very heavy with guerrilla actions	France eventually concedes independence to Algeria
OAS in Algeria	Communal (ethnic) and ideological (rightist)	Keep Algeria French	Moderate	French government continues with negotiations and Algeria becomes independent under majority rule
…dian…	Communal (religious)	Drive out minority religious groups	Extremely heavy	Virtually all Hindus leave Pakistan and many Muslims leave India
…ia and …ogroms	Communal (ethnic and religious)	Ethnic cleansing of Ibos in the north	Heavy	Surviving Ibos flee to their home area
…nesia	Communal (ethnic) and Ideological (anti-Communist) with some state support	Attacks against local communists and Chinese	Very heavy	PKI destroyed as mass political organization and Chinese community reduced in numbers

Continued

Continued

Group	Type	Objectives	Casualties	Success
Neo-Fascists in Italy	Ideological	Force government to move to right and become authoritarian	Relatively few	Government remains democratic even though plot to "strengthen" government discovered and defeated
KKK in United States	Communal	Prevent Blacks from exercising their rights	Moderate	Civil rights victories won by Black Americans and KKK in decline
Duvalier regime in Haiti	Instrumental	Keep Francois Duvalier in power	Heavy	Government survives while Duvalier lives
Venezuela (MIR and FALN)	Ideological (leftist)	Overthrow capitalist democracy and establish leftist system	Moderate to heavy	Government survives and leftist groups are defeated

CHAPTER NINE

The Rise of the New Left and the Failure of Communism: Increasing Terrorism on a Global Scale

From 1967 and 1968 to the beginning of the 1990s, terrorism in the world was characterized by the appearance of large numbers of groups of leftist dissidents willing to use violence to achieve their goals. Western democracies were frequently, but not exclusively, the targets for this violence. The U.S. involvement in Vietnam fueled the unrest, but that was not the sole reason for the discontent. Students in Europe were also opposed to the U.S. involvement in Vietnam, and they often saw it as part of a broader capitalism plan to control and exploit countries and workers around the world. In 1967, the Israeli Defense Forces triumphed over the armed forces of Egypt, Syria, and Jordan. It was clear to the Palestinians that conventional military warfare was not going to lead to a Palestinian state, thus, the Palestinian Liberation Organization (PLO) opted to rely on terrorism as an additional weapon in its struggle to create this state. The period of the New Left terrorism largely ended with the collapse of Communism in Europe and the end of the Cold War. In addition, the long-simmering discontent of some Irish over the British presence in Northern Ireland erupted, and there were a variety of other dissident organizations that began to rely on terrorism.

A Rising Tide of Terrorism

There were a few dissident terrorist groups active in previous years that continued their activities in this period. The KKK was still suffering major declines in strength in the United States, but it had not completely disappeared.[1] The Italian neo-Fascist groups were still present. The neo-Fascists did not end their attacks, including false flag attacks; they continued them in an effort to increase the pressure on the Italian government to adopt more authoritarian policies to deal with the violence. The attacks undertaken by the neo-Fascists were limited in numbers, but they were often more deadly that any individual attacks launched from the left.[2] The Nivelles Group in Belgium also launched false flag attacks in an effort to incriminate the left and to lead the government into adopting more authoritarian practices in order to deal with the terrorist threat.[3] Right-wing groups other than the KKK were beginning to appear in the United States. These groups would become more widespread and dangerous in the 1990s (and many are discussed in chapter ten as a consequence). The Silent Brotherhood, commonly called The Order, appeared at this time. It was an overtly racist, anti-Semitic, and anti-government group that appeared in the Pacific Northwest in 1983. By 1985, local authorities had arrested most members of the group and its leader was killed in a gun battle with the police.[4] Another right-wing group opposing its government operated in Nicaragua where the Contras launched a guerrilla and terrorist campaign to overthrow the Sandinista regime that had brought down the Somoza regime. The guerrilla efforts largely failed, as the Sandinista army was able to defeat incursions from neighboring countries. The Contras then began to terrorize supporters of the regime. They also launched campaigns of assassination against local officials in the countryside.[5] The Sandinistas were able to contain the Contra threat, but they could not eliminate it. The struggle ended when the government lost the free elections in 1990.

More widespread was the general opposition appearing from groups on the left to the capitalist economic system and the U.S. involvement in Vietnam. For many critics capitalism and the war were intertwined as part of a broader neocolonialism, where the capitalist countries controlled and exploited developing countries in the world. These critics from the left relied on the doctrines and writings of Marx, Lenin, Trotsky, Mao, and others. These ideas proved especially attractive to students throughout the world who were disenchanted as a result of the injustices that they saw. These circumstances were conducive to many students who were questioning the prevalent social, economic, and political systems. Eventually, many of the students joined organizations that were willing to use terrorism to bring about the political changes that seemed so necessary, especially when the political systems were unresponsive to less violent forms of protest. The left-wing theories that the students were following suggested an indirect approach to changing the system in the event the direct assault failed. In the face of constant attacks on the status quo, governments would adopt more repressive methods to maintain control. These measures would then alienate the working class and the population in general, leading to a popular revolt to overthrow the capitalist system.[6]

Leftist groups committed to using violence appeared in most European countries. The Communist Combat Cells (CCC) in Belgium, Direct Action (AD) in France, the First of October Anti-Fascist Popular Forces (GRAPO) in Spain, and the Popular Forces—April 25 in Portugal undertook occasional violence, which was directed against local and multinational businesses, government officials, and U.S. military stations or U.S. diplomatic facilities.[7] These organizations were not able to maintain any long-lasting campaigns against their governments or pose a real threat. The Baader–Meinhof Gang in West Germany, later known as the Red Army Faction (RAF), also was more of a nuisance than a real threat, but it had a great flair for publicity. The group, composed largely of student radicals, regarded the parliamentary democracy of West Germany as a façade. To them it was simply a continuation of the Nazi political system.[8] The group often chose the targets for its attacks for their visibility, and the group was successful in publicizing its political objectives through the issuance of communiqués. American military personnel and military bases were often a favorite target for the attacks of the RAF.[9] The group was relatively unique among the smaller leftist organizations since it was able to replace its leadership. Andreas Baader and Ulrike Meinhof were captured rather early in the campaign, and they eventually committed suicide in prison. Baader and Meinhof were replaced by a second group of leaders after the suicides, and when these leaders were captured, a third generation of leaders appeared.[10] The ability of the group to develop new leaders gave it the staying power, notwithstanding its relatively small size.

The Greek and Italian leftist groups were ultimately more effective in their use of terrorist groups than the Baader–Meinhof group, even though their styles of organization were distinctly different from each other. Unlike the RAF, the Red Brigades were a large organization that made its mark by the large number of attacks that it mounted. At the beginning of the 1990s, when the organization had largely disappeared, the group had been responsible for more than 14,500 incidents in which 419 people had died and more than 14,000 had been injured.[11] The Red Brigades initially began with nonlethal attacks.[12] The violence, however, soon escalated. The Red Brigades began the practice of shooting their targets in the kneecaps. Such assaults, which came to be known as kneecapping, displayed the audacity of the groups since the attackers had to get close enough to the victims to wound without killing, demonstrating the vulnerability of the victims and the impotence of the system. The Red Brigades, and other dissident leftist groups that broke away also began to use more lethal techniques as indicated by a death toll of over 400. In 1977, the Brigades made a major effort to disrupt the legal system when captured members were being put on trial. They targeted judges, prosecutors, and defense lawyers. The legal system was virtually paralyzed and many jurors were afraid to serve.[13] At one point, 8,000 security personnel were necessary to protect the courthouse where the trials were taking place.[14] The most spectacular single attack was the kidnapping and eventual execution of Aldo Moro, a former prime minister and then the president of the Christian Democratic Party at this time. His execution, however, mobilized and unified public opinion against the dissidents and led to greater, and more successful, government efforts to control them.[15]

In Greece, a number of radical left groups arose. The 17 November Organization was the most important and longest-lasting terrorist group of dissidents. It shared opposition to global capitalism and the role of the United States in the world. It began as a group opposed to the military junta that was in power in Greece in the 1970s. It took its name from a date in 1973, when security forces killed at least 30 people and injured more than 800 persons who were protesting against the government and its policies.[16] The group launched its first attack in 1975, and it was not until 2002 that the first members of the organization were identified. The group lasted for over 25 years, but it was only able to mount a limited number of attacks. The targets were prominent Greeks, multinational corporations, U.S. and British military personnel in Greece, and the CIA section chief in Athens.[17] The Greek dissidents copied the Red Brigades in that they adopted the technique of kneecapping selected individuals.[18] The group carefully avoided compromising the identity of its members, which was one of the reasons for its longevity. The Greek security forces, even with the help of the British and the Americans, failed to break the organization. The security forces only managed to identify a member of the group when he was injured in a premature bomb explosion. His capture permitted the police to interrogate him and track down some other members of the group.

Even though the Vietnam War helped to trigger the terrorist violence from the left in this period, no major leftist group developed in the United States. The Weathermen or the Weather Underground launched attacks on property but shied away from lethal attacks. The Symbionese Liberation Army (SLA) generated an immense amount of publicity when it kidnapped Patricia Hearst, but local police authorities quickly dealt with what was otherwise a marginal dissident group. Japan had to deal with more active radical leftist groups, including the Japanese Red Army (JRA). The Japanese government, through the use of informants and effective policing, was able to disrupt Japanese leftists within the country without too much difficulty.[19] The JRA then began to use attacks outside of Japan, including hijackings of international flights and attacks on embassies abroad in efforts, frequently successful, to gain concession from the Japanese government.[20] After being forced out of Japan, the JRA reconstituted itself as an international Marxist group.

Violent leftists appeared in India in West Bengal in the form of a group known as the Naxalites, attacking landlords and capitalists in West Bengal.[21] The Naxalites were not effective in generating a major revolt against the government. Nearby, Sri Lanka also saw the rise of leftist groups committed to the use of violence. Student leftists formed the Peoples' Liberation Front (Janatha Vimukthi Peramuna—JVP), a Troskyite party committed to its own version of Marxism.[22] In 1971, the leaders of the party decided to attempt to take over control of the country through a brief, violent campaign of urban guerrilla activity.[23] The attempted insurrection did not plan on an extensive campaign of terrorist activity since the dissidents expected a quick victory, but the government was quickly able to contain the attempt. In the late 1980s, the JVP made a second attempt to gain control of the government. This time the party used a campaign of terrorism and assassination directed against state employees, politicians from the governing party and other parties, police and members of the armed forces and their families, and political opponents of the JVP.[24] In addition to the leftist ideology, the JVP also had a very nationalistic tone. The party opposed the attempted secession of the Tamils since it threatened the integrity of the Sri Lankan nation.[25] This second attempt was much more serious; consequently, it took the government more than two years to control the situation, and more than 30,000 people lost their lives in the struggle.[26]

Other leftist groups appeared in Latin America, drawing upon some of the same ideologies and views as their European and Asian counterparts, and they also had the earlier Venezuelan examples. Most Latin American leftists saw the United States as an ever present evil that supported non-leftist governments, democratic or otherwise, and that supported U.S. companies, which had alliances with local capitalists. In El Salvador in the early 1970s, leftists began a guerrilla struggle against the state.

Eventually, different groups of dissidents united in the Farabundo Marti National Liberation Front (FMLN). This group was somewhat unique in that it directed the terrorist actions that complemented guerrilla actions primarily against the economic resources of the state.[27] After more than a decade of conflict, the group reached an agreement with the government for peaceful participation in the political system.

In Peru radical leftist terrorism was associated with the Shining Path (*Sendero Luminoso*) guerrilla movement and Tupac Amaru Revolutionary Movement (MRTA)—named for Tupac Amaru II discussed in chapter five. Both groups gained greater strength from their association with the Indian communities in the interior of the country that had largely been ignored by successive governments in Lima. The Marxist ideology of the dissidents led them to see the Indian problems as a reflection of capitalism. The dissident organizations blended together, at least somewhat effectively, ideological and communal concerns. A local university professor in the interior formed Shining Path in 1980, and the core of the movement drew heavily upon students. Shining Path was the more active of the two groups, combining guerrilla operations with terrorist attacks, especially against local functionaries. Police, local officials, landowners, and the clergy were targets for attacks, and in some areas local government virtually ceased to exist, providing an opportunity for the leftists to set up governing structures.[28] The Shining Path activities provided a serious challenge to the government for many years, but the effort to overthrow the government and establish a new leftist system was faltering. The leaders of the movement decided on an urban terrorist campaign to complement the activities in the countryside. They hoped that the urban terror would lead to a military coup that would further polarize the Peruvian population and generate more support for the dissidents.[29] The urban campaign did not generate the expected coup, although the civilian government of President Alberto Fujimoro did establish a more repressive system. The urban campaign led to the capture of key leaders and many rank and file members, and the group had largely been contained by the end of 1992.[30] MRTA, which was always less of a threat to the government, was also in decline by the early 1990s. In December 1993, its last major action was a spectacular one when members of the group captured the Japanese embassy in Lima and held many persons hostage for months. The event did not generate the anticipated public uprising, and Peruvian forces in a carefully staged operation managed to recapture the embassy. The embassy capture was the last gasp of the group, and it has not undertaken any other major attacks since that seizure.[31]

Colombia also faced leftist violence in this period. A number of different groups appeared in the mid-1960s, including the National Liberation Army (ELN), the Popular Liberation Army (EPL), the April 19 Movement (M-19), and most importantly the Revolutionary Armed Forces of Colombia (FARC). The different groups, especially the ELN and FARC were able to benefit from the disruption that occurred with *La Violencia*. Government structures in the countryside had been destroyed, giving alternative political groups an opportunity to establish themselves.[32] FARC, and to a lesser extent the ELN, were able to establish rural zones that they controlled, and they complemented their guerrilla activities with assassinations, kidnappings, and other types of terrorist actions, including attacks on economic targets.[33] The M-19 group was always more of an urban movement, and it was particularly active in Bogotá. Militants seized the embassy of the Dominican Republic in 1980 and the Palace of Justice in 1985. The 1980 occupation ended peacefully, but the incident in 1985 ended badly when government troops attempted a rescue. Over a hundred people died—dissidents, soldiers, and hostages, including eleven members of Columbia's Supreme Court.[34] M-19 could not maintain its momentum in the urban areas and disbanded as a guerrilla and terrorist group in 1989.[35] FARC and the ELN continued to be very active into the next era.

The leftists in Peru and Colombia eventually formed alliances with those involved in the narcotics traffic. The leftists and the drug dealers formed an alliance since neither one wanted an effective government presence in the area. The profits from the drug traffic in Peru helped to finance Shining Path's operations against the government.[36] The Shining Path and MRTA were actually competing for control of the coca areas that provided a key source for funds for guerrilla activities and terrorist operations.[37] With the availability of secure funding there were instances where the Shining Path guerrillas were better armed than the Peruvian police or the soldiers that they faced.[38] The drug operators in Colombia also formed alliances with FARC and ELN, but that arrangement was solidified after 1990. One group of drug producers, the Medellin Cartel, tried to use terror to intimidate the government on its own. The Cartel used car bombs in the streets of Bogotá and other cities; judges, political leaders—including three presidential candidates, and journalists were assassinated; other judges and police officials were threatened.[39] A Colombian airliner with 130 people on board was blown up to kill the informants that were on board.[40] The drug cartel was trying to coerce the government leaders, civil servants, and the population in general in order to get the government to stop interfering with the narcotics traffic. The conflict resulted in a bloody war between the police and the drug cartels, often with no quarter being given by either side.[41] The direct confrontation with government ended when key leaders of the cartel were killed or imprisoned.[42]

Brazil, Uruguay, and Argentina also faced terrorism by leftist groups. The dissidents in Brazil attempted an urban guerrilla campaign, but the military government in power had little difficulty in dealing with the threat.[43] The Uruguayan Movement of National Liberation, usually called the Tupameros (after Tupac Amaru II) presented a greater threat. Most of the Tupameros were students and young idealists, who robbed banks to finance the movement and even took over towns briefly to embarrass the government.[44] Like other leftist groups, the Tupameros hoped to push the ostensibly democratic government into showing its true colors by becoming more repressive.[45] In this case the dissidents succeeded. The inability of a weak and disorganized political leadership to deal with the activities of the leftists led directly to a military takeover. The military, once in power, was quite willing and able to take the necessary repressive measures and quickly eliminated the Tupameros from the scene. Those who were not killed or captured went into exile.

In Argentina, a military regime had taken power in 1966. In 1969, popular protests occurred in Cordoba, but they were put down with force, resulting in deaths and casualties.[46] Many Argentineans became radicalized, and a number of leftist dissident groups organized to challenge the government, including the Montoneros and the more radical People's Revolutionary Army (ERP). These groups became very adept at using kidnapping for ransom—especially of foreign businessmen—to finance the purchase of arms to attack the government and political opponents. The financial support from the kidnappings ran into the millions.[47] The dissidents also used assassinations and other attacks against the military government that was in power, frequently targeting government officials in an effort to demonstrate that the government could not even protect its own.[48] Some of the leftists joined with other political groups in efforts to let former president Juan Peron return from exile in Spain. Eventually, the military withdrew from power under pressure and permitted elections that resulted in Peron's return to power. While Peron welcomed the support of the left, when he was forced to choose between those on the right and those on the left, he chose the right. He had begun to move against the more radical ERP when he died in 1974.[49] The government of his widow and Vice President, Isabel, continued to attack on the left, leading to a new round of violence by the dissidents.[50] Isabel Peron's government proved to be ineffective in dealing with protests and demonstrations and violence, so the military staged another coup in 1976. This military government was willing to use more repressive procedures and was able to crush the ERP and the Montoneros (see below).

Turkey also faced violence perpetrated by leftist student groups in this period. The leftists regarded Turkish democracy as a cover for the continued exploitation and manipulation of the masses by the elite.[51] The leftist dissidents regarded violence as quicker than working through the democratic process, and perhaps the only sure way to gain power.[52] There were many violent leftist groups that formed and became involved in campaigns in the cities. In addition to these groups the Marxist Kurdish Workers Party (PKK) appeared in this period, initially stressing the need for the government to adopt a socialist structure and policies to address the needs of the Kurds.[53] The leftist doctrines and ethnic components were mutually supportive for the PKK. It was later that the party became more of a communal dissident group willing to use violence to achieve its ends (see chapter ten). These dissident Turkish groups had to face not only government security forces but also right-wing groups that were willing to use violence against the leftists. These right-wing terrorists stressed the idea of Turkish identity and Sunni orthodoxy in their efforts to defend the states against the dissidents who gained support from religious, ethnic, and ideological minorities.[54] The democratic Turkish state thus faced escalating violence directed against the government and increasing turmoil in the streets as a consequence of violence between the left and the right. Thousands of people died in these struggles.[55] The military intervened in 1980 to take over control of the government. The military government cracked down on the violent groups, especially on the leftists, and terrorist incidents declined precipitously.[56] In neighboring Iran the overthrow of the Shah led to a power struggle between the clerics on the one hand and the middle class and leftists, including many students, on the other. The different groups had cooperated to overthrow the Shah, but in the contest for power after his fall the clerics won. The leftists and members of the secular middle class coalesced in the Mujahedin-e-Khalq (MEK) and launched a series of attacks against the Islamic Republic. Bombs killed the Speaker and other members of the Parliament, high-ranking officials, and government supporters. Over a thousand members of the government and supporters died.[57] A few members of the MEK even undertook suicide attacks.[58] After an 18-month terrorist campaign of bombings and assassinations, the MEK was defeated, and the surviving members retreated into exile.[59] The group gained a new lease on life when the Iraqis invaded Iran.

The MEK gained the active support of Iraq.[60] With the end of the war, however, it became much less effective and no longer constituted a major threat against the Islamic Republic.

There was also communal violence in this period. There were sporadic attacks by Puerto Rican nationalists and Croat separatists. There was a brief upsurge of nationalist violence by those seeking an independent French-speaking Quebec.[61] France had long faced disgruntled inhabitants in Corsica, but when the Front for the National Liberation of Corsica (FLNC) was formed, the nationalists became more violent in the late 1980s. There were hundreds of bombs set off per year, mostly against property, on the island and in mainland France.[62] In the late 1960s, the Euzkadi ta Askatasuna (ETA—Basque Homeland and Freedom) had been formed in Spain with the objective of gaining freedom for the Basque provinces. While Franco's authoritarian regime was in power, the ETA was able to launch only a few attacks, although it did manage to assassinate the prime minister toward the end of the Franco regime. The technique used in the assassination involved tunneling under a street and setting off explosives when the prime minister's vehicle passed over—a technique introduced by the Russian anarchists in one of their failed attempts to assassinated the Tsar.[63] The ETA continued its attacks after the creation of a functioning democratic system in Spain since the Basque region was still not independent. More moderate Basque nationalist parties had contested elections while the ETA continued its violence, providing Basque nationalists with multiple avenues of political activity. The ETA initially relied on attacks on property, but the group has been responsible for more than 500 assassinations, kidnappings, bombings, assaults, and robberies.[64] It had focused its violent attacks on government officials for the most part, but at times uncooperative Basques have become targets, especially for refusing to pay "revolutionary taxes."[65] The ETA had used leftist rhetoric at times in order to attract support, but the essence of the group's objectives had always been communal.[66] The ETA had survived a number of splits within the group due to disagreements over ideology, tactics, and long-term strategies.

The situation in Northern Ireland exploded in 1969. In emulation of the U.S. experience, Catholics in Ulster undertook a civil rights campaign to improve their economic and political position in the province. The local government, dominated by Protestants, refused to give ground and resorted to repression.[67] The conflict escalated, and the IRA began to organize in support of the local Catholic population. British troops arrived in an attempt to contain the situation and provide neutral enforcement of the laws. Over time, however, the British soldiers antagonized the Catholic minority, and other mistakes were made, including the incident on Bloody Sunday (January 30, 1972) when British soldiers on crowd control killed 13 unarmed demonstrators.[68] Very quickly the British, in addition to the Protestants, became targets for a terrorist campaign. The IRA at this time split. The Official IRA had adopted a leftist ideology that argued for working within the political system, and it was unwilling to resort to violence. The Provisional IRA, or Provos, opted to use the tried and true techniques and to use a terrorist campaign to try to force the British out. The Official IRA faded into insignificance, and the Provos in effect became the IRA. IRA militants attacked local police, the British army, government officials, and the Protestant population in general. The IRA violence also led to the formation of Protestant groups that used terror against the Catholic population and suspected IRA members in retaliation. By 1990, thousands of people had been killed in the violence (by the security forces, the IRA, and Protestant groups formed to combat the IRA).[69] In addition to the IRA, the Irish National Liberation Army (INLA) operated against the British. This group combined leftist ideology with a willingness to use violence and terrorism in the struggle for Irish unification. While separate from the IRA, its actions effectively supplemented the activities of the IRA.[70] The IRA was so effective in intimidating the local population that the British had to dispense with jury trials for cases involving IRA members. Witnesses and jurors were too frightened to appear or convict.[71] The IRA and INLA carried the attack to Britain itself, launching bombing campaigns against military targets, political foes, and the British population in general. INLA militants were able to assassinate a close friend and a confidant of Prime Minister Thatcher, while an IRA unit set off a bomb at the annual meeting of the Conservative Party in 1984 and used remote control mortars to fire at a cabinet meeting at No. 10 Downing Street when John Major was prime minster.[72] The increased level of violence in England itself led the British Parliament to pass more stringent measures to deal with terrorists.

There was communal terrorism elsewhere in the world. When the Philippines gained its independence, a variety of Muslim separatist groups appeared, of which the Moro National Liberation Front (MNLF) was the most prominent in this period. These groups fought an ongoing guerrilla battle against the government, and they also relied on the use of terrorist actions to supplement their other activities.[73] Extensive violence also appeared in Sri Lanka between the Sinhalese majority and the Tamil minority (in addition to the violent attempts of the JVP to seize power). The Sinhalese leaders began to promote the position of their group by making Sinhala the national language in 1956 and progressively imposing limits on Tamil representation in the professions, universities, the bureaucracy, and other areas. Communal violence began to appear in 1981, and in 1983 massive riots targeting Tamils broke out after Tamil dissidents killed 13 members of an army patrol. Two to three thousand Tamils were killed in the rioting, and the high property losses that occurred were almost exclusively Tamil.[74] These riots, in turn, triggered a major increase in violence by Tamil dissident groups.[75] The Tamil dissidents were initially divided into a number of different organizations. Some of the groups advocated increased autonomy, while others wanted complete independence for the Tamil areas of the island. The Liberation Tigers of Tamil Eelam (LTTE), commonly called the Tamil Tigers, have continuously pursued the maximalist goal of an independent Tamil state on the island. The LTTE eventually became the dominant dissident organization by eliminating or absorbing the other groups.[76] The group has undertaken daring and effective terrorist actions and has assassinated a number of prominent political leaders in the country.[77] It has also targeted the Sinhalese population in general with attacks that have included a bomb on a Sri Lankan airliner and one in the central bus station in Colombo that killed more than a hundred people.[78] The Tigers have also practiced ethnic cleansing in Tamil areas. Non-Tamils found in villages or on buses have been executed while the Tamils were unharmed.[79] These massacres have had the desired effect in getting other non-Tamils to flee the areas.

India also faced terrorist groups in this period. In 1980, Sikh dissidents in Punjab began to attack Indian officials and local Sikhs allied to the government in an attempt to gain an independent Sikh state in the area. The dissidents used guerrilla attacks, assassinations, bombs, and other typical techniques in their struggles. There were eventually well over a hundred groups participating on the Sikh side in the conflict.[80] One of the largest dissident groups took over the complex of the Golden Temple of Amistrar, which was the holiest site for the Sikh religion, as its headquarters. It continued its terrorist and guerrilla campaigns from this sanctuary. Finally, in 1984 Prime Minister Indira Gandhi ordered the military to assault the complex. Many dissidents were killed, but a large number of pilgrims died on the temple grounds and the temple itself was damaged.[81] In retribution for the assault on the temple, Gandhi was assassinated by two of her Sikh bodyguards. Her assassination in turn led to riots around the country in which thousands of local Sikhs were killed. The violence in Punjab also included ethnic cleansing activities as the dissidents attacked Hindus in efforts to drive out "foreign" groups from the area.[82] By the early 1990s, the violence in the region had been largely contained, and all but a handful of the dissidents had been dealt with.[83] By 1990, India was also beginning to face terrorist problems in Jammu and Kashmir. The largely Muslim population of Kashmir either desired incorporation into Pakistan or independence. Both local groups and guerrillas from Pakistan began to rely on terrorism in campaigns that carried over into the 1990s.[84]

An unusual case of communal terrorism involved two Armenian organizations, the Armenian Secret Army for the Liberation of Armenia (ASALA) and the Justice Commandos of the Armenian Genocide (JCAG). These two groups were not seeking an independent Armenia, instead they wanted to focus world attention on the forgotten genocide of the Armenians that occurred in 1915. They also wanted the government of Turkey to admit guilt for the genocide and to provide reparations to the Armenian people. These two groups launched attacks against a variety of Turkish targets around the world, including diplomats.[85] These actions did gain the desired attention about the earlier genocide, but it failed to gain a Turkish admission of guilt or reparations. By the end of the 1980s the two groups had disappeared, perhaps because the unusual nature of their demands made a permanent following hard to attract.

Some of the most publicized terrorist actions in this period involved the efforts of the Palestinians to win a homeland. After the defeat of the Arab armies in 1967, the PLO began to use terrorism to support continuing guerrilla raids into Israel. This choice of the terrorist strategy was not completely accepted until Yassir Arafat was elected Chairman of the PLO, since he and his organization, *Fatah*, favored the use of both terrorism and the guerrilla raids.[86] The PLO actually adopted the structure of the Irgun as one of the organizational models for the struggle since they saw the Irgun as a useful and effective example to follow.[87] The Popular Front for the Liberation of Palestine (PFLP), one of the component units of the PLO, began airline hijackings to publicize the Palestinian cause. In 1972, came the attack on the Israeli athletes at the Munich Olympics by Black September—a group that was no longer part of the PLO. Through the next two decades PLO members and members of groups that were not part of the PLO undertook a variety of attacks on targets in Israel and on Israeli targets abroad. The United States, by this time the major supporter of Israel, also became a target for some attacks by Palestinian groups. Some external groups like the Abu Nidal Organization would mount attacks in efforts to disrupt peace discussions between Israel and the Palestinians.[88] Despite the internal conflicts and disagreements over tactics, the PLO held together. By 1990, the PLO had renounced terrorist actions against Israel and its allies, although other Palestinian groups in Israel and the Occupied Territories continued to use terrorism.

Various Palestinian groups were joined in operations by other terrorist organizations, including European leftist groups and leftists elsewhere. Many leftists regarded Israel simply as an extension of global or U.S. capitalism and colonialism and as a mechanism for exploitation and control of the Middle East and its resources. The PFLP, which had a Marxist orientation as well as the commitment to a Palestinian state, found it easy to cooperate with other leftist groups. The PFLP in conjunction with German and other leftists took many prominent hostages at an OPEC meeting in Vienna in 1975.[89] A joint operation between the RAF and the PFLP led to the hijacking of an Air France flight that finally landed at Entebbe Airport in Uganda. In another operation members of the JRA flew into Lod Airport with hidden weapons and attacked the passengers in the terminal.[90] The PFLP and the JRA also collaborated in launching an attack on the Shell Oil facilities in Singapore as part of a battle against capitalist interests.[91] These cooperative activities not only provided the Palestinians and the leftists with opportunities for publicity for their causes, but it also provided the Palestinians with a support net-work for actions undertaken on their own in Europe.

The Palestinian operations also led to a reappearance of terrorist groups among the Jewish population of Israel. Some Jewish groups wanted to expand Jewish settlements into the Occupied Territories, especially the West Bank (or Judea and Samaria) and force the Palestinians out.[92] One group of extremists plotted to blow up the Muslim holy sites in Jerusalem, but they were caught before they could do so.[93] These extremists wanted to avenge the attacks launched by the Palestinians, to deter attacks on the Jewish settlers in the Occupied Territories, and some even hoped that escalating levels of violence would eventually prevent the evacuation of the Sinai Peninsula as specified in the Camp David Accords.[94] They even used violence against peace activists, as well as those protesting the invasion of Lebanon in 1982.[95] Most of the members of these groups were arrested by Israeli security forces, brought to trial for their actions, and given long prison sentences. Later governments, however, commuted their sentences, and many returned to positions of leadership in groups supporting the expansion of settlements.[96]

Lebanon in the 1970s and 1980s was a country plagued by terrorism and violence. Lebanon had a wide variety of communal groups.

The communalism was based on religious differences since virtually the entire population was Arab. While the most basic division was between Muslims and Christians, there were divisions within each group as well and alliances across the religious divide. The involvement of outside countries exacerbated the existing differences and contributed to the Lebanese civil war and breakdown of the government. In the struggles of the civil war, the use of terrorism became widespread. Westerners were killed or kidnapped by the more militant groups, especially the Shi'ite Hizballah that was backed by fellow Shi'ites in Iran. It was in Lebanon that the car bomb came into prominent use. Shi'ite groups supporting Iran used one against the Iraqi embassy in Beirut after the invasion of Iran by Iraqi forces.[97] The U.S. embassy was also a target for car bombs as were Israeli military forces in the country after the 1982 invasion. In 1983, Hizballah suicide bombers killed more than two hundred U.S. marines and nearly a hundred French paratroopers in Beirut.[98] Attacks were not limited to foreign targets. One such car bomb killed newly elected president, Bashir Gemayel. It is estimated that over 8,000 people, the vast majority of whom were Lebanese, died as a consequence of Hizballah attacks.[99] This technique, like any other that has proven to be effective, came to be widely copied by groups elsewhere in the world. The various militias in Lebanon also practiced communal cleansing during the various conflicts. The massacres of civilians served to drive out members of other groups so that more homogeneous and defensible areas could be created.[100]

As was also the case in the past, there were times when governments contributed to attacks against some of their own citizens. There are indications that the mobs targeting the Tamils in Sri Lanka in 1983 were organized or at least supported by Sinhalese government officials.[101] Similarly, in India the mobs that attacked Sikhs after the assassination of Indira Gandhi were sometimes encouraged by local political leaders, and in some cases police or military units did choose to intervene to stop the violence.[102] In the case of Jewish extremists there is at least the possibility that they were able to carry out vigilante attacks on Palestinians with little fear from the authorities, or even the courts.[103] The fact that the prison sentences of convicted extremists were considerably shortened also implied government support.

Death squads and government sanctioned paramilitary groups often appeared in Latin American countries as part of the battle against leftist dissidents. El Salvador has frequently been cited as a country where death squads ran rampant. In actual fact, the death squads resulted in relatively few deaths compared to military actions by the armed forces or security units.[104] Guatemala saw much more of this type of activity by government supported groups against suspected leftists or guerrillas or the Indians that were thought to favor the guerrillas. In fact, Guatemala had as many casualties from this kind of terror as the rest of Latin America.[105] The military regime in Brazil and Uruguay did not need to rely on death squads to control dissidents. In Colombia, paramilitary groups were beginning to appear at the time and attack leftists, but a more active role for these groups was in the future. Argentina became one of the most infamous users of death squads. Under Isabel Peron, the Argentine Anti-Communist Alliance (AAA) was responsible for the assassinations of hundreds of presumed enemies of the state.[106] When the military seized power from Isabel Peron, they greatly increased the use of such squads. Anyone suspected of sympathy to the ERP, the Montoneros, or other leftists groups was picked up and interrogated. In almost all the cases, the victims were never seen again. They became known in Argentina as "The Disappeared Ones." The total casualties of this dirty war against actual and potential dissenters were somewhere between 15,000 and 30,000 individuals.[107] The victims did not have to be left on public display in town squares; their disappearances on such a scale were sufficient to induce terror.

The use of death squads was hardly limited to Latin America. South Africa under the white minority regime and the associated apartheid system resorted to death squads to deal with opponents, blacks and white. The government also helped to organize vigilante groups that attacked dissenters opposed to the minority political system.[108] The Spanish government created the Antiterrorist Liberation Groups (GAL) to murder Basque terrorist leaders and ETA members in France. When the activities of the unit came to light, the group was quickly disbanded.[109] The government of the Philippines had encouraged self-defense groups in the southern parts of the country to deal with the threat from the Muslim separatists. These groups combined with government death squads to take a toll of Muslim separatists and innocent civilians.[110] The government of Sri Lanka also used death squads during the second JVP uprising, targeting not only JVP members but sympathizers as well.[111] Indonesia faced problems with an independence movement when it attempted to incorporate the former Portuguese colony of East Timor. The Indonesians used a variety of methods to deal with the unrest, including repression by the military and security forces, torture and death while in custody, and rape as a means of demoralizing the indigenous population.[112] When these methods failed to defeat the independence movement, the Indonesian authorities used death squads made up of police or military personal out of uniform and paramilitary groups and militias trained by the military.[113] Casualties among the East Timorese were high, and by the end of the period of Indonesian occupation, more than 200,000 of the East Timorese, approximately one-third of the population in 1974, had been killed.[114] India also used death squads to deal with dissidents during the struggle with the Sikhs. Suspected dissidents would disappear into the jails, but many of them would later be announced as casualties in battles with the security forces or otherwise listed as killed in conflict.[115] These extrajudicial executions played a role in defeating the Sikh separatists.

Foreign nations were also active in supporting terrorist groups operating in other countries. Iraq supported the MEK. Virtually every Arab country provided the PLO or other Palestinian groups with funding and support, as did the Soviet Union and other states. Libya supported groups elsewhere in the world, including Muslim separatists in the Philippines and even the IRA.[116] Iran provided important assistance to Hizballah for its activities in Lebanon.[117] Other Lebanese groups had outside backers as well. Israel provided clandestine aid to some Christian groups, and the Syrians had favored groups as well. India and Pakistan provided support to dissident groups operating in each other's territory, including at least some Pakistani support for some Sikh and Kashmiri groups.[118] The Cold War was still ongoing throughout this period, and it was reflected in patterns of support. Cuba provided support for leftists groups in Latin American when it could. The dissidents in El Salvador received aid from Cuba and the Soviet Union while the United States in turn supplied significant aid to the Contras. The United States gave significant aid to the guerrillas in Afghanistan as part of the Cold War competition as well. Many of the leftist groups operating in Europe in this period received some support from Communist countries.[119] The Soviet Union and its allies did not control these groups, but they saw the obvious benefits in contributing to instability in the Western democracies.

Outside support came from sources other than governments. The diaspora populations continued to be financially important for the IRA, the Tamils in Sri Lanka, and the Palestinians.[120] The PLO was able to establish training camps in a variety of Arab countries, especially Lebanon, Syria, and Libya. These camps trained not only Palestinian fighters but also members of many other groups. More than 40 organizations sent individuals to these training camps, including leftists, the IRA, the ETA, and Corsican nationalists.[121] The links established at these camps helped to facilitate the joint operations undertaken by the Palestinians and the others. North Korea also ran a number of training camps or provided advisors for camps elsewhere. These camps also served groups from many different countries, and they provided the meeting place for the JRA and the Palestinians to create their alliance.[122] The existence of these camps in relatively safe territory provided an opportunity for terrorists and guerrillas to learn new techniques generally secure from the threat of attack. These arrangements were basically ad hoc ones, and they did not lead to the appearance of any transnational terrorist grouping.[123]

The Indian intelligence service initially provided some support to the Tamils in Sri Lanka in deference to the 69 million Tamils in the Indian state of Tamil Nadu just across a narrow strait from Sri Lanka.[124] As the severity of the Sri Lankan conflict increased, however, India became more supportive of the central government. In 1987, India served as a guarantor of an agreement between the government and the LTTE and sent a peacekeeping force to Sri Lanka. The Tamil Tigers did not disarm as expected, and they used the lull in the fighting to entrench themselves. Eventually the Indian troops became involved in fighting the Tamil rebels. They fared no better than the Sri Lankan government forces and eventually withdrew without having helped to resolve the civil war. One direct consequence of the Indian involvement and fighting was that in 1991, a Tamil suicide bomber assassinated Rajiv Gandhi, who had been prime minister in 1987.

Objectives and Causes

As the above discussions have indicated, ideology was an important factor explaining terrorism in this period. Leftists groups willing to use violence were very prevalent in much of Europe and Latin America. One of the weaknesses of these groups was their commitment to their ideologies, for there was a tendency for the groups to splinter over theoretical issues. The Red Brigades were one of the largest leftist terrorist organizations in Europe, but the groups in Colombia, Argentina, and Peru were also substantial. Leftist influences were present within the Palestinian nationalist movement, and they were quite important for joint operations that were undertaken, but they were not able to dominate that movement. The Palestinian leftists also had the same tendency to splinter over ideological issues. In addition to all the leftists groups there were right-wing ideological groups in this period, but their activities paled by comparison with the efforts of the left. Groups like the Order were beginning to appear in the United States and were willing to use violence to reach their objectives, but their activities were limited. The Contras were more important for events in Nicaragua.

Communal groups were also present in the period, although not as extensive as the leftists. The IRA, ETA, Corsicans, Armenian groups, the Quebec dissidents, and the Palestinians were basically ethnic nationalists. Communalism rooted principally in religious identities appeared with the Sikhs in their struggles within India. The dissident groups in the Philippines were based on religion, as was true for most of the groups practicing terrorism in Lebanon. The dissidents that were beginning to become active in Kashmir combined national feelings with religious ones, and the Israeli extremists that resorted to terror relied on a mixture of religious and Zionist (i.e., nationalist) rationales for their actions. In other cases, there were combinations of objectives. In Sri Lanka, the largely Hindu and Christian Tamils were not only ethnically different from the Buddhist Sinhalese but religiously differentiated as well. While the Shining Path and MRTA were overwhelmingly ideological for the leaders and cadres, they also managed to tap into the communal feelings of the Indian populations.

The reliance on the use of death squads or paramilitaries by governments often involved mixed motives. Death squads by their very nature are part of an instrumental use of terrorism by the state. While the government terror was instrumental, it also had ideological and communal components. The governments in India, the Philippines, and Sri Lanka (in reference to the Tamils) were attempting to prevent secessionist movements from succeeding—essentially a communal goal. In Central and South America the dissidents were rooted in Marxist ideology or variations of Marxism, so the death squads were inevitably ideologically to the right. The death squads in South Africa represented both the opposition of right-wing ideologies to the vague leftist orientations of the majority population and the communal efforts to maintain white minority rule. While death squad activity often involved instrumental goals, the terrorist campaign by the Medillin Cartel to coerce the government of Colombia provides the most obvious example of almost pure instrumental terrorism. The drug lords were seeking increased profits by coercing changes in government policies.

Globalization and modernization played a role in the terrorism that appeared in this period. Most groups on the left saw global capitalism as being responsible for problems in their countries and the world. They identified with the Palestinians and other groups as victims of imperialism that was part of an expanding global capitalism. Other terrorist groups reflected the effects of globalization. The ETA and Corsican nationalists were fighting against increasing integration of their areas into broader national units and the loss of local identity. The Basques had even become a linguistic minority in their core provinces as migrants from elsewhere in Spain had moved into the region.[125] In Corsica, the attacks had been principally on foreign owned property and thus constituted a reaction to the entrance of outside groups.[126] Violence in Turkey and Greece reflected the problems inherent in the transition from a rural to a more modern urban society.[127] Other communal groups do not appear to have been reactions to globalization. The Tamils in Sri Lanka, the PLO, the Armenians, and the Sikhs were not anti-modern or anti-global. In fact, the Sikhs were relatively cosmopolitan and their diaspora has carried them around the world to positions of economic influence. The Sikhs were reacting to some extent to movements within Hinduism that sought to elevate the Hindu religion to a state religion and incorporate Hindu values into state law (Hinduvata). It was the Hinduvata activists who were anti-global since they wished to expunge foreign influences.[128] There was little evidence of terrorism linked to clashes of civilizations in this period. The activities of the leftists (and responses by governments using death squads) were all within the same cultural area, as were many of the communal groups. Only a handful of cases might qualify. The residual activities of the KKK represented extreme cultural exclusivism. The conflicts in the southern Philippines and East Timor had elements of clashes between different religious areas. The conflict between Palestinians and Israeli Jews and between Hindu Tamils and Buddhists Sinhalese might qualify as well. Overall, these cases are a small minority of all the situations in which there was active terrorism. Huntington in his argument, of course, did suggest that such actions would occur after the end of the Cold War.

Weak states played a greater role as a contributing factor to terrorism in this period. Most of the Western democracies that were the scene of leftist violence were not weak, except in the eyes of right-wing extremists. The Greek security forces were somewhat inept since they lacked the training, motivation, or expertise to deal with terrorist groups, but the Greek political state, however, was not especially weak.[129] Italy had some difficulties in dealing with the Red Brigades, in part because the security forces had been reorganized because of right-wing conspiracies that involved high-ranking members.[130] Ironically, the right-wing groups had helped to create the very weaknesses that they feared. Over time, however, the Italian political system recovered and was able to deal with the terrorists. Japan was very effective in dealing with violent leftist dissidents. The Israeli state was never weak, and Israel has not shied away from retaliation and effective responses to terrorism. Turkey provides a contrary example in that the democratic government in power was unable to deal with the terrorist activities, and the failure to control the first violent groups no doubt led other groups to adopt violent techniques to achieve political objectives.

The states that faced terrorism in Latin America were often weaker states. In Uruguay it took a shift from a weak democratic system to a military regime to provide enough strength to defeat the dissidents. Argentina also displayed strengths and weaknesses. When the ERP, the Montoneros and other leftists first challenged the military regime in power, that regime was losing support. Leftists groups were not the only ones involved in the struggles to change the system, and the weight of opposition overwhelmed the military, permitting Peron's return. When Juan Peron was in power, the system became stronger, only to weaken significantly after Isabel Peron became president. The military regime that replaced Isabel Peron was strong enough to decisively defeat and destroy the leftists with its own brand of terror. Both Uruguay and Argentina demonstrate that state weakness need not be a chronic condition—it could be temporary. Guatemala and El Salvador are intermediate cases. Both states had obvious weaknesses but they managed to deal with the dissidents over time. Colombia and Peru are examples of states that demonstrated more chronic weaknesses. The government of Peru let the activities of Shining Path and MRTA catch it unawares, partially because weak governments had ignored the region.[131] It proved to be difficult for the government to regain control of the countryside, and the possibility that the leftists have begun to reappear and that they may constitute a threat again is another sign of chronic weakness. The Colombian government for a long time has not controlled significant parts of its own territory. FARC has safe areas and has been able to negotiate almost as an equal with different governments.

Weak state systems contributed to terrorism elsewhere. In Iran the government dominated by the clerics was vulnerable to the attacks of the secular groups. The period of vulnerability, like that for many new regimes, however, was limited and the campaign failed. Before the coup in 1980, the Turkish government had clearly been incapable of dealing with the combined terrorist violence of the left and the right.[132] The government in the Philippines was never able to gain effective control of the Muslim areas. Guerrilla raids and terrorism were always present. The willingness to sanction actions by local paramilitary groups was a sign of weakness on the part of the government.[133] Indonesia was unable to defeat the independence movement in East Timor through regular military action and had to resort to the unofficial actions by the militias and death squads. Lebanon probably provides an exemplar of a weak state. The government was never very strong, in part because the local elites preferred a weak state that left them greater freedom of action.[134] The weakness and then the collapse of the state meant that terrorist organizations were relatively free to operate (at least in areas not controlled by outside actors).

Successes and Failures

The great wave of leftist terrorism in Europe failed for the most part in terms of the objectives of creating greater equality and disrupting capitalism (in either the local or global variations). Even in Italy, which was the most affected, there were few changes in policies. The dissident groups were defeated or contained. When communism collapsed in the Soviet Union and Eastern Europe, the remnants of the groups disintegrated since their model had failed.[135] While neither was ultimately successful in challenging the regime in power, the Red Brigades and 17 November reflect opposite poles as to how leftist groups attempted to challenge the system in Europe. The Red Brigades launched more than 10,000 attacks, kidnapped a former prime minister, and paralyzed the legal system at times. The group mobilized more than a thousand followers and many more sympathizers—many of whom it lost with the execution of Aldo Moro. The size of the group, however, helped to contribute to its downfall. The government offered captured members of the Red Brigades reduced sentences in exchange for information on other members of the group. The process worked in terms of breaking up the organization and led to the capture of most of the members.[136] The 17 November group was just the opposite. It was a small group that was able to maintain the security of the organization and to prevent discovery by the police. In a 1992 communiqué, the group actually indicated that it had learned valuable lessons on maintaining secrecy from the negative experiences of the Red Brigades.[137] The negative side of this approach is that while 17 November had a continuous terrorist presence of over 25 years, it was only able to undertake a few attacks in any of those years. The group was small enough to protect its anonymity but was too small to effectively challenge the Greek political system.[138]

The leftists groups were defeated in Sri Lanka, Iran, Turkey, and Brazil without accomplishing much. In Peru the government did assume a more forceful posture and impose more limits, but the military did not intervene to stage a coup as the dissidents hoped, and the government was able to defeat both the Shining Path and MRTA. The Tupameros were eminently successful in forcing an authoritarian government to take power in Uruguay, but the new government was quite capable of quickly dealing with the dissidents and eliminated them in short order. In Argentina the Montoneros were successful in a number of ways. The attacks of the leftists in conjunction with other efforts played a role in the decision of the military government to step down in 1973 and to permit Juan Peron to return. When faced with a more determined military government willing to use death squads and extreme measures the left in Argentina ultimately failed. In El Salvador the combination of guerrilla activity and terrorism, however, led to negotiations and a peace settlement with the government that guaranteed the leftists a role in the political system. In Colombia by 1990, FARC had maintained control of important areas of the country and kept the government weak, providing opportunities for gains in the future.

The communal dissidents in this period survived to remain active into later years. In 1990, the Corsican nationalists, the LTTE, the IRA, the Muslim separatists in the Philippines, and the dissidents in Kashmir had been successful enough to survive. Their successes over the longer period are considered in chapter ten. The Sikhs were defeated in their effort to create an independent state. The Armenian terrorist groups did generate some attention to the forgotten genocide during World War I, but they did not get an admission of guilt from the Turkish government or reparations. It is difficult to assess the results for Lebanon. In this multisided conflict, many different groups relied on violence, including terrorism. In such circumstances, both the winners and the losers (however determined) were often using the same techniques. Thus, to some extent terrorism was both successful and a failure at the same time. The situation in Israel and the Occupied Territories involved many forms of terrorism by many groups. The Palestinians were able to obtain some tactical objectives. A Palestinian attack in 1973 in Austria, for example, convinced the government to close a transit camp that was being used by Soviet Jews immigrating to Israel.[139] At least some of the major actions focused global attention on the Palestinian cause. The terrorist struggle also helped to provide an element of unity among the Palestinian dissidents, and it gave the Palestinian nationalists activities that they could identify with and support.[140] The PLO was eventually successful in bringing Israel to the negotiating table. By the beginning of the 1990s the PLO had been accepted in the Oslo Accords as the spokesman for the Palestinians. When the Palestinian Authority was created to help govern the West Bank and the Gaza Strip, the PLO became the major political group in power. The PLO as an organization had forsworn terrorism along the way, but it is unlikely that Israel would have even made the concessions that it did had there not been the terrorist activity for the preceding quarter of a century.[141] The efforts of the Jewish extremists group to prevent negotiations or to neutralize the Palestinian leadership, on the other hand, had failed when the agreement in Oslo was reached.

A variety of terrorist groups, including Palestinian groups, had achieved other successes. There have been many cases of Western governments not apprehending known terrorists or bringing terrorists to trial for fear of reprisals from the group.[142] France for a period of time followed a doctrine of sanctuary. As long as terrorist organizations operating internationally did not launch attacks in France, they would have nothing to fear from the French authorities.[143] By 1990, the French had changed to a policy of accommodation, making deals with specific groups to prevent attacks on French soil.[144] In 1973, then prime minister Aldo Moro had come to an informal understanding with the PLO and the Abu Nidal group that Italy would not interfere with the transit of Palestinian operatives as long as Italians or Italian interests were not targeted.[145] These deals, which many considered to be unwise, were at least limited successes for the terrorist organizations. They had gained tactical advantages from Western governments because politicians feared terrorist campaigns.

The few ideological groups from the right that operated in this period were somewhat successful. The right-wing Turkish groups obviously succeeded in attaining some of their goals when the military regime came into power. This government reflected at least some of their values and it greatly limited the power of the leftist groups in Turkish society. The neo-Fascists and the KKK accomplished little, and local police eliminated the Order. The Contras in Nicaragua with major support from the United States did play a role in undermining the Sandinista government. The elections held, and lost, by the government may not have occurred if the Contras had not been a threat. The government lost the election in part because it could not fight the Contras (and the United States) at the same time it was attempting to create a new government and new programs to serve the population.[146] The government-supported terror that occurred was often more effective since the groups involved did not have to fear arrest or interference from the authorities. It was most effective in Argentina, Guatemala, and against the Sikhs. In India once the security forces had gained an edge, Sikhs—even family members of the dissidents—refused to support the dissidents out of the fear of the death squads.[147] The GAL in Spain did manage to murder a number of Basque leaders before exposure led to its being disbanded. The death squads were less effective in Sri Lanka and the Philippines, and in East Timor their use did not succeed in perpetuating Indonesian control. In South Africa, majority rule did occur despite the activities of the death squads.

Summary

David Rapoport noted that the period discussed in the chapter constituted the third wave of terrorism in the form of attacks from the left.[148] It is clear that groups committed to some version of leftist terrorism dominated this period. Most of the industrialized countries faced some violence from such groups. Latin America was also home to many such groups. When terrorists groups were not present in Latin America, there were often leftist guerrilla movements (Guatemala, the Sandinistas in Nicaragua). After the collapse of communism the leftist groups lost much of their steam although many of the groups had already failed or had begun to fail. FARC with its links to the drug cartels was one of the few leftist survivals. Small left-wing groups in Asia continued as well. It might be assumed that ideological terrorism from the left would now be relegated to the dustbin of history, but that may not be true. Religion was once considered to have disappeared as a major political force in the world, but the expectation of its demise was premature. Fascism was discredited in 1945, but it has since reappeared at times. The same could happen in the future with Marxism. It would be premature, and even dangerous, to assume that terrorism rooted in ideologies of the left is a thing of the past.[149] It would have been expected that right-wing movements would decline since so many of them appeared to battle the left, but as chapter ten will make clear, such has not been the case.

Communal terrorism remained present in this period and continued on; thus, this form of terrorism demonstrated more staying power in the latter part of the twentieth century. Some of the communal movements, both ethnic and religious, carried over into the next period since they would be less affected by the demise of Communism than leftist movements. The end of the Cold War did remove potential patrons and supplies for some communal movements. The groups that have had the most persistence are those with ethnic bases since these identifications are often the most deep-seated. Ethnic concerns were somewhat more prominent than religious communalism in this period. The communal movements were often the most costly in terms of the loss of life.

A number of other patterns were apparent in the occurrences of terrorist activity in this era. The trafficking in narcotics was beginning to bring terrorist organizations and criminal groups together. It was most obvious in the connections between cocaine production and leftists in Colombia and Peru. This alliance also meant that the guerrillas and terrorist were becoming better armed. Death squads were active in more countries in this period. The Argentine example was one of the most prominent, but death squads were active in many parts of the world. Paramilitary groups that used terrorism were also becoming more prevalent in this period as governments relied on widely varying sources of support. It is possible that the extent of terrorist activity in this period explains, at least in part, the willingness of governments to rely on death squads and other irregular groups. Finally, the success rate of the terrorist organizations in this period was lower than that of the preceding period when so many anti-colonial struggles had at least some successes. The successes of the earlier periods would appear to have encouraged many groups to try to duplicate the achievement of political goals, but the organizations adopting the previously successful strategy were dealing with new situations in different political and social environments.

Group	Type	Objectives	Casualties	Success
Neo-Fascists (Italy)	Ideological (right-wing)	Force Italian government to become more authoritarian	Moderate from small number of attacks	System remains democratic
Nivelles Group (Belgium)	Ideological (right-wing)	Force Belgian government to become more authoritarian	Few although limited attacks are bloody	System remains democratic
Right-wing groups in Turkey	Ideological (right-wing)	Force Turkish government to become more authoritarian	Heavy	Military coup occurs in response to terrorism from left and right but government sides with right
KKK	Communal (ethnic)	Maintain white supremacy in southern United States	Moderate but for a long time period	Fails as national legislation extends voting rights and other rights to Blacks

Continued

Continued

Group	Type	Objectives	Casualties	Success
The Order	Ideological (right-wing) with racist overtones	Undermine U.S. government	Very few	Quickly destroyed
Contras in Nicaragua	Ideological (right-wing)	Undermine Sandinista government	Moderate from terrorism, moderate from guerrilla activity	Sandinista party loses election; public dissatisfaction linked to Contra activities in part
Baader–Meinhof Gang (Red Army Faction)	Ideological (left-wing)	Undermine democratic government in West Germany	Few	Fails to change government policies but does generate significant publicity
Red Brigades	Ideological (left-wing)	Undermine democratic government in Italy	Moderate (heavy over course of 20 years)	Fails, but severely tests the Italian political system (and democracy)
17 November Organization	Ideological (left-wing)	Undermine democratic government in Greece	Few	Fails, but generates publicity by selective attacks and survival
CCC, Direct Action, GRAPO, and others in Europe	Ideological (left-wing)	Undermine democratic governments	Few	Never a threat but able to generate publicity in context of leftist activity elsewhere in Europe
Weathermen and others in United States	Ideological (left-wing)	Undermine government, attack capitalism, and end war in Vietnam	Few	Limited, peaceful agitation and protest more effective in anti-war movement
Left-wing groups in Turkey	Ideological (left-wing)	Undermine democratic government in Turkey	Heavy	Military coup occurs in response to terrorism from left and right but government sides with right
Japanese Red Army	Ideological (left-wing)	Undermine democratic government in Japan and attack capitalism internationally	Moderate from relatively few attacks	Fades from scene without creating significant changes in Japan or elsewhere

Continued

Continued

Group	Type	Objectives	Casualties	Success
JVP	Ideological (left-wing)	Undermine democratic government in Sri Lanka	Few from terrorism in first attempt, heavy in the second	Government survives and JVP reintegrated into political party system
Farabundo Marti National Liberation Front	Ideological (left-wing)	Undermine government in El Salvador and create more rights for poor	Few from terrorist activity, moderate from guerrilla actions	FMLN negotiates agreements bringing about change and place for left in government
Tupameros	Ideological (left-wing)	Undermine democratic government in Uruguay	Few	Democratic government collapses, replaced by military regime, leftists defeated, no popular uprising
Shining Path, MRTA	Ideological (left-wing)	Undermine democratic government in Peru	Moderate to heavy from terrorism, heavy from guerrilla actions	Government becomes more authoritarian, leftists defeated, political system left weaker
FARC, ELN, and others	Ideological (left-wing) and instrumental	Undermine democratic government in Colombia	Moderate to heavy from terrorism, heavy from guerrilla actions	Leftists survive, well-financed by allying with drug lords
Medellin Cartel	Instrumental	Force government in Colombia to permit drug trade	Heavy from bombings and assassinations	Medellin Cartel destroyed, but other drug cartels continue
Brazilian leftists	Ideological (left-wing)	Undermine military government in Brazil	Few	Easily defeated by government
Montoneros and others	Ideological (left-wing)	Undermine series of governments in Argentina	Moderate	Helped to bring down one military government, forced new military government, decimated by security forces

Continued

Continued

Group	Type	Objectives	Casualties	Success
Mujahedin-e-Khalq	Ideological (left-wing and secular)	Undermine Islamic Republic in Iran	Heavy	Government triumphs and clerics solidify power
Corsican separatists	Communal (ethnic)	Autonomy or independence	Few	Property attacks continue
Quebec separatists	Communal (ethnic)	Independence	Very few	Virtually no effect
ETA★				
IRA★				
Muslims in Philippines★				
Tamil Tigers★				
Sikhs	Communal (religious)	Independence or greater autonomy	Heavy	Communal groups defeated with minor policy concessions made
Kashmir★				
ASALA and JCAG	Communal (ethnic and religious)	Publicize Armenian genocide, acknowledgment from Turkey	Light to moderate	Publicity gained, but no action from Turkish government
PLO and others	Communal (ethnic), some groups with leftist views as well	Independent Palestinian state	Heavy	Negotiations in Oslo lead to creation of Palestinian Authority and possible state in future
Jewish extremists	Communal (ethnic and religious)	Prevent negotiations with Palestinians	Few	Oslo Accords signed
GAL in Spain	Instrumental death squad	Defeat ETA	Few	Government discredited when GAL discovered, ETA survives
India	Instrumental death squads	Deal with Sikh dissidents	Heavy	Help government to defeat dissidents

Continued

Continued

Group	Type	Objectives	Casualties	Success
Argentina	Instrumental death squads	Deal with leftist groups	Very Heavy	Leftists and supporters decimated
South Africa	Instrumental death squads	Prevent majority rule	Moderate	Majority rule eventually achieved
Sri Lanka	Instrumental death squads	Deal with leftist guerrillas and sympathizers	Heavy	Leftists defeated
Guatemala	Instrumental death squads	Deal with leftist groups and sympathizers	Heavy	Governments survive series of threats
Philippines	Instrumental death squads and paramilitary groups	Deal with Muslim separatists	Moderate	Muslim separatists groups continue to operate
East Timor	Instrumental death squads and paramilitary groups	Attempt to eliminate independence movement and keep East Timor in Indonesia	Heavy from irregular forces, heavy from military	East Timor eventually gains independence
Lebanon—multiple groups	Left-wing, right-wing, communal (religious), and instrumental	Gain power at expense of other groups operating in Lebanon	Very heavy from terrorism, also heavy from civil war	At least partially effective for some of the groups using terrorism as part of broader strategies

Note: ★ These groups are included in table at the end of the next chapter. All of them survived and were present at the end of the time period covered in this chapter.

CHAPTER TEN

From Marxism Back to Communalism

The economic and political failures of Communism and then its collapse largely put an end to the widespread presence of violent leftist dissident groups, especially in the countries of West Europe and Latin America, where they had been so prominent. The 17 November Movement in Greece is one of the few groups that continued on into the 1990s and later, but this group had avoided connections with any of the existing Communist states. The collapse of the Soviet Union also meant that the Cold War had ended and some state supported terrorism disappeared. The end of the Cold War did not make terrorism redundant, and it has in many ways "become even more complex, multifaceted and lethal."[1] The attacks of September 11, 2001 were in some ways the culmination of this trend of increasing casualties. In the years after 1990, communalism— especially based in religion—reappeared as a major source of dissident terrorism. Violence also was associated with the breakup of empires, a phenomenon seen earlier in time. In this period, it was the disintegration of the Soviet Union and Yugoslavia. The 1990s also saw a significant increase in terrorist activities by right-wing groups including neo-Nazis, skinheads, and other "visionaries" seeking to recreate some former or future ideal political state.

New Movements with New and Old Techniques

The 1970s and 1980s were the era of the New Left, but only a few groups survived into the 1990s. There were still some occasional terrorist attacks by Marxist dissidents in India, but they were few and to date have not constituted even the beginnings of a threat. The PKK in Turkey evolved from a radical leftist party into a much more consciously nationalist group and will be discussed below. FARC in Colombia was the most prominent leftist group. It not only survived into the 1990s, but it was still a very effective organization, which continued to challenge the government of Colombia. It was able to build and gain strength by forming an even deeper alliance with the drug cartels operating in that country. The defeat of the Medellin Cartel convinced the surviving drug lords that they could not defeat the government on their own. The profits from the drug trade have permitted FARC to develop a solid financial base from which it could purchase the weapons it needed to arm its guerrilla forces and materials to be used in terrorist actions. The dissidents have been able to buy sophisticated arms, including surface to air missiles.[2] The leftists conducted a very effective campaign of assassinations as a means of undermining the government.[3] The constant struggles between the government and the dissidents and drug cartels contributed to Colombia having the highest murder rate in the world.[4] Between 1989 and 1999, at least 700 government officials or elected politicians were assassinated.[5] At the beginning of the twenty-first century, FARC had not only been able to maintain its position, but it also had been able to negotiate with the government on truces that recognized FARC authority in large areas. The negotiations have not yet been successful in ending the violence, in part because it would appear that the dissidents have no real incentive to give up on guerrilla activity and terrorism since it has served them so well.[6]

A variety of communal groups continued their campaigns. The Corsicans remained a problem for the French government. There have been more than 10,000 violent acts and more than 200 deaths over the decades of dissident violence.[7] The ETA continued to be active in Spain and there appears to have been little decline in the activity level of the ETA from the 1980s to the 1990s. The Spanish government has actually granted the Basque region greater local autonomy, but the ETA has continued to press for total independence for Basque speakers in Spain and neighboring areas of France. There has been some concern that the core of the ETA has become so conditioned to violence that it finds it difficult to move beyond the process of fighting, resulting in a culture of violence that is self perpetuating.[8] The IRA continued its campaigns into the 1990s as well, and the violence included attacks against targets in England and Europe as well as in Northern Ireland. Some of the attacks outside Northern Ireland may have been related to the presence of vulnerable targets.[9] The IRA had used bombs in English cities to demonstrate its ability to do so when it pleases. By the end of the twentieth century the violence had subsided as representatives of the IRA and the British government met to consider political solutions to the issue of Northern Ireland, and there has been at least some hope that an eventual settlement could be reached. The peace negotiations have spawned splinter groups from the IRA—the Real IRA and the Continuity IRA. It is somewhat ironic that the Provisional IRA (the current IRA) split from the Official IRA over questions of tactics and the use of violence, and now the process has repeated itself. The appearance of the splinter groups may also suggest that the violence may continue for some time to come since they have rejected compromise with the British.[10]

While there were many leftist dissident groups operating in Turkey in the 1970s, by the 1990s only a few remained. The PKK was the major survivor, but it became primarily a communal dissident organization, emphasizing the rights of the Kurdish population, and it was particularly strong in southeastern Turkey where there were concentrations of Kurds.[11] The party became involved in major guerrilla activities in the region, and used terrorist attacks to supplement the guerrilla activity. More than 30,000 Turkish troops, insurgents, and Kurdish villagers caught in the middle of the conflict died.[12] As the government gained the upper hand, the PKK also resorted to suicide attacks to continue the struggle and to raise the morale of the party members and their supporters.[13] The PKK lost much of its impetus for continuing the terrorist and guerrilla campaigns in the aftermath of the capture of its leader, who was convicted in a court of law, and sentenced to death. He has called for an end to PKK violence, apparently in exchange for the commutation of the death sentence. While not all PKK attacks have ceased, the group has become much less active.[14]

The Tamil Tigers continued their campaign into the 1990s and the twenty-first century. The group continued to utilize a variety of terrorist tactics in addition to guerrilla warfare and even conventional battles to control territory. There were attacks against the Sinhalese civilian population with major casualties, spectacular attacks against major targets, and the continuing campaign of assassinations against leading Sri Lankan politicians.[15] The Tigers also continued to use suicide bombings, and the LTTE was the single most active terrorist group in terms of such attacks. There have been some recent indications that the LTTE might negotiate some sort of settlement with the central government whereby Tamil areas would receive a significant amount of autonomy, but such hopes have been dashed before.

Right-wing groups were important in both Europe and the United States in the 1990s. These groups, usually referred to as neo-Nazi or neo-Fascist given their ideological links with the past or their glorification of earlier right-wing movements, did not disappear with the demise of communism; they have increasingly focused on a new enemy. The new danger was the presence of "foreign" groups within their societies. Some of the groups identified the danger as a continuing "Jewish threat."[16] More frequently these groups assumed anti-immigrant and racist stances as a consequence of the appearance of guest workers from Africa and the Middle East and refugees and asylum seekers from these areas, Asia, and East Europe. Frequently, Gypsies—whether migrants or indigenous to the countries—were also considered to be a foreign element that threatened local cultures and racial purity.[17] The antipathy toward foreigners increasingly assumed violent forms. Beginning with the end of the 1980s and carrying over into the 1990s, there was a clear increase in violent attacks, especially in Germany after the reunification.[18] By the mid-1990s it was estimated that there were more than 80 such groups in Germany with over 40,000 members, and that over 6,200 of these had been involved in violent activities.[19] While Germany may have seen the largest increase in such dissident organizations, there was increased activity in the United Kingdom and significant increases in anti-immigrant actions in Scandinavia as well.[20] While many of the organizations were very much secular groups and did not rely on religious principles, they were opposed to foreign religions, including Islam, since they are an important part of the foreign cultures.[21] The attacks by Al Qaeda on September 11 and in Madrid in 2004, have increased the negative view that these groups have about Islam. These extremist groups have formed alliances of convenience with the less ideological European skinheads. The skinheads are not necessarily an integral part of most of the neo-Nazi groups, but the more ideological racists can readily mobilize them for attacks on foreigners.[22] The various groups on the right share one other aspect of their Fascist and Nazi models, one that sets them apart from the extreme right in the United States. They do not fear or mistrust the government, and they often see a stronger government as an essential defense against outside influences.[23] Similar types of right-wing parties have appeared in the fledgling democracies of East Europe. The local skinheads have developed ties to the neo-Nazis just as their counterparts in West Europe did.[24] Extreme nationalists have targeted those that they consider to be foreign elements, including Jews, Turks (i.e., Muslims) in Bulgaria, and Gypsies virtually everywhere.[25] These groups have been as violent as the racist and highly nationalistic organizations in Western Europe with whom they share many of the same prejudices.

Similar extremist groups had been present in the United States, but in the 1990s the United States experienced an increase in the number of violent right-wing groups and the number of hate crimes went up as well.[26] The Order proved to be a precursor of a much greater trend. There was a multitude of different groups that operated. Many of them were anti-Semitic and opposed to what they called the Zionist Occupation Government—what they saw as the Jewish dominated national government. Virtually all of them had racist overtones and were opposed to immigrants who differed from the group's perception of a White, Christian (Protestant) country. While not all the groups had a religious base, many of the groups adhered to ideas of Christian Identity, which viewed Christianity as the preserve of the white race.[27] Their anti-Semitism and more recently anti-Islamic views were at times rooted in opposition to foreign cultures and what they regarded as foreign races. They have come to see the current political and cultural system in the United States as illegitimate, decadent, racially polluted, and dominated by foreign elements that will eventually enslave true Americans.[28] The presence of such groups became much more obvious, in part because of the rise of the militia movement in this decade with its emphasis on gun ownership, unusual interpretations of the Constitution, and resistance against government laws that the groups considered oppressive. As a consequence, some of these militia organizations also came to be called Christian Patriot organizations. Unlike earlier right-wing groups, they are willing to attack government agencies and officials.[29] The various groups regard personal gun ownership as the most important constitutional right, and resist any efforts by the government to limit ownership of weapons. A number of these organizations have also had a fascination with poisons like ricin and biological weapons that they planned to use against government officials.[30] The organizations saw the incidents with Randy Weaver and his family at Ruby Ridge in Idaho and the Branch Davidians in Texas as examples of overbearing government.[31] The idea of leaderless resistance has taken root within these groups. Formal organization has often been eschewed in favor of providing broad direction to the militants in the militia and Christian Patriot movements and racist organizations.[32] Timothy McVeigh's bombing in Oklahoma City fit within this framework. The number of militias and militia members declined after the Oklahoma City attack in 1995, but the units that have survived have become more extreme and active.[33]

Terrorist violence also appeared in the United States in the context of the struggle over abortion. For most of the activists religious principles fueled their opposition to abortion, but this religious feeling lacked the communalism of other groups. The activists agreed on the principle that abortion was not acceptable, but they were divided on most other theological issues. The militants normally confined themselves to property attacks—glue in locks, vandalism of clinics or cars of the workers, and arson attacks or bombs at clinics after working hours.[34] A small number of activists, however, took more extreme measures or supported those that did. Websites that provided addresses of clinic workers and inflammatory rhetoric were designed to "encourage" individuals to use violence to stop the abortions. There were assaults against workers at the clinics and even murders. A shadowy organization lacking formal structure called the Army of God appeared to provide some direction to the violence—an example of rather effective leaderless resistance.[35] The violence was not justified as revenge or retribution for performing abortions but as a deterrent to the future provision of abortion services.[36]

New violent communal groups appeared to complement the organizations that survived from the 1980s. Most of these communal terrorist groups involved some religious difference with the target state. Indonesia has faced a number of such situations, including the East Timor rebellion and a conflict in Papua (Irian Jaya or the former Dutch New Guinea) where largely Protestant Papuans have used terrorist guerrilla tactics.[37] At the other end of the country, the central government had recurring problems in Aceh, on the northern end of Sumatra. The Aceh sultanate was one of the last indigenous states to be subdued by the Dutch, and there have been groups that have sought to reestablish the old state. The Acehenese have followed a stricter and purer version of Islam that separates them from other Muslim Indonesians. In the 1980s, there was conflict in Aceh, but the Aceh Sumatra National Liberation Front (GAM) relied on guerrilla tactics. By 1991–92, when the guerrilla activity had been largely contained, the GAM began a terrorist campaign.[38] Foreign investments in the natural resources of Aceh became a major target for attack.[39] The appearance of a democratic government in Indonesia in 1998 led to an increase in dissident violence since the new government was weaker than the military regime it replaced.[40] The military government under General Suharto and then the civilian democratic government that replaced it both encouraged Javanese migrants to move to the region to dilute the local population (and to reduce land pressure in densely populated Java). The rebels also increasingly targeted these Javanese migrants.[41] These attacks, basically a form of ethnic cleansing by the dissidents, have been rather effective in convincing the Javanese to return home.

A form of communal ethnic cleansing occurred on Borneo (Kalimantan). As part of its ongoing efforts to ease overcrowding on the central islands, the Indonesian military government in the 1980s encouraged the inhabitants of Madura, an island on the north coast of Java, to migrate to Borneo. The native Dayak population, largely Christian, protested the migration since the Muslim Madurese were taking traditional Dayak lands. The Dayaks eventually resorted to violence and began to terrorize the Madurese to force them out. Madurese were murdered, their homes were burnt, and their other properties were destroyed. Between 1997 and 2001, approximately 1,100 people were killed in separate waves of violence and more than 100,000 were driven from their homes. This conflict was primarily ethnic or regional rather than religious. The Dayaks did not attack the other Muslim communities in Borneo, and, in fact, some long-term Muslim residents on the island joined in the attacks on the Madurese.[42] Violence also broke out in Ambion (Malaku Province) and in the Northern Malakus (including Sulawesi and Halmahera) between Christian and Muslim groups in Indonesia. Muslims drove out Christians where they could, and Christians practiced ethnic cleansing against Muslims.[43] The end of the military regime led to an increase in the violence. The conflict was further exacerbated by a declining economy that created greater pressure for access to fewer resources.[44] Muslim communities elsewhere in Indonesia formed paramilitary groups to help, including Laskar Jihad, created by the veterans of the wars in Afghanistan.[45] This aid was effective in some cases in helping the local Muslims win some of the confrontations with the Christians.[46]

Communalism centered on religious and ethnic differences that appeared in the successor states of Yugoslavia. In Bosnia and Herzegovina, ethnic cleansing became very common where the differences between the Slavic groups were basically religiously defined for the Muslim Bosniaks, Orthodox Serbs, and Catholic Croats. Local majorities of Croats, Serbs, and Muslims drove out members of the other groups in particular areas, although Serb forces used the practice much more widely than the other two groups.[47] The Serbs in Bosnia felt especially vulnerable in many ways since they were no longer the largest group. The Serbs feared that now they would lose access to jobs and other positions that they had been favored for in the past. The ethnic cleansing and terror by Serb paramilitary forces were often in those areas where the Serbian portion of the population had declined the most.[48] The Serbs in Bosnia received supplies of arms and other support, unofficially, from the remainder of Yugoslavia (Serbia and Montenegro) under the leadership of Slobodan Milosevic. Serb militias used mass killings and rape as ways to terrorize Muslims into abandoning their homes and claims to territory.[49] Serbian shelling and sniper fire directed against Muslims in the Bosnian cities were often designed to cause civilian casualties, and there were some indications that children were intentionally targeted to increase the fear and panic among the Muslims.[50] By the time the situation had stabilized toward the end of the 1990s well over a third of the population of Bosnia had been displaced from their old homes.[51]

The breakup of Yugoslavia led to problems for Serbia in Kosovo and for the new government of Macedonia with their Albanian populations. The majority of Albanians historically had a cultural link to Islam and also spoke a non-Slavic language. The Serb nationalism of the government in Belgrade under Milosevic, led to an effort to change the ethnic balance in Kosovo from one favoring Albanians to one favoring Serbs. These government efforts resulted in the formation of Kosovo Liberation Army (KLA) to fight back against the government forces. Attacks were directed against police, Serb civilians, and Albanians considered to be collaborating with the government.[52] Serb police became a special target for the dissidents, and it reached the point where Serbian police came to regard a transfer or assignment to Kosovo as tantamount to a death sentence.[53] The KLA also planned attacks to generate reprisals from the government security forces and the military. They fired on patrols from villages to encourage retaliation, used bombs against the Serb population, and tortured prisoners. The KLA was successful in driving a wedge between the population and the government; consequently, the government in Belgrade opted to try its own form of ethnic cleansing by driving most of the Albanian population out of the country by claiming they were not citizens but illegal residents. The attempts at forced migration finally engendered a response from the Western countries that resulted in the eventual withdrawal of Serb forces from the province, the return of the refugees, and the creation of an autonomous provincial government dominated by Albanian politicians. The success of the Albanians in Kosovo led to increased demands by the Albanian minority in Macedonia for greater autonomy and more rights in that new state. The Albanian dissidents in Macedonia attempted some of the same tactics as their counterparts in Kosovo. The Macedonian forces did react in the expected way in a few cases, but the response of the government was more controlled than was the case in Kosovo. Problems and tensions between the two groups, however, do remain.

Al Qaeda (The Base) was, of course, the terrorist group that came into worldwide prominence in the 1990s. The activities of this group have focused much more attention on terrorism. Al Qaeda is a modern transnational operation, consisting of an international network of loosely connected cells receiving some direction from the central leadership.[54]

Organizations in many countries are linked to it, permitting joint operations, the provision of local contacts for the different groups, and aid in money laundering.[55] The group also has been willing to support independent operations. A council would review proposed plans submitted by a variety of groups, and if it approved the plans, it would fund and support the operations.[56] These operations have permitted the groups to operate at relatively low costs as part of a terrorist campaign against the United States and its allies, including the ones in the Middle East. Al Qaeda has in effect been waging a global guerrilla war against the West, and especially the United States.[57] The lack of a rigid command structure makes Al Qaeda more difficult to defeat.[58] This network of terrorist organizations has proven to be one of the most dangerous groups in the world, striking wherever it sees opportunities. It had a hand in the bombings in Saudi Arabia, attacks on U.S. forces in Somalia in 1993, the attacks on the U.S. embassies in Kenya and Tanzania in 1998 that killed over 200 people, the suicide attack against the USS Cole in Aden, the September 11 attacks on the World Trade Center and the Pentagon, and the bombings of commuter trains in Madrid just before the Spanish general election in 2004. It appears to have been involved in the attack on Bali directed at Western tourists in 2002 and recent attacks on tourist hotels in Kenya that catered to Israeli tourists. One of the characteristics of Al Qaeda that sets it apart is that it has no set style of attack. The major attacks of the group have been innovative, hard to detect and deadly, all of which makes the group very dangerous indeed.[59]

Al Qaeda effectively got its start with the fighting in Afghanistan against the local communist regime and the Soviet troops sent to prop up the regime. Estimates vary, but there appear to have been as few as 10,000 and as many 17,000 such volunteers from more than 25 countries present in the ranks of the Afghan mujahedin.[60] Bin Laden had a chance to meet many of the individuals involved in the fighting either while he was in Afghanistan or in rest areas that he supported in Pakistan. Face-to-face contact is important—and even essential—in many Middle Eastern cultures, and the conflict in Afghanistan provided a unique opportunity for such contacts by bin Laden with individuals from a wide range of countries. The participation in the Afghan wars against the Soviets was essential for the links that have made Al Qaeda such a powerful organization.[61] Bin Laden's displeasure with the United States has resulted from U.S. support for Israel, support for Arab governments that are insufficiently religious, and the fact that the of U.S. troops on the soil of Saudi Arabia demonstrates the weakness of Muslim states in the face of a Western superpower.[62] The destruction of the Taliban regime in

Afghanistan removed a useful support for Al Qaeda, but it has been able to survive and continue to mount attacks. There are some indications that many of the key leaders of the group have relocated to Southeast Asian countries where they can find support in local Muslim communities and blend in with the local populations to at least some extent.[63]

A number of groups have benefited from Al Qaeda support for their operations. Notwithstanding the rhetorical emphasis given to the presence of Israel as a Western state in the Middle East, the organization seems to have had few, if any, links with Palestinian groups. In Egypt, the Islamic Group (Al Gama'a al Islamiyya), descended from the Muslim Brotherhood, had created significant problems for the government. Many of the members of the group fought in Afghanistan, and Egyptians are the most numerous national group of Al Qaeda operatives.[64] The group provided personnel for the attacks on the U.S. embassies in Kenya and Tanzania in 1998. In Egypt, the dissidents have also attacked government officials and facilities, and it had launched attacks on tourists, such as the one at Luxor in 1997. While not all the Islamic dissident groups operating in Egypt have links to Al Qaeda, the support has been quite important for some of them, and they in turn have helped Al Qaeda operations. In the Philippines the conflict between the Moros and the Christians has continued. The Muslim dissidents created new organizations in the 1990s that began to place greater stress on religious themes, including the need to implement Islamic law in an independent Moro state.[65] The most violent Islamic group has been Abu Sayyaf. The core of this group was the 300–500 Muslim Filipinos that had fought in Afghanistan; the group has links with Al Qaeda and has received support from that organization.[66] The group has been violently anti-Christian, and it has opposed any accommodation with the Christian population in the southern Philippines.[67] There are some indications that the group has evolved into a criminal organization focused on gaining income from such kidnappings.[68]

Violent Islamic groups have been very active in Algeria in the 1990s. The authoritarian government decided to permit relatively open elections that it thought it could win, but the military intervened to postpone the legislative elections when it became clear that the Islamic parties were going to win a substantial majority of the seats. The militant supporters of the Islamic parties then turned to guerrilla and terrorist violence, forming the Islamic Army Group (GIA), the Islamic Movement Army (MIA), and smaller groups. Many of the most militant dissidents in the two groups were Algerians who had fought in Afghanistan, and there appears to have been some support for the dissidents from Al Qaeda.[69]

The Islamic dissidents attacked those it broadly defined as supporters of the government, including bureaucrats, educators and other officials, journalists whose stories were considered to be pro-government, and even the families of members of the armed forces and security.[70] Algerians who were considered to be too European also became targets, including prominent women personalities and even schoolgirls who did not wear Islamic headscarves.[71] Foreigners also became targets.[72] Since the French government was supporting the government of Algeria throughout the violence, the Islamic dissidents began a bombing campaign in France, but the French intelligence agencies were able to capture many of those involved in the violence.[73] In a bold action, the Algerian dissidents even hijacked an Air France airliner in 1995. Their intent was to fly the plane to Paris and crash it into the city, probably with the Eiffel Tower as a target. The plan failed when French commandos stormed the plane while it was on the ground in Marseilles, freeing the passengers and killing the Algerian terrorists.[74] In addition, the more extreme dissidents launched a series of attacks on villages where the inhabitants were massacred, often in a very brutal fashion, in a an effort to spread even greater fear among the Algerian population.[75] The goal of such attacks was to demonstrate to the population in general the inability of the government to defend its own people or to punish villages for siding with the government. The death toll from terrorism, guerrilla attacks, and government actions in the 1990s surpassed 100,000 people, making the Algerian situation one of the most deadly conflicts in this period. At the turn of the century, there were some indications that a more open political system and reforms had weakened the insurgency and that the government was slowly regaining control of the country.

Communal terrorism continued in Kashmir in the 1990s. The violence increased as new groups appeared, either seeking an independent Kashmir or one attached to Pakistan. Thousands of militants from Pakistan and Afghanistan infiltrated into Kashmir.[76] By the late 1990s, the level of violence had increased and India was forced to commit additional resources to maintain control—security forces totaled 250,000 persons by the turn of the century.[77] In the increasing violence, the insurgents even practiced ethnic cleansing. The Muslims attacked Hindus in districts with Muslim majorities, and Hindus began fleeing from these areas.[78] Communal terrorism also appeared in Nigeria. Muslims and Christians began fighting each other in cities where the two groups were intermingled between the Muslim north and the more Christian south. More than 10,000 persons died in communal conflicts between 1999 and 2003 (not all due to fighting between Muslims and Christians).[79]

The groups involved in the violence between Christians and Muslims appear to have responded to local leaders rather than national ones. The communal violence has resulted in some effective ethnic cleansing in some areas.

Terrorism reappeared in Israel/Palestine, but the context and actors had changed somewhat. The PLO had renounced terrorism before the Oslo Accords, and after the Palestinian Authority had been set up, it was not in the PLO's interests to continue to use terror attacks. New groups that were willing to use terrorism, however, appeared. Hamas was by far the most important new group, but Islamic Jihad was involved in terrorist attacks as well. Both groups wanted to destroy Israel and create an Islamic Palestinian state. This emphasis on Islam has placed them partially at odds with the more secular PLO. Hamas and Islamic Jihad had earlier used terror attacks, including suicide bombings, in an effort to prevent the implementation of the Oslo agreements. They began the suicide attacks again in the late 1990s, and they have continued because they have proved to be cost-effective and relatively successful in inflicting damage on Israel.[80] While it was the religious organizations that initially used such attacks, secular groups like the Al-Aqsa Brigades, an offshoot of Fatah, have also begun to use them.[81] Israeli reprisals for the suicide assaults have led to a cycle of attack and retaliation, and retaliation for the retaliation, and so forth, that has increased casualties on both sides.[82] The Jewish extremists have used terrorism against the Palestinians and even other Israelis. Baruch Goldstein's attack on the worshippers at a mosque in Hebron was the most obvious. Yitzak Rabin's assassin apparently acted alone, but he was operating within a context in which many were suggesting that it was treason for any political leader to make peace with the Palestinians. Rabin's assassin and Goldstein are considered heroes by some in Israel.[83]

Violence has appeared in many of the successor states of the old Soviet Union. Some of this violence is guerrilla actions or conventional battles but some groups have relied on terrorism. In former Soviet Central Asia, the Islamic Movement of Uzbekistan (IMU) has sought to create a more Islamic state and opposed the secularism of President Islam Karimov (effectively a dictator). It attempted to assassinate Karimov and has set off bombs in the major cities.[84] While the Taliban was in power the IMU had support from Afghanistan and Al Qaeda, including many Chechen operatives. Chechnya has proven to be a major problem area for Russia as dissidents have fought a lengthy guerrilla campaign against the Russians in the province resulting in significant casualties on both sides. The Chechen dissidents have taken advantage of the opportunities that terrorism has provided for attacks against their adversary. Their actions have included car bombs, suicide attacks, hostage seizures, and kidnappings, both in Chechnya and neighboring provinces, major Russian cities, and abroad.[85] The raids that have involved hostage taking have often been very deadly. They have occupied a hospital in southern Russia, a Moscow theater in 2002, and a middle school in the Caucasus in 2004 in which hundreds of children and adults, taken as hostages, died. The Chechen dissidents are seeking separation from Russia on a variety of grounds. Some are nationalists that seek an independent state for their people. Others are religiously committed to creating an Islamic state in Chechnya.[86] Another group in the mix is the Chechen criminal groups, which are among the best organized of the criminal elements operating in Russia. These criminal groups would prefer to deal with a weak Chechen state rather than a stronger Russian one. Other dissidents have aided the Chechens in some cases. Some of the attacks, including ones involving hostages, may have been launched by non-Chechen Muslim dissidents sympathetic to their cause or by groups with links to Al Qaeda.[87]

The last part of the twentieth century saw the appearance of new groups willing to use terrorism. Aum Shinrikyo (Supreme Truth) in Japan was an unusual religious cult that combined beliefs from a number of religions. It was rooted in the messianic vision of its leader, Shoko Asahara, who believed that an apocalypse was required to cleanse the world of unbelievers and that the current Japanese government had to be destroyed and a theocratic state created in its place.[88] Asahara attracted many devoted followers, and he was able to build a significant financial base for the group. The Japanese government after World War II traditionally accepted unusual cults in the country, providing Aum with the opportunity to grow and to prepare weapons for the apocalypse.[89] The group attempted to gain access to nuclear technology and some of its members developed biological and chemical weapons.[90] When Japanese authorities began to investigate the group, Asahara decided to use the biological and chemical weapons to deflect the investigations.[91] The culmination of Aum's activities was the use of the sarin gas in the Tokyo subway system in 1993. While only a handful of people died, many thousands became ill. The actual objective of the attack was to kill thousands and spread terror throughout the city. Many of the intended victims would have been government employees; therefore, a successful attack with high death rates could have seriously disrupted the government.[92] Since the deaths were limited, however, the Japanese government was able to respond effectively and to arrest Asahara and other key members of the group.

A new type of violent group has appeared with the rise of environmental consciousness, especially in the Western world. Environmental groups, such as the Earth Liberation Front (ELF) and Earth First, began to attack property to protest or attempt to stop activities that they felt damaged the environment. They spiked trees, damaged logging or construction equipment, burned down ski lodges or homes intruding into areas previously clear of such structures, and vandalized gas-guzzling sport utility vehicles (SUVs) and all terrain vehicles (ATVs).[93] Animal rights groups, broadly part of the environmental movement but separate in some ways, have attempted to protect animals from exploitation and to keep them from being killed whenever possible. Organizations such as the Animal Liberation Front (ALF), which is most active in the United Kingdom and the United States, have used property terrorism to defend animals with attacks on labs using animals for research, fur operations, and clothing stores with products that required animals to be killed. Such attacks began in the 1980s, but increased in the 1990s.[94] The ALF has also promoted leaderless resistance by documenting successful operations on its web pages. More extreme groups, like the Animal Rights Militia (ARM)—which may be a front group for segments of the ALF, have assaulted researchers and workers, have been willing to use bombs in efforts to achieve their goals, even if the lives of the workers in the targeted facilities are endangered.[95] While the environmental and animal rights groups have normally sought to avoid harming anyone, attacks on individuals have occurred.[96]

Environmental issues and ethnic concerns have come together in the Niger Delta region of eastern Nigeria, which contains the oil resources that are so important for Nigeria. Most of the wealth from the oil has flowed to the central government, where admittedly much of it has been wasted on government projects or for corrupt politicians. The oil drilling operations have not only disrupted the local communities with few rewards, they have actually harmed the local environment because of pollution. Livelihoods from fishing and farming have been threatened, and there has been land loss because of the activities of the oil multinationals.[97] The opposition has been rooted in particular ethnic groups because they have been most affected by the environmental degradation. When normal political channels provided little satisfaction, dissidents resorted to launching attacks on the state and oil companies, with sabotage of pipelines being quite frequent.[98] The response of the government, however, has largely been one of repression by the military and security forces, including the destruction of whole villages and reprisals against the ethnic community for the actions of the dissidents.[99]

Governments still remained involved in terrorist activity in this period. India and Pakistan were still willing to support dissidents on the other side of the border. There is evidence, for example, that Pakistan's intelligence service supported rebels in Assam and India in turn fostered unrest in Pakistan.[100] The Taliban regime in Afghanistan cooperated with Al Qaeda in supporting groups in other countries. Iran maintained camps in the Sudan that have been used to train and support radical Islamic groups in a variety of countries, including Algeria.[101] Probably more important than external government aid was support from private groups. As noted above, Al Qaeda provided funding and assistance to a number of groups in the Middle East, Indonesia, and the Philippines in a mutually beneficial relationship. FARC in Colombia has formed connections with other groups in order to access outside expertise. Members of the IRA and the JRA have been brought to Colombia to train FARC cadres so that an urban bombing campaign could be launched.[102] Diaspora groups continued to be important sources of funding for groups in a number of countries.

Asian governments have continued to support unofficial groups that have been operating against dissident groups. Christian vigilante groups in the Philippines have been opposed to Muslim autonomy and have continued to undertake operations against suspected dissidents, probably with the aid of at least some local officials.[103] In Indonesia, it has been the Christian communities that have been disadvantaged by indirect support for Muslim groups as local officials and the military have helped Muslim militias like Laskar Jihad move to the areas of communal confrontation.[104] India has also seen the continued use of death squads and other forms of violence that is at least tolerated by some government officials. The military and security forces have used the techniques that it pioneered during the Sikhs rebellion in other parts of the country, especially Kashmir. The death squads have targeted not only dissidents but also human rights activists and other critics of the government.[105] Rape has been prevalent among the Indian forces operating in Muslim areas and appears to have been used as a means of terrorizing the potentially dissident population.[106]

Elsewhere in India there have been outbreaks of communal violence. Proponents of Hinduvata have sought to purify the country and have been willing to use violence to achieve their ends. Hindu extremists reclaimed a Hindu holy site at Ayodhya where a Muslim mosque existed after violent confrontations with Muslims. The violence at Ayodhya sparked violent outbreaks in many other areas of India, with Hindus attacking Muslims and Muslims retaliating and vice versa.[107] Much of the violence has been generically anti-Muslim as was particularly apparent in anti-Muslim riots that occurred in Mumbai (Bombay).[108] Hindu extremists have also attacked Christians, including missionaries, as an unwanted foreign influence.[109] Local police have often ignored these attacks in some cases, while local politicians have encouraged such attacks or failed to actively prosecute Hindus who are responsible for the actions.[110] It has been suggested that the Hindu nationalists and their political organizations are a form of middle-class authoritarianism that have characteristics very similar to the fascists parties operating in Europe prior to World War II.[111] The nationalistic fervor of these groups is obviously on par with that of the various fascist parties that appeared in the earlier era, and there may well be an increasing similarity in the emphasis on violence.

In Zimbabwe, the government of President Mugabe has tolerated the actions of paramilitary groups that have supported his party. Opposition politicians and their supporters have faced violence, intimation and murder from members of the government party and other militants.[112] Further, the paramilitaries and party militias have also attacked white farmers as part of a campaign to take over their landholdings and distribute them to government loyalists. Mugabe refused to let the police enforce court injunctions against those illegally occupying the farms or to provide any protection for the farmers.[113] Government involvement in terrorism has also appeared in Colombia. The Self Defense Forces of Colombia (AUS) were formed to deal with the threats from drug cartels and leftists. The government has tolerated the activities of the AUS, which was formed because of the inadequacies of the armed forces in dealing with threats to the state. The AUS has grown to the point that it has been able to mobilize as many as 8,000 active fighters. They have become part of the reasons why the government has lost control of its own territories since they have increasingly been able to operate on their own.[114]

Governments have also supported efforts at ethnic cleansing in a number of situations. In the Sudan, the government has given free rein to local militias in its war with the non-Muslim south. Militias have also been attacking the inhabitants of Darfur without any meaningful intervention by officials—and in reality with their apparent support. There is also evidence that earlier the government practiced ethnic cleansing against Nubians by supporting similar militias.[115] As noted earlier, ethnic cleansing was practiced by the Serbs with the support of their quasi-governmental leadership. Ethnic cleansing has also occurred in Kosovo after the forces of Yugoslavia were withdrawn. The Albanians, in de facto control of the province, began to force out the remaining Serbs and

Gypsies.[116] Violence against the Gypsies in other former Communist countries has been ignored by police and local authorities in many cases.[117] Local police in Germany have also failed to intervene at times when attacks against refugees and asylum seekers have taken place.[118]

Rwanda also saw communal violence between the Hutu and Tutsi carried to extremes. In Rwanda the majority Hutus controlled the government shortly after independence. Party militias attached to some of the ruling parties murdered opposition politicians and their supporters in early years, and there had been some earlier massacres of Tutsis and killings carried out by death squads and the security forces.[119] In 1994, Rwanda's president negotiated a power-sharing arrangement with Tutsi rebels who had invaded the country. A SAM missile, probably launched by Hutu extremists, shot down his plane as he was returning to the capital after the negotiations.[120] Hutu extremists in the government used the presence of the rebel forces and the death of the president as excuses to launch attacks on the minority Tutsi population in the country. Hutu party militias, sometimes supported by troops, massacred the Tutsis wherever they could be found.[121] The government hid news of the massacres in order to reduce the likelihood of foreign intervention and to limit Tutsi flight so that the victims would be easier to find and kill. There were also instances of government officials delaying the refugees at the border until they could be killed.[122] These actions indicate that the Hutu extremists intended to commit genocide and that the attacks were not simply ethnic cleansing. Somewhere between 500,000 and a million Tutsis, well over half of the Tutsi population, died in the massacres in Rwanda.[123] There have also been periodic outbreaks of communal violence in neighboring Burundi where the minority Tutsis had managed to stay in power in the years since independence.[124] The victims have been Hutus who have been attacked at random as the Tutsi groups attempt to control the majority group in the population by terrorizing them.

Objectives and Causes

Whereas the previous period had seen large numbers of leftist groups using terrorism, the underlying causes for terrorism in this period were more mixed. There were a few leftist groups that remained active, but only in Colombia were they major contributors to terrorism in this period. Right-wing ideological groups in the form of skinheads, neo-Nazis, and other racist groups were much more prevalent. Environmental groups were also ideological dissidents who were willing to use violence. These groups are closer to the left since the environmental groups are usually anti-capitalist since unrestrained growth is a major cause of the environmental degradation.

Communal violence was more prevalent relative to ideological terrorism during this time. Some of the communal terrorism was ethnic as in the case of the Dayaks, ETA, Corsicans, Aceh, and the Albanians (both as targets and perpetrators). The government terrorism in Burundi and the genocide in Rwanda were ethnic as well. The IRA and LTTE continued to reflect a mix of ethnic and religious factors. The ethnic cleansing in Bosnia and elsewhere also reflected varying mixes of ethnicity, cultural identity, and religion. Many of the other communal terrorist groups operating in this period were primarily religious. The dissident movements in the southern Philippines, Algeria, Kashmir, Uzbekistan, and Christians and Muslims in Malaku and Ambion, both Christians and Muslims in Nigeria, and Al Qaeda were largely rooted in religious communalism. Aum Shinrikyo was the exemplar of religious communalism. The Jewish extremists in Israel were also more driven by religious views than ethnic ones. Religion was the dominant factor in the antiabortion terrorism that occurred in the United States, but it was not really communal.

The antiabortion groups combined ideology and religion in an instrumental way since they were devoted to accomplishing a single objective. There were a few other cases of instrumental terrorism in this period. As was the case for earlier chapters, the governmental support of terrorism by paramilitaries or militias against citizens frequently had elements of instrumental terrorism. It was probably strongest in Zimbabwe where the overriding goal of Mugabe appears to have been staying in power. Instrumental terrorism was becoming more relevant in Colombia. Increasingly FARC has been more concerned with maintaining control of the drug producing and processing areas in the country with the concomitant wealth. Similarly, the AUS has increasingly been corrupted by drug money.[125]

The weakness of states has clearly contributed to the appearance of terrorism and in some cases to its success just as it has in the past. The government of Colombia has continued to lack control over much of its territory. At times it has been a spectator in the struggles between FARC and the AUS. The breakup of empires left weaker states and increased vulnerability. Both Indonesia and the Philippines have been weak as states in part because they are colonial creations that lack historical connections or identification.[126] There are areas of both states where the government lacks authority and control.[127] Faced with insurgencies in many areas, the government has been short of resources. East Timor was able to finally gain its independence in part because Indonesian forces were spread thin in response to terrorism and uprisings elsewhere in the island. The attack on the tourist facilities in Bali in 2002 was probably also facilitated because the government lacked the resources to monitor all the potentially dangerous groups in the country. The military has been able to control the situation in Aceh so far, but that has meant fewer resources elsewhere in the country.

The state supported terror in Zimbabwe resulted from the weakness of the regime. Mugabe could not automatically count on the support of more militant elements in the ruling part, and thus he had to defer to them on issues like the farm invasions.[128] The government in Nigeria has not been strong enough to prevent the violence between Muslims and Christians in the cities where the two groups previously had lived together amicably. The weaknesses or even the lack of government in Bosnia and Kosovo facilitated the ethnic cleansing activities that occurred in those two areas. The regime in Uzbekistan is actually solidly established in some respects, but it clearly has lacked the strength that was present in the Soviet era when dissidents were dealt with swiftly and effectively. The problems that Russia has had with Chechnya are another example of state weakness facilitating outbreaks of terrorism. It must be noted, however, that stronger states can still be the scene of terrorism. The United States, the United Kingdom (Northern Ireland), France (Corsica), Israel, and Japan (Aum Shinrikyo) have all seen major terrorist problems, and none of them would qualify as weak states.

Globalization and modernization have been important factors in the appearance of some of the terrorist movements. The religious communal groups were often reacting to changing circumstances. Many of these groups are opposed to Western secular values and have recognized the danger that local cultures can disappear in a more homogenous world.[129] Aum Shinrikyo attracted young Japanese who were unhappy with the materialist orientation of their society.[130] The ideas behind Hinduvata include opposition to the intrusion of foreign religions and ideas. Many of the Jewish extremists fear Western materialism because it interferes with religious practice.[131] Many Islamic groups, including Al Qaeda, have been opposed to the intrusion of foreign Western values, modernization, and secularism.[132] The Muslim dissidents in Algeria have been something of an extreme case in their attacks on anyone and anything that appears to reflect the cultural contamination of the West.

Many of the right-wing groups also constitute a reaction to modernization and globalization. The groups in the United States have been opposed to the presence of nonwhite immigrants and outside influences.

The anti-Semitism often present in these groups is another reflection of opposition to globalization and the diversity that it brings. The religious ideas of some of the groups lead them to oppose the secular humanist ideas of the modern world, which they see as a threat to basic religious tenets and a moral society.[133] The neo-Nazi groups in Europe share many of the same orientations toward modern society. The religious and cultural differences that have been obvious with the presence of the new migrants and guest workers are one outcome of an increasingly global society.

Other groups have reacted negatively to globalization in this period. The Corsican dissidents have clearly reacted to the increasing presence of outside groups, sometimes defined to include French from the mainland. Basque and Irish nationalists have in part also reacted to urbanization and industrialization that have threatened the rural economies and the local system of cultural values that are valued.[134] The environmental activities have also been responding to globalization and the damage that can be done to the environment and to animals. These reactions as well as the actions of the dissidents in the Niger Delta and the attacks of ALF and ELF are the more extreme forms of protest. Deindustrialization, less pollution, preservation of nature, and similar objectives espoused by these groups can be seen as antithetical to increasing global integration.

This period also provided some evidence for Huntington's ideas about the clash of civilizations, but then he formulated his ideas with this period in mind. The conflicts in Nigeria, the Philippines, Bosnia, Kosovo, Macedonia, and the communal fighting in Malauku and Ambion all center on interactions along or across the borders between Western Christianity or Eastern Orthodoxy and Islam. Bosnia, of course, was the place where all three met. The right-wing movements in Europe and in the United States were reacting to the presence of foreign cultures as well. While the Chechen dissidents were also nationalist, the conflict in this area was exacerbated by the different religious cultures involved. The conflicts in Kashmir, Lebanon, and Sri Lanka are similar in this regard. In fact, in this era there are a significant number of conflicts involving groups in different civilizations or cultures. Of course, other conflicts were within specific civilizations. While fracture lines between civilizations may explain some of the outbreaks, or perhaps the severity of the outbreaks of terrorism, they hardly explain all of them.

Successes and Failures

There were successes and failures with the terrorist organizations. In some cases it is difficult to judge the ultimate outcome of the struggles of some of the groups, but many of them have at least managed to survive. In other cases there have been at least some partial successes. The Turkish government did make some concessions to Kurdish groups in an effort to undercut support for the PKK.[135] The Corsican dissidents and the ETA have managed to survive even if they have not convinced the parent states to grant them independence. The ETA, however, has been successful indirectly. Because of its activities, the Spanish government has conceded greater autonomy to the Basque region. Moderate political groups have gained reforms that probably would not have been granted with the terrorism of the ETA.[136] A similar conclusion can be drawn about Northern Ireland. The IRA managed to eventually bring the British to the negotiating table. In Macedonia, the Albanian minority did gain some concessions from the government as well. As one dissident leader noted for both Kosovo and Macedonia, more concessions were gained with a few months of armed struggle than in a decade of peaceful politics.[137] The Dayaks were probably the most successful since their attacks drove out the majority of the Madurese migrants and dissuaded others from even attempting to move to the area. The ethnic cleansing undertaken by the various groups in Bosnia also succeeded in forcing out minority groups. At the end of the struggle, the Serbs controlled slightly over half of the territory—more than they controlled before the outbreak of the violence. The violence was effective for the Bosnian Serbs since it permitted them to secure additional land within a system of effective self-governance.[138] The results of the communal violence in Nigeria are too recent to be able to tell the extent to which minorities have left the areas of violence.

Elsewhere, groups have frequently adopted the tactic of using "indiscriminate" acts of terror to generate harsh countermeasures by the government that will polarize ethnic communities.[139] This polarization is a practical step toward the goal or independence or autonomy since it would create a greater likelihood of ethnic separation. Such polarization has occurred in Sri Lanka.[140] Extremists in India used violence and terrorism to unify the Hindu community and separate it from the Muslim population.[141] The KLA in Kosovo was very successful with this tactic. The activities of the Albanian dissidents in Macedonia have increased the polarization between the Macedonian and Albanian communities, making compromise in a multiethnic state less likely rather than more likely.[142] This tactic of polarization is a modern variation of the tactics used in the Balkans by the Christian populations in the Ottoman Empire. Of course, if the international intervention does not occur, the polarization can lead to heavy casualties among the ethnic group. There is now greater religious separation between Muslims and Christians in Indonesia. In the Philippines and Aceh, the separatists continue to persist in their struggle, denying their governments the opportunity to eliminate them.

The Islamic dissidents in Egypt and the IMU in Uzbekistan have accomplished relatively little to date. Some actions have embarrassed the governments or even cost them revenues, but there has been no major threat to the political systems. The Chechens have mounted a more serious threat with their guerrilla and terrorist activities. The dissidents control some territory in the province, and they have demonstrated the capacity to strike at Russian interests in Chechnya, the North Caucasus, and in Moscow (and therefore anywhere). It does not appear likely that the Chechens will be defeated any time soon, and they may eventually win the right to negotiate and gain concessions from a weary opponent. The same situation could occur in Kashmir, although both India and Russia, as heterogeneous states, may be loath to create a precedent of granting autonomy to one area under the threat of continuing violence since that could prompt similar tactics from other groups. In Algeria it would appear that the threat from the Islamic groups has been defeated for the moment. On the other hand, the military now has a reduced role in the current government, reforms have occurred, and the more moderate Islamic parties have been operating within the system. The groups operating in Israel/Palestine have also achieved some of their goals. At various times, Jewish extremists and Muslim dissidents have disrupted peace negotiations. Both groups of extremists see success in essentially negative terms at the present time. As long as they can prevent a definitive peace settlement there is hope of achieving the maximum goals. Of course, the goals are mutually incompatible; thus, at least one set of extremists is bound to lose. If peace does occur, then both groups seeking the maximum objectives will have lost.

Aum Shinrikyo clearly failed in its terrorist campaign. The biological and chemical attacks failed to prevent investigations and the group has been severely weakened as a consequence of prosecutions for the subway attacks. The success of Al Qaeda is more difficult to evaluate. Its spectacular attacks have generated increased opposition to the West in at least some parts of the Middle East. The response of the United States and others to the 9/11 attacks increased alienation between the West and many Muslims in the world, an event that may be exactly what bin Laden hoped to accomplish. Whether or not a clash of civilizations is actually going on, bin Laden has clearly seen the conflict in those terms and has done all within his power to increase the conflict between the West and the Muslim world.[143] The attacks and responses may well make future confrontations more likely. This outcome would be a clear victory in the eyes of the key leaders of Al Qaeda, one more important than the damage done by the attacks themselves. The bombs in the commuter trains in Madrid, in 2004, were quite effective in demonstrating that the organization was still operating, and the attacks contributed to an election victory by parties willing to remove Spanish troops from Iraq.

The ideologically motivated terrorist groups were often successful in achieving some of the their objectives. The vandalism and violence of antiabortion activists have deterred some, who might otherwise provide the procedure. Overall, abortions have become harder to obtain in some areas of the country as a direct result of these activities.[144] In the United States, the groups of the extreme right have had a nuisance value but they have had no real influence on national policy even though they continue to survive. The same is true for the many European groups. The European neo-Nazis have been more successful, however, in terms of influencing policy. In addition, a number of European countries recently have made emigration more difficult and restricted the use of guest workers.[145] The longer-term objectives of gaining control of the government or changing the political system have not yet been obtained.

FARC in Colombia has been eminently successful in maintaining their base and destabilizing the government with a combination of guerrilla warfare and campaigns of terrorism. While they have not imposed a leftist regime in Colombia, the government has no likelihood in the immediate future of defeating them and gaining effective control of the countryside. The environmental and animal rights groups have also accomplished some of their goals. Logging has been made more expensive, and it is possible that some development activities have been canceled. Some companies no longer use animals for product tests, and some firms that supplied animals for testing no longer do so. The groups in the Niger Delta have managed to gain some changes from the oil companies as a consequence of their attacks.

The efforts by governments in support of terrorism and ethnic cleansing have succeeded all too well in most cases. When government support is present, the paramilitaries and others have sufficient resources and do not have to fear arrest; thus, the damage they can do is much greater. The Indian practices in Kashmir and elsewhere may ultimately prove to be counterproductive, but in the short term the lid has been kept on. Since death squads and extra-legal activities worked in Punjab, the government is unlikely to consider changing what has to be regarded as a winning strategy. Mugabe has been able to keep himself in power in Zimbabwe, although the situation in that country has gotten progressively worse and his support for militants may ultimately backfire. The ethnic cleansing in Kosovo by the Serbs failed since it triggered outside intervention. The AUS in Colombia has managed to damage the leftist at times and has supported the government, but the paramilitary groups have become something of a threat in their own right. Efforts at ethnic cleansing supported by the government in the Sudan have been very effective. Many in the targeted groups have been killed, and many others have fled. The genocide in Rwanda eliminated large numbers of Tutsis in the country, but ultimately the Hutu militants lost power to the rebel Tutsi group. Interestingly enough, the three clearest cases of genocide in the twentieth century by the Ottoman Turks, German Nazis, and Hutu extremists have been undertaken by regimes that could not manage to survive the conflicts they were engaged in.

Summary

The end of the twentieth century and the beginning of the twenty-first was characterized by a large number of groups that still used terror. There may have been somewhat fewer incidents, but there was no clear decline in the number of victims. Some of the terrorist campaigns—including Algeria, Sri Lanka, Chechnya, and Bosnia—and the genocide in Rwanda were very deadly. Suicide attacks also became more prevalent in this period, which led to increased casualties. The attacks on the World Trade Center towers and the Pentagon were the most obvious examples of committed terrorists willing to die and to inflict significant casualties on a general target population supporting a government with policies contrary to the desires of the terrorist group.

Communal groups were the most common in this period while left-wing terrorism declined. While right-wing terrorism increased, it was not to levels where ideological terrorism was as great as in the previous period. Among the communally based groups, religious communalism appears to have increased somewhat relative to ethnic varieties. Al Qaeda was an explicitly religious terrorist organization, and it was the most innovative group to appear in terms of tactics and techniques. Its loose network structure was also relatively rare but quite successful in permitting the organizations and most of its leaders to survive even when it was the target of the security agencies and military forces of the United States and many other countries. One of the commonalties that many of the groups in this period shared, whether they were ideological (right or left) or communal (religious or ethnic) was opposition to globalization.

Another factor that came into play in this period with greater salience was the increasing involvement of drug traffickers with different terrorist groups. The importance of such connections was most obvious in the case of Colombia and Peru when the Shining Path and MRTA were at their most threatening, but the insidious influence of the drug trade has affected others as well. The prevalence of these linkages has increased and have involved a wide variety of dissident groups, including the Chechen rebels, the PKK in Kurdistan, Al Qaeda. various groups in Lebanon and Afghanistan over the years, by Uzbek dissidents, the KLA in Kosovo and by other groups in the Balkans, and the LTTE in Sri Lanka.[146] Another indication of how lucrative, and corrupting, the drug trade can be is the fact that the Pakistani intelligence services have funded many of their operations in the region, including aid to dissident groups in India, with the proceeds from the drug trade.[147]

One final point to note is that this period was characterized by a substantial number of terrorist groups that were at least partially successful. Of course, an even larger number of other groups appeared very briefly on the political scene, and when they failed, they were never heard of again. The groups that lasted long enough to make effective statements or to mount attacks over a period of time did obtain at least some of their goals with regularity. They publicized the cause and caused some discomfort to the government. The groups, however, generally did not achieve their ultimate political objectives in terms of new governments or new states. Ethnic cleansing activities were more successful in at least some cases in clearing areas of minority population and creating more homogenous areas. Such operations succeeded with government collaboration and at times by independent efforts of local populations. These successes are likely to lead to the continuing use of the technique in the future.

Group	*Type*	*Objectives*	*Casualties*	*Success*
PKK	Communal (ethnic) and ideological (left)	Create an independent Kurdish state with Marxist government	Terrorism and guerrilla struggle result in very large numbers of casualties	Capture of leader has disrupted the group's efforts, at least temporarily
FARC	Ideological (left) and instrumental	Create leftist government and protect source of drug profits	Terrorism and guerrilla efforts have led to moderate number of deaths	Leftists have survived and control significant parts of Colombia, including drug-producing areas

Continued

Continued

Group	Type	Objectives	Casualties	Success
ETA	Communal (ethnic)	Create an independent Basque homeland	Deaths have mounted as a consequence of a struggle lasting more than 30 years	Basque region has greater autonomy and central government has made many concessions, but not independence
IRA	Communal (ethnic and religious)	Join Northern Ireland to the Republic	More than a thousand dead in 30 years of struggle	British government has made concessions, but Northern Ireland still part of United Kingdom
Tamil Tigers	Communal (ethnic)	Independent Tamil state in Sri Lanka	Terrorism and guerrilla actions had led to major casualty totals	Independence not achieved, but central government cannot defeat LTTE
Neo-Nazis and others in Europe	Ideological (right) with communal overtones	Create right-wing governments and purge "foreign" influences (ethnic and religious)	Deaths relatively few, but many assaults and injuries	European governments have restricted immigration and changed policies in response to violence
Militia movement et al in United States	Ideological (right) with communal overtones	Create right-wing government and purge "foreign" influnce (ethnic and religious)	Thousands of assaults, no major attacks with casualties before Oklahoma City in 1995	Little discernible effect but pressures to reduce immigration have appeared
Antiabortion in United States	Communal (religious) but single-issue	Prevent abortion or at least reduce availability	Relatively few deaths, some injuries, property damage	Abortions have become harder to obtain
Aceh Sumatra National Liberation Front	Communal (ethnic and regional with religious overtones)	Re-create independent state of Aceh	Moderate casualties from various forms of violence	Central government has been able to maintain control
Dayaks on Borneo	Communal (ethnic)	Drive out Madurese migrants	Moderate casualties, many displaced	Most Madurese have left and further migration discouraged

Continued

Continued

Group	Type	Objectives	Casualties	Success
Christians versus Muslims in Ambion and Malaku	Communal (religious)	Cleansing of areas of members of other faith	Fairly heavy casualties from communal violence	Many areas cleansed
Hinduvata groups in India	Communal (religious)	Drive out foreign religious influences (Islam, Christianity)	Heavy from communal fighting	Foreign influences still present but under threat
Serbs in Bosnia	Communal (religious and ethnic)	Attempt to attach Serb areas of Bosnia to Serbia	Heavy from terrorism, fighting, and ethnic cleansing	Serb areas remain in Bosnia, but Serbs have autonomous control of more territory
Serbs in Kosovo	Communal (ethnic and religious)	Repopulate Kosovo with Serb majority	Relatively few deaths, many Albanians temporarily displaced	Outside intervention stops effort, and Kosovo gains autonomy from central government
KLA	Communal (ethnic and religious)	Create independent Albanian state or join Kosovo to Albania	Relatively few deaths	Violence triggers government attempt at ethnic cleansing, foreign intervention, autonomy for Kosovo and probably independence in the future
Albanians in autonomous Kosovo	Communal (ethnic and religious)	Ethnic cleansing of Serbs and Gypsies	Relatively few deaths but many assaults	Serbs and Gypsies have fled from many areas
Albanians in Macedonia	Communal (ethnic and religious)	Greater rights for Albanians or join Albania	Relatively few	Some concessions and policy changes made by government
Al Qaeda	Communal (religious)	End Western influence in the Middle East and overthrow pro-Western regimes	Heavy from a small number of major attacks plus support for other dissidents using terrorism	Supporters mobilized and a number of regimes threatened, ultimate effects unknown
Islamic Group (Egypt)	Communal (religious)	Establish Islamic regime in Egypt	Moderate	Regime has damaged the dissidents but has not been able to eliminate them

Continued

Continued

Group	Type	Objectives	Casualties	Success
Abu Sayyaf, Moro National Liberation Front	Communal (religious with ethnic overtones)	Establish a Moro state in the southern Philippines	Very heavy through years of fighting and terrorism	Government has made little headway but dissidents have gained little
Algeria (GIA, MIA)	Communal (religious)	Create an Islamic state	Very heavy from fighting, terrorism, massacres	Dissidents threatened the state, and political system has become more open, dissidents have been losing ground
Kashmir	Communal (religious and some ethnic)	Create an independent Kashmir or join Kashmir to Pakistan	Heavy from terrorism and guerrilla warfare	Dissidents have survived and prevented India from consolidating control
Hamas and others	Communal (religious with ethnic overtones)	Create an independent, Islamic Palestinian state	Moderate, including large number of suicide attacks	Uncertain what portion of area will be governed by Palestinians and under what conditions
Chechens	Communal (ethnic and religious)	Independent Chechnya, perhaps Islamic	Heavy from guerrilla fighting and terrorism	Uncertain, area still in turmoil, but Russian control weak
Islamic Movement of Uzbekistan	Communal (religious)	Overthrow regime and create Islamic state	Light from terrorism and guerrilla activity	Little immediate effects but unrest remains
Aum Shinrikyo	Communal (religious)	Create a theocratic state in Japan	Few, but attempt to kill thousands	Leaders in jail, and movement weakened
ELF, ALF	Ideological (general left-wing)	Preserve environment and rights of animals	Most attacks directed against property, only a few injuries	Businesses have changed some practices, greater awareness, dissidents still present
India	Instrumental death squads	Defeat uprising in Kashmir, deal with dissidents elsewhere	Heavy	Situation in Kashmir still not controlled by government

Continued

Continued

Group	Type	Objectives	Casualties	Success
Philippines (Government)	Death squads, support for paramilitary groups	Defeat continued efforts to create Moro state in southern Philippines	Heavy	Muslim separatist groups continue to operate
Zimbabwe	Instrumental	Preserve Mugabe regime	Moderate	Regime has retained control, but country political and economically weak
Self Defense Groups of Colombia	Ideological (right-wing) and Instrumental	Eliminate leftist threat to Colombia, tacitly supported by government	Heavy, including campaigns against presumed supporters of FARC	Somewhat effective in weakening FARC, but corrupted by drug money
Rwanda	Communal (ethnic)	Genocide	Very heavy	Over half of Tutsi population killed
Burundi	Communal (ethnic)	Paramilitary attacks to keep Tutsi minority in power	Heavy from random violence against Hutus and some major massacres	Tutsis remain in control but future of regime uncertain
Niger Delta	Ideological (environmental) and Communal (ethnic)	Gain greater control of natural resources, stop destruction of environment, local autonomy	Few from dissident attacks	Some apparent concessions from government, future uncertain

CHAPTER ELEVEN

Conclusions

Terrorism has been a problem for governments at least since the time of the Greeks and the Romans and has been more common than is commonly thought. Additional cases from the past will become known as historical investigations analyze earlier violent group activities from perspectives that take into account the possibility that dissident groups used terrorist tactics to achieve their political goals. This volume may even serve to encourage some research using new perspectives. Terrorism has occurred in virtually all parts of the world and in all types of society. Even the totalitarian states that avoided or eliminated dissident violence were responsible for state terrorism against their own citizens. Some types of groups or forms of terrorism have been more frequent in different historical periods. No one cause for outbreaks of terrorism was obvious in the preceding chapters, but terrorism was more likely to occur under some circumstances. Since there is no single cause for terrorism, it is unlikely that there can be any single response that is guaranteed to prevent or overcome the dissidents that rely on terrorism.

Frequency and Severity over Time

Chapters nine and ten indicates that the use of terrorism has become more prevalent in the period after 1970. The increase in terrorist activity may have occurred because increasing global communications made the use of terrorist techniques known to more and more groups. Dissidents in earlier times did not need to rely on terrorism since rebellions could work. Terrorism increased in the 1700s and 1800s based on the available evidence, but much of the violence in these years still relied on conventional revolts and insurgent armies. By the 1900s, however, weaponry had given an edge to government forces in many cases, leaving terrorism and guerrilla warfare as more viable options than attempted armed revolts. The Boxers fared better when they used terror and intimidation than when they relied on conventional military tactics against Western troops. By the end of the twentieth century the disparity of weaponry between governments and potential dissidents was such that armed revolts against reasonably powerful states were increasingly difficult (although not impossible) to mount.

The preceding chapters thus provide reasonable evidence that terrorism by dissident groups has become more common, although it is not completely certain that such violence peaked in the twentieth or early twenty-first centuries. There have been peaks and valleys through time, and peaks and valleys in different regions. At least locally there was a peak in the United States around the time of the Civil War (anti-Mormon actions, Kansas, Indian removals, and the activities of the first KKK). On a global scale, the fascist and right-wing terrorism of the 1920s declined in the 1930s when authoritarian governments were established. After World War II, there were the activities of the national liberation groups that peaked in the late 1950s. For nearly the whole of the next decade there were fewer attacks and then the resurgence occurred in the later 1960s and early 1970s with the appearance of leftist movements throughout much of Europe and Latin America. This higher level of activity has continued into the present time. There may have been a small decline in the levels of terrorism with the end of the Cold War, but the levels increased again, making the last 30 years of the twentieth century one lengthy peak of activity involving many different groups. Given the variations in the past, a downturn in the future may not be a prelude to steady declines but could simply be a temporary drop in the level of violent activity.

The types of movements utilizing terrorism for political ends followed no clear patterns. Before the 1700s, communal terrorism was most frequent, but instrumental terrorism was present (Rome during the Republic, the Byzantine factions, the Italian cities). Ideological groups were relatively rare, and when ideology was present it was often combined with other factors. The communal identity that was more relevant normally was rooted in religion. In the Age of Revolutions, ideology and ethnic communal identities began to appear as more important factors identifying terrorist groups. Religious community and instrumental terrorism declined in a relative sense. In the 1800s, there was perhaps the greatest mix of underlying types with religious communalism

(Muslim suicide attacks, anti-Mormonism), ethnic communalism (the first KKK, the Cherokee removals, IMRO), ideology (Kansas, the anarchists), and situations involving a mixture of factors (the Boxer Rebellion, the Turks and Armenians). After World War I, ideology—largely the right-wing variety—and ethnic communalism (sometimes joined together) were the driving forces. After World War II, on the other hand, the ethnic groups in national liberation struggles were more important until the late 1960s when left-wing ideologies drove many of the organizations that resorted to terrorism. Religious communalism was beginning to reappear in the 1980s (the Sikhs, the Moros), and then became much more important in the following years. In the last 15 years ethnic and religious communalism or combinations have dominated. Ideological violence from the left has faded, but the extreme right has remained active and even increased its activities. Instrumental terrorism as a primary focus was somewhat infrequent after World War I. It has appeared most often with the governments that supported death squads or paramilitary groups utilizing terrorist techniques. The Medellin Cartel's attacks on the political system in Colombia was one of the few purely instrumental terrorist campaigns discovered in the previous chapters that did not involve government support of domestic groups. Criminal and drug groups have cooperated with dissidents for instrumental reasons in other cases, and instrumentalism would appear to be increasingly important as a motivation for FARC in Colombia.

While there were trends, or at least tendencies, in some periods of time in terms of the types of groups that resorted to terrorism, it is also obvious that none of the major types has totally dominated any era and no one type has disappeared. Religious communal terrorism was less important for a period but it recovered as a basic motivation at the end of the twentieth century. Religion or religious conflicts have increased as a cause of conflict and nonreligious motivations have declined in a relative sense since the end of the Cold War, an observation borne out by chapters nine and ten. Ethnic communalism has remained important, and ideology has been ever present as a primary or secondary factor. While somewhat less prevalent in recent years, ideology has not disappeared. Instrumental terrorism has been rare but never totally absent, and most common in the actions of government death squads and irregulars. What has appeared as a new form of terrorist activity in terms of the extent of its use has been the practice of ethnic cleansing. Its use has expanded in scope, perhaps because the direct conquest of territory is much less acceptable today. Ethnic cleansing, as a consequence, has become an alternative mechanism for territorial consolidation.[1]

The religiously based communal terrorist groups involved all the world's major religions. Al Qaeda and other groups in the Middle East, of course, have been Muslim. The targets for such groups have often been fellow Muslims who are not fervent enough or too secular. Christianity has a played a role in antiabortion movements and for many right-wing groups in Europe and the United States in the twentieth century. Religion played a role in some of the interwar fascist movements, especially the Iron Legion in Rumania. Groups supporting Hinduvata and the Sikh extremists have been religiously motivated, and religion has played a supporting role in Sri Lanka. Orthodox Serbs practiced ethnic cleansing in Bosnia in 1990s, and so did the Catholic Utashe in Croatia in the 1940s. Confucianism in China helped to set the Boxers apart from their Christian targets in that country. Jewish terrorists were present in British Palestine and later in Israel/Palestine. Religious differences have separated perpetrator and victim in government supported terror in the Holocaust, the Armenian genocide, Christian vigilantes in the Philippines, and Muslim ninjas in East Timor. No major religion has been proof against the attractiveness of terrorism as a technique to achieve political goals. Terrorist activities have also known very few geographic restrictions. All areas of the world have been affected by domestic attacks. American or European interests abroad have been targeted. Tourists, foreign investments, business officials or technicians, or diplomats have become convenient targets for communal, ideological, or instrumental reasons. Terrorism has been truly international in its scope and in its effects.

On average, the severity of terrorist attacks would appear to have increased through time as well. The Jewish Revolt was an especially bloody affair, but not all the deaths were from terrorism. Political violence in the Roman Republic, by the Assassins, and in the Italian city-states, while important at times, was not massive. Relatively few died in these cases, although the violence with terrorist overtones or the battles that resulted from terrorist violence in the Byzantine Empire were very bloody. The Assassins targeted the leaders not the masses, a practice adopted by the anarchists and the Social Revolutionaries. Deaths in Bloody Kansas and in the anti-Mormon attacks were relatively few in number. The Muslim suicide attacks in Malabar, the Dutch Indies, and the Philippines only involved a few casualties. The activities of the KKK after the Civil War and the Boxer Rebellion, on the other hand, were movements that involved higher levels of casualties and more victims. The chaos of the French Revolution also resulted in thousands of deaths. The anticolonial terrorism in the Thirteen Colonies and by

Tupac Amaru II prior to open hostilities had few fatalities, although the resulting wars resulted in significant losses of life. In Haiti, however, the death toll was much higher from terrorism and from military campaigns. Even with the noted exceptions, however, the periods before World War I saw relatively few cases of terrorism that resulted in large numbers of deaths, even relative to the smaller populations present in these earlier periods.

It was not until the twentieth century that casualties regularly increased, when terrorist groups began targeting larger groups of individuals, although many groups that maintained ongoing terrorist campaigns did not seek or generate high body counts. Clearly the genocides against Armenians, Jews and Gypsies, and Tutsis accounted for millions of deaths. The Soviet repression and state terrorism under Stalin also killed millions. Casualties from terror and terror combined with guerrilla activities were heavy in Algeria (both in the 1950s and the 1990s), in Israel/Palestine since 1948, in the Punjab and Kashmir in India, in Sri Lanka, in the Philippines, in Colombia and Peru, and in Chechnya. Government death squads and government-supported paramilitaries were especially deadly in Argentina, Guatemala, and East Timor, but deaths were high elsewhere as well. Dissident attacks and government involved with paramilitaries combined to increase casualties in cases such as the Philippines. Cumulative casualties could be high as in the case of Turkey with the ideological groups of the left and the right and the PKK, the ETA in Spain, and the Mujahedin-e-Khalq in Iran. Aum Shinrikyo attempted to kill thousands or even tens of thousands but failed to achieve its goal. Some of the attacks of Al Qaeda have resulted in heavy casualties, especially the September 11 and the East African embassy attacks. Not all twentieth-century groups, however, were responsible for large numbers of deaths; some were active, even for significant periods of time, with lower levels of fatalities. The street violence of the Nazis and Fascists between the wars actually did not result in large numbers of dead, although there were thousands and even tens of thousands of injuries. The Italian Fascists and their opponents actually lost more supporters in the street battles than was the case with the more famous confrontations in Nazi Germany. Many leftist groups of the 1970s and 1980s undertook attacks in ways that minimized casualties among bystanders. The kneecapping technique of the Red Brigades was virtually guaranteed to prevent excessive deaths. The Montoneros were careful only to attack security personnel or the military and avoided indiscriminate bombing campaigns. Deaths from terrorism and guerrilla activities were not particularly high in Cyprus, Palestine, and Malaya, yet, two of these liberation movements succeeded.

Foreign support for terrorists in other countries declined by the beginning of the twenty-first century.[2] Terrorism has, however, become more internationalized over time. Domestic groups are more likely to launch attacks from abroad, to embarrass their governments. They may also feel that the source of their problems originates from abroad, when a foreign government supports their government, when secularism or a foreign religion threatens their society, when a foreign economic system or way of doing business intrudes, or when they see foreigners as an enemy civilization. The many different groups, including those from the outside, attacking American, allied, and Iraqi forces in Iraq in 2004, are just one of the most recent examples of such actions. Support of terror by states against their own citizens, however, still continued and generated higher death tolls, and there were some indications that governments were relying more on terror and less on repression in the twentieth century. Government or quasi-official support has increased the casualties resulting from ethnic cleansing in the Sudan, Kosovo, Bosnia, and East Timor. Even in situations where governments have not been involved, ethnic cleansing by local groups has been among the bloodiest incidents. The partitions in India resulted in a massive loss of life that was not supported by either the government of India or Pakistan. The increase in activities by religious dissidents has also been associated with more deadly attacks. Religious groups have been less constrained in terms of causing casualties, apparently since unbelievers are involved.[3] Not all mass casualty attacks that have been launched in recent years, however, have involved religious groups.[4] Casualties do appear to be higher when religion reinforces ethnicity.[5] The casualties from ethnic dissident groups can mount over time since nationalists have a stronger base, and, consequently, their activities will last longer.[6]

There currently has been great concern that at least some terrorist groups would be able to procure and use weapons of mass destruction. To date, Aum Shinrikyo has been the only group that attempted to use a chemical weapon to inflict mass casualties. The anthrax attacks in the United States did not cause major casualties, and were unlikely to do so given the delivery method that was chosen. No other group has used such weapons for mass casualties—so far. The future, of course, is more uncertain. Biological weapons are potentially the deadliest, but they are also the most difficult to control. A plague will not stop at national boundaries, recognize ethnic groups, or afflict only members of certain religions. Chemical weapons or dirty bombs causing death by radiation poisoning are probably a great threat only if the target population is separate from the attackers. The Palestinians, ideological groups, and the Muslim dissidents in Algeria and Egypt will be unable to use some weapons because there is no target population that is separated from potential supporters of the group. The IRA could use some devices in England or the ETA in other parts of Spain, but the political fallout from such actions would probably be disastrous to their causes. Aum Shinriyko and Al Qaeda have been the most dangerous of the groups interested in weapons of mass destruction. Both had sufficient financial resources to obtain the weapons and the acquisition of such weapons was important to their ultimate objectives—cleansing the world for Aum and forcing the United States to concede to demands for the future of the Middle East.[7] In this context, having the weapons could be tantamount to using them. These weapons may be more likely to be used in cases where the terrorism corresponds to Huntington's clash of civilization examples if geographic separation of the target population is present. Al Qaeda launching such an attack in Europe or North America or a Chechen attack in Moscow with such weapons would be possibilities. When all is said and done, however, most terrorist groups will still seek more controlled violence.[8] Weapons of mass destruction are also only relevant as an option if mass casualties are one of the goals of the dissidents.[9] Terrorist groups also have tended to rely on established techniques, in part because they know that they work.[10] Al Qaeda has used conventional weapons that have had the best chances of success for the group instead of relaying on untried chemical, biological, or nuclear weaponry.[11] Even the attacks of September 11 were variations on conventional methods. Perhaps, of more immediate concern than weapons of mass destruction have been suicide bombings. The use of this type of attack has spread, and it could be the technique of the future because such attacks are difficult to detect or to prevent. A suicide bomber can also attack targets that are largely inaccessible to a terrorist who hopes to remain alive.[12] These attacks have become increasingly effective as more and more groups have used the tactic. The availability of suicide bombers, however, would also make it easier to use a biological, chemical, nuclear, or radiological weapon since protection or survival of the dissident members would no longer be a concern. In addition, the most deadly attacks, identified in the previous chapters, have occurred with government involvement in terror against its citizens. Governments do not need weapons of mass destruction to accomplish their goals.

Causes of Terrorism: The State of the Field

This rather exhaustive survey of terrorism over the millennia offers very few conclusions that hold true for all or even most circumstances. State support for terrorist groups in other countries has declined, partially as a consequence of the end of the Cold War. In fact, such state support may be at its lowest level in 50 years, but it has not disappeared. There were no clear-cut answers as to the causes of terrorist activity that was present. Communal, ideological, and instrumental factors underlay the use of terrorism by different groups, but there were many ideological and communal groups, some perhaps more committed to their causes than the terrorists, and those seeking instrumental gain that did not choose terrorism as a course of action. Many of these other groups did not resort to violence, even when they failed to achieve their political objectives through peaceful methods. These groups either continued to try non-violent means to achieve their goals or they gave up on attempting to achieve such goals. It was difficult to detect any patterns to explain why the violence broke out when it did. The contention between slavery and non-slavery forces resulted in campaigns of violence in Kansas. The violence could have occurred somewhere else earlier in time but it did not. Specific reasons can actually be constructed for the violence in Kansas—including geographic proximity to the slave state of Missouri, the passage of the Kansas–Nebraska Act, the breakup of the major parties on a sectional basis, the Dred Scott decision, and the weak administration of Presidents Pierce and Buchanan. None of these reasons, however, provide much insight on the outbreak of terrorist violence in other places and other times.

Weak states provided greater opportunities for terrorist groups. While the presence of a weak state does not mean terrorism will occur, it does mean it may be more likely and that when it does occur it will be more difficult to deal with. Even though weak states may provide fertile ground for groups that fail to obtain their objectives to resort to violence, some weak states do not face any terrorist threat or they have to deal with other types of political violence (coups, peasant uprisings, civil wars, and so on). Democratic states face institutional "weaknesses" (which are also the strengths of democracy) vis-à-vis the violent terrorists. Ultimately democracy proves to have more benefits than disabilities, but democracies will still be prone to suffer terrorist attacks as one of the costs of this system of government. Similarly, states in transition can be especially vulnerable as they shift from one form of government to another, since government capabilities are usually more limited during such periods. Globalization has clearly generated tensions and stresses that have contributed to terrorism. The examples range from the Maccabees and Zealots to Al Qaeda. Modern terrorism is a conflict between secular globalization leading to ethnic and religious fragmentation that in turn results in both ethnic and religious fundamentalism that help to fuel violence.[13] Not all the terrorist movements that have appeared over time have been a consequence of globalization or the problems that it brings. Ethnic and religious fragmentation has not automatically followed secular globalization. As a consequence, however important globalization may be in some cases, it cannot be considered the underlying cause for all terrorism any more than any other single factor. Similarly, it is obvious that Huntington's thesis can only be a partial explanation, but his views have provided important insights, and they do help to explain at least some instances of violent conflict and the appearance of terrorist groups.

Somewhat unique events can obviously play a role in the occurrence of terrorism. A conjunction of circumstances can come into play. The French Revolution resulted from economic stresses and the resulting insecurity, an expanding population, new political ideas, and financial instability resulting from France's participation in the American Revolution against England. The wars of the Revolution and Napoleon set in motion events leading to outbreaks of violence and occasionally terrorism elsewhere. The turmoil after World War I—economic, social, and political—generated conditions that were conducive to the use of terrorist techniques that were widely, but not universally, practiced. After World War II, the weakened European colonial empires provided opportunities for national liberation movements willing to use terrorism and guerrilla warfare or just terrorism in their efforts to establish independent states. In 1968, the stress of economic changes in the world and the Vietnam conflict came together to generate a wave of leftist violence that was reinforced and supported by the Palestinian struggle for an independent state. The struggle of the Afghans against the Soviet Union and local communists provided a setting for the creation of the Al Qaeda network that has become so deadly. A more recent concern has been the increasing links between terrorist organizations and criminal groups, especially drug operations. Both benefit from weak states and have worked together to prevent effective states control most notably in Colombia. It is feared that such a "narco-terrorist" path could be a threat to many Southeast Asian countries.[14] Each of these sets of circumstances was different and none of them is likely to be repeated in the future.

Of course, some other conjunction of events not yet anticipated can have similar effects as the ones from the past.

Of course, there were still other terrorist movements that operated outside these conjunctions of circumstances or which occurred independently of globalization (at least in any obvious sense), weak states, or the decline of empires. What drove at least some of the groups to adopt terrorist techniques and which then contributed to the associated waves of terrorism were perceptions of the successes of the previous groups. One of the myths of analyses of terrorism is the idea that terrorism does not succeed, but it actually does.[15] The preceding chapters have demonstrated that sometimes terrorism has been very effective in relationship to the main objectives of the groups involved. In other cases the organizations adopting the use of violence achieve at least some important objectives, including tactical goals such as group polarization, reinforcement of dissident solidarity, or the disruption of peace negotiations. Ethnic cleansing has been especially effective for the ethnic cleansers. They have often been rewarded with gains from boundaries officially redrawn or new boundaries separating ethnic or religious groups that have been at the expense of the victims.[16] It is also important to note that ideological groups (both left and right), communal groups (both ethnic and religious), and instrumental groups have had successes. Success has not been limited to one type of group. Of course, terrorism has also often failed, but potential terrorists are much more aware of the successful uses from the past than all the failures. It is precisely those terrorist groups that have constituted the greatest threat to political systems or that achieved the most obvious results that have been the best known to potential or future dissidents. The dissidents of the future focus on the successes; the many failures are often unknown. Clearly the failures outnumber the successes, but a group desperate enough to resort to terrorism is more likely to be motivated by the fact that sometimes terrorism has been successful or at least appears to have been successful than by the fact that the violence may fail. Since terrorism is a weapon of the weak, the possibility of failure is always present.

One final point that is worth reemphasizing is that terrorism is a technique available to all kinds of groups with all kinds of objectives. The fact that it is a technique rather than a defining characteristic of the organizations involved in its use is one of the factors that makes causal prediction so difficult.[17] Almost any committed group of dissidents can, and have, used it. Modern inventions have expanded the ways in which the basic technique can be used. Dynamite made the anarchists more dangerous, and chemical fertilizers have been a boon to many groups.

If a group has dedicated members willing to undertake suicide attacks to support the causes, the group becomes much more dangerous, instills greater fear, and is generally more effective. The possible availability of weapons of mass destruction has the potential for generating even greater fear for the groups willing to use it. Ethnic cleansing may be increasingly used by groups to create homogenous home territories and to drive out minorities. What may be the most important recent change in terrorist activity is not related to underlying causes, the types of weapons that can be used, or how lethal they are. What is relatively new is the increasing reliance on less hierarchical organizational styles.[18] Leaderless resistance is one relatively new form, even though its functional equivalent existed with the *pagabsil* attacks in colonial Asia. One of the difficulties that the government and American forces have had in Iraq is the fact that the dissidents represent many different groups and for some of them, there is no organizational structure to attack. The network structure of Al Qaeda has also presented greater challenges to agencies seeking to prevent terrorism, especially since it has developed sophisticated financial operations, has the ability to use modern communication facilities, and has access to high technology data and information sources.[19] The most obvious conclusion from the preceding pages is that terrorism will continue because it has worked in the past, because it requires few resources, and because it can be a very flexible technique. Circumstances such as weak states, globalization, and interactions with drug cartels will play a key role in at least some cases in facilitating the appearance and continuation of terrorist groups. The relative weight of ideological, communal, and instrumental violence as the underlying factors behind groups changed from period to period in the past and is likely to change in the future, because "history shows that the inspiration for a terrorist wave may dry out in time, and that resistance can destroy organizations or make them ineffectual. But, alas, it also demonstrates that terrorists regularly invent new ways to conduct their activities."[20] Terrorism will continue, and it cannot be prevented at the present time, only contained, and not very well at that!

NOTES

Chapter One   Terrorism Today and Yesterday

1. John Deutch, "Terrorism," *Foreign Policy*, No. 109 (1997), p. 11.
2. Albert Parry, *Terrorism: From Robespierre to Arafat* (New York: Vanguard Press, 1976).
3. Roland Gaucher, *The Terrorists: From Tsarist Russia to the O. A. S.*, Paula Spurlin, trans. (London: Secker & Warburg, 1968); V. Khoros, "The 'Crown', the 'Roots', and the 'Climate' of Terrorism," *Russian Politics and Law*, Vol. 41, No. 2 (2003), p. 70; Walter Laqueur, *A History of Terrorism* (New Brunswick, NJ: Transaction Publishers, 2001), p. 11; and Gregory A. Raymond, "The Evolving Strategies of Political Terrorism," in Charles W. Kegley, Jr. (ed.), *The New Global Terrorism: Characteristics, Causes, Controls* (Upper Saddle River, NJ: Prentice Hall, 2003), p. 77.
4. Bruce Hoffman, "The Emergence of the New Terrorism," in Andrew Tan and Kumar Ramakrishna (eds.), *The New Terrorism: Anatomy, Trends and Counter-Strategies* (Singapore: Eastern Universities Press, 2002), p. 45.
5. Peter C. Sederberg, "Global Terrorism: Problems of Challenge and Response," in Kegley (ed.), *The New Global Terrorism*, p. 269.
6. Isabelle Duyvesteyn, "How New Is the New Terrorism?" *Studies in Conflict and Terrorism*, Vol. 27, No. 5 (2004), p. 442.
7. Farish A. Noor, "Globalization, Resistance and the Discursive Politics of Terror, Post-September 11," in Tan and Ramakrishna (eds.), *The New Terrorism*, p. 159.
8. Bernard Lewis, *The Assassins: A Radical Sect in Islam* (New York: Basic Books, 1968), p. 128.
9. David C. Rapoport, "The Four Waves of Rebel Terror and September 11," in Kegley (ed.), *The New Global* Terrorism, p. 36–52; and Paul Wilkinson, "Why Modern Terrorism? Differentiating Types and Distinguishing Ideological Motivations," in Kegley (ed.), *The New Global Terrorism*, pp. 106–38.
10. Wilkinson, "Why Modern Terrorism?" p. 124.

Chapter Two   Definitions, Classifications, and Causes

1. Alex P. Schmid, *Political Terrorism: A Research Guide to Concepts, Theories, Data Bases, and Literature* (New Brunswick, NJ: Transaction Books, 1983).
2. Michael Dartnell, "A Legal Inter-Network for Terrorism: Issues of Globalization, Fragmentation, and Legitimacy," in Max Taylor and John Horgan (eds.), *The Future of Terrorism* (London: Frank Cass, 2000), pp. 199, 204; Brian M. Jenkins, "International Terrorism: The Other

World War," in Kegley (ed.), *The New Global Terrorism*, p. 19; and Paul R. Pillar, *Terrorism and U.S. Foreign Policy* (Washington, DC: Brookings Institution, 2001), p. 13.
3. David Claridge, "State Terrorism? Applying a Definitional Model," *Terrorism and Political Violence*, Vol. 8, No. 3 (1996), pp. 47–63; Bruce Hoffman, *Inside Terrorism* (New York: Columbia University Press, 1998), Chap. 1; and James M. Lutz and Brenda J. Lutz, *Global Terrorism* (London: Routledge, 2004), p. 10.
4. David E. Long, *The Anatomy of Terrorism* (New York: Free Press, 1990), p. 5; and Gary G. Sick, "The Political Underpinnings of Terrorism," in Charles W. Kegley, Jr. (ed.), *International Terrorism: Characteristics, Causes, Controls* (New York: St. Martin's, 1990), p. 51.
5. Thomas J. Badey, "Defining International Terrorism: A Pragmatic Approach," *Terrorism and Political Violence*, Vol. 10, No. 1 (1998), p. 93.
6. J. Browyer Bell, *Transnational Terror* (Washington, DC: American Enterprise Institute, 1975), p. 8; Alex P. Schmid, "The Response Problem as a Definition Problem," *Terrorism and Political Violence*, Vol. 4, No. 4 (1992), pp. 10–11; and Thomas Perry Thornton, "Terror as a Weapon of Political Agitation," in Harry Eckstein (ed.), *Internal War: Problems and Approaches* (Glencoe, IL: The Free Press, 1964), p. 79.
7. Bruce B. Campbell, "Death Squads: Definitions, Problems, and Historical Context," in Bruce B. Campbell and Arthur D. Brenner (eds.), *Death Squads in Global Perspective: Murder with Deniability* (New York: Palgrave Macmillan, 2000), p. 2; and Khoros, "The 'Crown'," p. 70.
8. Michael T. Klare, "The New Face of Combat: Terrorism and Irregular Warfare in the 21st Century," in Kegley (ed.), *The New Global Terrorism*, p. 31.
9. Peter Chalk, *West European Terrorism and Counter-Terrorism: The Evolving Dynamic* (Houndsmill, Basingstoke: Macmillan, 1996), p. 13; Hoffman, "The Emergence of the New Terrorism," p. 45; Khoros, "The 'Crown'," p. 71; Long, *Anatomy of Terrorism*, p. 139; and Paul Wilkinson, *Terrorism and the Liberal State* (London: Macmillan, 1977), p. 81.
10. Gaucher, *The Terrorists*, p. 298.
11. David A. Charters, "Introduction," in David A. Charters (ed.), *The Deadly Sin of Terrorism: Its Effect on Democracy and Civil Liberty in Six Countries* (Westport, CT: Greenwood Press, 1994), p. 2.
12. Michael Radu, "Terrorism after the Cold War," *Orbis*, Vol. 46, No. 2 (2002), p. 276.
13. Jenkins, "International Terrorism," p. 22.
14. Badey, "Defining International Terrorism," pp. 90–107; Chalk, *West European Terrorism*, p. 17; and Khoros, "The 'Crown'," p. 71.
15. Bruce Hoffman, " 'Holy Terror': The Implications of Terrorism Motivated by a Religious Imperative," *Studies in Conflict and Terrorism*, Vol. 18, No. 4 (1995), p. 281; and Harvey W. Kushner, *Terrorism in America: A Structural Approach to Understanding the Terrorist Threat* (Springfield, IL: Charles C. Thomas, 1998), pp. 82–83.
16. Bruce Hoffman, "Change and Continuity in Terrorism," *Studies in Conflict and Terrorism*, Vol. 24, No. 5 (2001), p. 418.
17. Martha Crenshaw, "The Causes of Terrorism," in Kegley (ed.), *The New Global Terrorism*, p. 97.
18. Peter Chalk, "Low Intensity Conflict in Southeast Asia: Piracy, Drug Trafficking and Political Terrorism," *Conflict Studies*, No. 305/306 (1998), p. 14. Cf. Paul Wilkinson, *Terrorism versus Democracy: The Liberal State Response* (London: Frank Cass, 2000), p. 13.
19. Lutz and Lutz, *Global Terrorism*, p. 209.
20. Chalk, *West European Terrorism*, p. 20; and Peter A. Sproat, "Can the State Be Terrorist," *Terrorism*, Vol. 14, No. 1 (1991), p. 24.
21. Campbell, "Death Squads," p. 5.
22. Ray Abrahams, *Vigilant Citizens: Vigilantism and the State* (Cambridge: Polity Press, 1988), p. 4.
23. Tore Bjorgo, "Introduction," in Tore Bjorgo (ed.), *Terror from the Extreme Right* (London: Frank Cass, 1995), p. 3.
24. Frank Chalk and Kurt Jonassohn, *The History and Sociology of Genocide: Analyses and Case Studies* (New Haven: Yale University Press, 1990), p. 23.

NOTES

25. Walter Laqueur, *A History of Terrorism* (New Brunswick, NJ: Transaction Publishers, 2001), p. 143.
26. David Veness, "Low Intensity and High Impact Conflict," in Horgan and Taylor, *The Future of Terrorism*, p. 11.
27. Crenshaw, "The Causes of Terrorism," p. 98; Ted Robert Gurr, "Terrorism in Democracies: When It Occurs, Why It Fails," in Kegley (ed.), *The New Global Terrorism*, p. 203; Hoffman, *Inside Terrorism*, p. 65; and Michael Stohl, "The Mystery of the New Global Terrorism: Old Myths, New Realities?" in Kegley (ed.), *The New Global Terrorism*, p. 87.
28. Bell, *Transnational Terror*, p. 10.
29. John K. Cooley, "Terrorism: Continuity and Change in the New Century," *Global Dialogue*, Vol. 2, No. 4 (2000), p. 12.
30. Cf. Crenshaw, "The Causes of Terrorism"; Charles W. Kegley, Jr., "The Causes of Terrorism," in Kegley (ed.), *International Terrorism*, pp. 99–101; Edward N. Muller and Mitchell A. Seligson, "Inequality and Insurgency," *American Political Science Review*, Vol. 81, No. 2 (1987), pp. 425–51; and Wilkinson, "Why Modern Terrorism?" pp. 106–38 among many others.
31. Walter Laqueur, "The Futility of Terrorism," in Kegley (ed.), *International Terrorism*, pp. 69–70.
32. Laqueur, *A History of Terrorism*, p. 119; and Sederberg, "Global Terrorism," p. 281.
33. Gurr, "Terrorism in Democracies," p. 202; Laqueur, *A History of Terrorism*, p. 11; and Wilkinson, *Terrorism and the Liberal State*, p. 122.
34. Crenshaw, "Causes of Terrorism," p. 94; and Feliks Gross, *Violence in Politics: Terror and Political Assassination in Eastern Europe and Russia*, Studies in the Social Sciences 13 (The Hague: Mouton, 1972), p. 90.
35. Laqueur, *A History of Terrorism*, p. 11.
36. Wilkinson, *Terrorism versus Democracy*, p. 24.
37. Samuel P. Huntington, "Political Development and Political Decay," *World Politics*, Vol. 17, No. 3 (1965), pp. 95–139.
38. Audrey Kurth Cronin, "Behind the Curve: Globalization and International Terrorism," *International Security*, Vol. 27, No. 3 (2002/03), p. 36.
39. Huntington, "Political Development," p. 95.
40. Michael Mousseau, "Market Civilization and Its Clash with Terror," *International Security*, Vol. 27, No. 3 (2002/03), pp. 16–17.
41. Stanley Hoffmann, "Clash of Globalizations," *Foreign Affairs*, Vol. 81, No. 4 (2002), p. 108.
42. Sean Kendall Anderson, and Stephen Sloan, *Terrorism: Assassins to Zealots* (Lanham, MD: Scarecrow Press, 2003), p. 13.
43. Klare, "The New Face of Combat," p. 30.
44. Samuel P. Huntington, "The Clash of Civilizations?" *Foreign Affairs*, Vol. 72, No. 3 (1993), pp. 22–49; and Huntington, *The Clash of Civilizations and the Remaking of World Order* (New York: Simon & Schuster, 1996).
45. Huntington, *The Clash of Civilizations*, p. 258.
46. Leonard B. Weinberg and William L. Eubank, "Terrorism and the Shape of Things to Come," in Taylor and Horgan (eds.), *The Future of Terrorism*, pp. 83–93.
47. Cf., for example, Jonathan Fox, "Religion and State Failure: An Examination of the Extent and Magnitude of Religious Conflict from 1950 to 1996," *International Political Science Review*, Vol. 25, No. 1 (2004), pp. 55–76; and Lavina Rajendram, "Does the Clash of Civilisations Paradigm Provide a Persuasive Explanation of International Politics after September 11th," *Cambridge Review of International Affairs*, Vol. 15, No. 2 (2002), pp. 217–32.
48. Max. Taylor and John Horgan, "Future Developments of Political Terrorism in Europe," in Taylor and Horgan (eds.), *The Future of Terrorism*, p. 85.
49. Crenshaw, "The Causes of Terrorism," p. 93; and Raymond, "The Evolving Strategies," p. 77.
50. Bell, *Transnational Terror*, p. 89; and Martin Shubik, "Terrorism, Technology, and the Socioeconomics of Death," *Comparative Strategy*, Vol. 16, No. 4 (1997), p. 407.

Chapter Three Terrorism in the Ancient World

1. Carl Glick and Hong Sheng-Hwa, *Swords of Silence: Chinese Secret Societies—Past and Present* (New York: Whittlesey House, 1947), p. 34.
2. Nick Fisher, "Hybris, Revenge and Stasis in the Greek City-States," in Hans van Wees (ed.), *War and Violence in Ancient Greece* (London: Duckworth and the Classical Press of Wales, 2000), pp. 83–123.
3. Anthony M. Burton, *Urban Terrorism: Theory, Practice & Response* (New York: The Free Press, 1975).
4. Fergus Millar, "The Political Character of the Classical Roman Republic, 200–151 B.C.," *Journal of Roman Studies*, Vol. 74 (1984), p. 2.
5. Alexander Yakobson, *Elections and Electioneering in Rome: A Study in the Political System of the Late Republic* (Stuttgart: Franz Steiner Verlag, 1999), p. 189.
6. Jurgen von Ungern-Sternberg, "The End of the Conflict of the Orders," in Kurt A. Raaflaub (ed.), *Social Struggles in Archaic Rome: New Perspectives on the Conflict of the Orders* (Berkeley: University of California Press, 1986), p. 374.
7. Kurt A. Raaflaub, "From Protection and Defense to Offense and Participation: Stages in the Conflict of the Orders," in Raaflaub (ed.), *Social Struggles in Archaic Rome*, p. 219.
8. Thomas W. Africa, "Urban Violence in Imperial Rome," *Journal of Interdisciplinary History*, Vol. 2, No. 1 (1971), p. 12; D. C. Earl, *Tiberius Gracchus: A Study in Politics*, Collection Latomus, Vol. 66 (Bruxelles-Bercham: Latomus Revue d'Etudes Latines, 1963), p. 81; and Fergus Millar, *The Crowd in Rome in the Late Republic*, Thomas Spencer Jerome Lectures 22 (Ann Arbor: University of Michigan Press, 1998), pp. 136, 149.
9. Wilfried Nippel, "Policing Rome," *Journal of Roman Studies*, Vol. 74 (1984), p. 25.
10. Millar, *The Crowd in Rome*, p. 150; and W. G. Runciman, "Capitalism without Classes: The Case of Classical Rome," *British Journal of Sociology*, Vol. 34. No. 2 (1983), p. 160.
11. Franklin L. Ford, *Political Murder: From Tyrannicide to Terrorism* (Cambridge, MA: Harvard University Press, 1985), pp. 55–58.
12. Nippel, "Policing Rome," p. 27.
13. A. W. Lintott, "Cicero and Milo," *Journal of Roman Studies*, Vol. 64 (1974), pp. 62–78; and A. N. Sherwin-White, "Violence in Roman Politics," *Journal of Roman Studies*, Vol. 46, No. 1/2 (1956), pp. 4–5.
14. John M. Allegro, *The Chosen People: A Study of Jewish History from the Time of the Exile until the Revolt of Bar Kocheba, Sixth Century B.C. to Second Century A.D.* (Garden City, NY: Doubleday, 1972), p. 84; and Shimon Applebaum, "The Zealots: The Case for Revaluation," *Journal of Roman Studies*, Vol. 61 (1971), p. 160.
15. Martin Sicker, *Between Rome and Jerusalem: 300 Years of Roman-Judean Relations* (Westport, CT: Praeger, 2001), pp. 17–18.
16. Rose Mary Sheldon, "Taking on Goliath: The Jews against Rome, AD 66–73," *Small Wars and Insurgencies*, Vol. 5, No. 1 (1994), p. 3.
17. Allegro, *The Chosen People*, p. 278.
18. Josepheus, *The Jewish War*, G. A. Williamson, trans., rev. ed. (New York: Dorset Press, 1981), p. 147.
19. Allegro, *The Chosen People*, p. 295; and Alexander Fuks, "Aspects of the Jewish Revolt in A.D. 115–117," *Journal of Roman Studies*, Vol. 51, No. 1/2 (1961), pp. 98–104.
20. Werner Eck, "The Bar Kokhba Revolt: The Roman Point of View," *Journal of Roman Studies*, Vol. 89 (1999), pp. 76–89.
21. John W. Barker, *Justinian and the Later Roman Empire* (Madison: University of Wisconsin Press, 1966), p. 59, and Constance Head, *Justinian II of Byzantium* (Madison: University of Wisconsin Press, 1972), p. 95.
22. Michael Whitby, "The Violence of the Circus Factions," in Keith Hopwood (ed.), *Organised Crime in Antiquity* (London: Duckworth with the Classical Press of Wales, 1999), p. 241.

Notes

23. Yakobson, *Elections and Electioneering in Rome*, p. 195.
24. Earl, *Tiberius Gracchus*, pp. 8, 104–07; and Runciman, "Capitalism without Classes," p. 166.
25. Whitby, "The Violence of the Circus Factions," p. 241.
26. Josephus, *The Jewish War*, pp. 168–69, and David C. Rapport, "Fear and Trembling: Terrorism in Three Religious Traditions," *American Political Science Review*, Vol. 78, No. 3 (1984), p. 669.
27. Fuks, "Aspects of the Jewish Revolt," p. 99.
28. Michael Grant, *Julius Caesar: A Bibliography* (New York: M. Evans & Co., 1992), p. 4.
29. Africa, "Urban Violence," p. 7; and Nippel, "Policing Rome."
30. Nippel, "Policing Rome," p. 23.
31. Sicker, *Between Rome and Jerusalem*, p. 23.

Chapter Four   The Middle Ages to the Renaissance

1. Farhad Daftary, *The Assassin Legends: Myths of the Isma'ilis* (London: I. B. Tauris, 1991), p. 35.
2. Rapoport, "Fear and Trembling," p. 663.
3. Lewis, *The Assassins*, pp. 106–07.
4. Daftary, *The Assassin Legends*, p. 34; and David C. Rapoport, "Religion and Terror: Thugs, Assassins, and Zealots," in Kegley, Jr. (ed.), *International Terrorism*, p. 150.
5. Wilkinson, *Terrorism versus Democracy*, p. 174.
6. Judith Hook, *Siena: A City and Its History* (London: Hamish Hamilton, 1979), p. 44.
7. Steven A. Epstein, *Genoa & the Genoese, 958–1528* (Chapel Hill: University of North Carolina Press, 1996), p. 81.
8. Lauro Martines, "Political Conflict in the Italian City States," *Government and Opposition*, Vol. 3, No. 1 (1967–1968), p. 80.
9. J. R. Hale, *Florence and the Medici: The Pattern of Control* (London: Thames and Hudson, 1977), p. 78.
10. Marvin B. Becker, *Florence in Transition: Volume I, The Decline of the Commune* (Baltimore: Johns Hopkins Press, 1967), p. 114.
11. Epstein, *Genoa & the Genoese*, pp. 325–27.
12. George Holmes, *Florence, Rome, and the Origins of the Renaissance* (Oxford: Clarendon Press, 1986), p. 4.
13. Yves Renovard, *The Avignon Papacy: The Popes in Exile, 1305–1403*, Denis Bethell, trans. (New York: Barnes and Noble, 1994, originally published in translation in 1970), pp. 28–29; and Daniel Waley, *The Papal State in the Thirteenth Century* (London: Macmillan, 1961), p. 248.
14. Raj Desai and Harry Eckstein, "Insurgency: The Transformation of Peasant Rebellion," *World Politics*, Vol. 42, No. 4 (1990), p. 449; and Heiko A. Oberman, "The Gospel of Social Unrest," in Bob Scribner and Gerhard Benecke (eds.), *The German Peasant War 1525—New Viewpoints* (London: George Allen and Unwin, 1979), p. 44.
15. Rudolf Endres, "The Peasant War in Franconia," in Scribner and Benecke, *The German Peasant War*, pp. 74, 78.
16. Lewis, *The Assassins*, p. 132.
17. Walter Laqueur, *Terrorism* (Boston: Little Brown, 1977), p. 9; and Lewis, *The Assassins*, p. 139.
18. Martines, "Political Conflict," p. 72.
19. Martines, "Political Conflict," p. 87.
20. Michael E. Bratchel, "Lucca, 1430–94: The Politics of the Restored Republic," in Thomas W. Blomquist and Maureen F. Mazzaoui (eds.), *The "Other Tuscany": Essays in the History of Lucca, Pisa, and Siena during the Thirteenth, Fourteenth, and Fifteenth Centuries*, Studies in Medieval Culture 34 (Kalamazoo, MI: Medieval Institute Publications, Western Michigan University, 1994), p. 25.
21. Hale, *Florence and the Medici*, p. 91.
22. Hale, *Florence and the Medici*, p. 16.

23. Martines, "Political Conflict," p. 71.
24. Lewis, *The Assassins*, pp. 136, 139; and Rapoport, "Religion and Terror," p. 152.
25. Hook, *Siena*, p. 173.

Chapter Five   Terrorism in the Age of Revolutions

1. R. J. Knecht, *The French Wars of Religion, 1559–1598*, 2nd ed., Seminar Studies in History (Harlow, Essex: Longman, 1996), pp. 48–50.
2. Cf. Peter Beresford Ellis, *Hell or Connaught! The Cromwellian Colonisation of Ireland 1652–1660* (New York: St. Martin's, 1975).
3. Benson Bobrick, *Angel in the Whirlwind: The Triumph of the American Revolution* (New York: Simon and Schuster, 1997), p. 75; and Division of Archives and History (State of New York), *The American Revolution in New York: Its Political, Social and Economic Significance* (Albany: The University of the State of New York, 1926), pp. 14–18.
4. Rapoport, "The Four Waves of Rebel Terror and September 11," in Kegley (ed.), *The New Global Terrorism*, pp. 37–38.
5. Bobrick, *Angel in the Whirlwind*, p. 62; Paul Bradley Davis, "American Experiences and the Contemporary Perception of Terrorism," *Small Wars and Insurgencies*, Vol. 7, No. 2 (1996), p. 224; and Robert Leckie, *George Washington's War: The Saga of the American Revolution* (New York: Harper Collins, 1992), p. 79.
6. For example, dissidents boarded a ship containing tea outside of New York City and dumped it into the ocean. Cf. Division of Archives and History, *The American Revolution*, p. 33.
7. Nicholas A. Robins, *Genocide and Millennialism in Upper Peru: The Great Rebellion of 1780–1782* (Westport, CT: Praeger, 2002), pp. 103–04.
8. Sinclair Thomson, *We Alone Will Rule: Native Andean Politics in the Age of Insurgency* (Madison: University of Wisconsin Press, 2002), p. 106.
9. Ward Stavig, *The World of Tupac Amaru: Conflict, Community, and Identity in Colonial Peru* (Lincoln: University of Nebraska Press, 1999), Chap. 5.
10. Sergio Serulnikov, *Subverting Colonial Authority* (Durham, NC: Duke University Press, 2003), pp. 140–42; and Thomson, *We Alone Will Rule*, p. 135.
11. Stavig, *The World of Tupac Amaru*, p. 224.
12. Laurent Dubois, *Avengers of the New World: The Story of the Haitian Revolution* (Cambridge, MA: Belknap Press of Harvard University Press, 2004), pp. 77–78.
13. C. L. R. James, *The Black Jacobins: Toussaint L'Ouverture and the Santo Domingo Revolution*, 2nd rev. ed. (New York: Vintage Books, 1963), pp. 96–97, 101.
14. Martin Ros, *Night of Fire: The Black Napoleon and the Battle for Haiti*, Karin Ford-Treep, trans. (New York: Sarpedon, 1994), p. 197.
15. Dubois, *Avengers of the New World*, p. 300; and Ros, *Night of Fire*, p. 197. The only general exceptions that were made were for Polish soldiers who deserted from the French (and allied) troops sent by Napoleon.
16. Karin Andriolo, "Murder by Suicide: Episodes from Muslim History," *American Anthropologist*, Vol. 104, No. 3 (2002), pp. 736–42; and Thomas M. McKenna, "Murdered or Martyred: Popular Evaluations of Violent Death in the Muslim Separatist Movement in the Philippines," in Jeffrey A. Sluka (ed.), *Death Squad: The Anthropology of State Terror* (Philadelphia: University of Pennsylvania Press, 2000), p. 193.
17. Stephen Frederic Dale, "Religious Suicide in Islamic Asia: Anticolonial Terrorism in India, Indonesia, and the Philippines," *Journal of Conflict Resolution*, Vol. 32, No. 1 (1988), p. 49.
18. Dale, "Religious Suicide," pp. 48–49.
19. Francois Furet, "Terror," in Francois Furet and Mona Ozouf (eds.), *A Critical Dictionary of the French Revolution*, Arthur Goldhammer, trans. (Cambridge, MA: Belknap Press, 1989), p. 148.

20. Paddy Griffith, *The Art of War of Revolutionary France, 1789–1802* (London: Greenhill Books, 1998), pp. 62–63.
21. George Rude, *The Crowd in the French Revolution* (Oxford: The Clarendon Press, 1959), p. 113.
22. James, *The Black Jacobins*, pp. 119–20.
23. Rude, *The Crowd in the French Revolution*, pp. 104–05.
24. Robins, *Genocide and Millennialism*, p. 2; and Thomson, *We Alone Will Rule*, pp. 169–70.
25. Robins, *Genocide and Millennialism*, p. 162.
26. Furet, "Terror," p. 147; Donald Greer, *The Incidence of Terror during the French Revolution: A Statistical Interpretation* (Cambridge: Harvard University Press, 1935), pp. 16–17; and Griffith, *The Art of War*, Chapter 4.
27. Ros, *Night of Fire*, pp. 23–24.
28. Dale, "Religious Suicide," p. 56.
29. Dubois, *Avengers of the New World*, p. 84.
30. Thomson, *We Alone Will Rule*, p. 240.
31. Stavig, *The World of Tupac Amaru*, p. 226.
32. Michel-Rolph Trouillot, *Haiti: State against Nation—The Origins and Legacy of Duvalierism* (New York: Monthly Review Press, 1990), p. 119.
33. Davis, "American Experiences," p. 224.
34. Parry, *Terrorism*, p. 51.
35. Furet, "Terror," p. 147.
36. Dale, "Religious Suicide," p. 47.

Chapter Six The End of the Napoleonic Wars to World War I

1. Dale, "Religious Suicide in Islamic Asia," p. 54; and McKenna, "Murdered or Martyred?" p. 193.
2. Guy Puyraimond, "The Ko-lao Hui and the Anti-Foreign Incidents of 1891," in Jean Chesneaux (ed.), *Popular Movements and Secret Societies in China, 1840–1950* (Stanford, CA: Stanford University Press, 1972), pp. 113–16.
3. William J. Duiker, *Cultures in Collision: The Boxer Rebellion* (San Rafael, CA: Presidio Press, 1978), pp. 33–34.
4. Duiker, *Cultures in Collision*, pp. 65–67, 103.
5. Leon Comber, *Chinese Secret Societies in Malaya: A Survey of the Triad Society from 1800 to 1900*, Monographs of the Association for Asian Studies No. 6 (Locust Valley, NY: J. J. Augustin, 1959), p. 271; and David Ownby, *Brotherhoods and Secret Societies in Early and Mid-Qing China: The Formation of a Tradition* (Stanford, CA: Stanford University Press, 1966), p. 182.
6. Comber, *Chinese Secret Societies*.
7. Comber, *Chinese Secret Societies*, pp. 77–78.
8. Marvin S. Hill, *Quest for Refuge: The Mormon Flight from American Pluralism* (Salt Lake City: Signature Books, 1989), pp. 93, 161; and Kenneth H. Winn, *Exiles in a Land of Liberty* (Chapel Hill, NC: University of North Carolina Press, 1989), p. 167.
9. Hill, *Quest for Refuge*, p. 105.
10. Annette P. Hampshire, *Mormonism in Conflict: The Nauvoo Years*, Studies in Religion and Society, Vol. 11 (New York: Edwin Mellen Press, 1985), pp. 243–45.
11. Hampshire, *Mormonism in Conflict*, p. 150; and Hill, *Quest for Refuge*, p. 182.
12. Hampshire, *Mormonism in Conflict*, p. 251.
13. Hill, *Quest for Refuge*, p. 181.
14. Jules Abels, *Man on Fire: John Brown and the Cause of Liberty* (New York: Macmillan, 1971), p. 47; Louis A. DeCaro, Jr., *"Fire from the Midst of You": A Religious Life of John Brown*

(New York: New York University Press, 2002), pp. 216–18; and Nicole Etcheson, *Bleeding Kansas: Contested Liberty in the Civil War Era* (Lawrence: University Press of Kansas, 2004), p. 57.
15. Abels, *Man on Fire*, pp. 48–49; and DeCaro, "*Fire from the Midst of You*," p. 219.
16. Stephen B. Oates, *To Purge This Land with Blood: A Biography of John Brown*, 2nd ed. (Amherst: University of Massachusetts Press, 1984), p. 146.
17. DeCaro, "*Fire from the Midst of You*," p. 220.
18. Oates, *To Purge This Land*, p. 158.
19. Abels, *Man on Fire*, p. 90.
20. Oates, *To Purge This Land*, p. 256.
21. Andrew Sinclair, *An Anatomy of Terror: A History of Terrorism* (London: Macmillan, 2003), p. 147.
22. Marvin Maurer, "The Ku Klux Klan and the National Liberation Front: Terrorism Applied to Achieve Diverse Goals," in Marius Livingston with Lee Bruce Kress and Marie G. Wanek (eds.), *International Terrorism in the Contemporary World*, Contributions in Political Science No. 3 (Westport, CT: Greenwood, 1978), p. 145.
23. Peter Alter, "Traditions of Violence in the Irish National Movement," in Wolfgang J. Mommsen and Gerhard Hirschfeld (eds.), *Social Protest, Violence and Terror in Nineteenth- and Twentieth-Century Europe* (New York: St. Martin's Press for the German Historical Institute, 1982), p. 137.
24. Peter Heehs, "Terrorism in India during the Freedom Struggle," *Historian*, Vol. 55, No. 3 (1993), pp. 469–82.
25. Rapoport, "The Four Waves of Rebel Terror and September 11," p. 40.
26. Peter Heehs, *Nationalism, Terrorism, Communalism: Essays in Modern Indian History* (Delhi: Oxford University Press, 1998), p. 4.
27. Gaucher, *The Terrorists*, pp. 164–66; and Duncan M. Perry, *The Politics of Terror: The Macedonian Liberation Movements 1893–1903* (Durham, NC: Duke University Press, 1988), pp. 125, 128.
28. Feliks Gross, *Violence in Politics: Terror and Political Assassination in Eastern Europe and Russia*, Studies in the Social Sciences, No. 13 (The Hague: Mouton, 1972), pp. 57, 122–29.
29. Hugh Poulton, *Who Are the Macedonians?* 2nd ed. (Bloomington: Indiana University Press, 2000), p. 53; and Perry, *The Politics of Terror*, p. 117.
30. Ivo Banac, *The National Question in Yugoslavia: Origins, History, Politics* (Ithaca, NY: Cornell University Press, 1984), p. 110.
31. The Russian government apparently was not informed of the assassination attempt on the Archduke, in part because they would have opposed the effort. It is not clear if Black Hand as an organization favored the attempt, although some members clearly did. Cf. Laqueur, *A History of Terrorism*, p. 113.
32. Laqueur, *Terrorism*, p. 44.
33. Andrew Bell-Fialkoff, *Ethnic Cleansing* (New York: St. Martin's Griffin, 1999), p. 149; Richard G. Hovannisian, "The Historical Dimensions of the Armenian Question, 1878–1923," in Richard G. Hovannisian (ed.), *The Armenian Genocide in Perspective* (New Brunswick, NJ: Transaction Books, 1986), p. 24; and Laqueur, *A History of Terrorism*, p. 44.
34. Laqueur, *A History of Terrorism*, p. 50.
35. Ford, *Political Murder*, pp. 208–09.
36. Parry, *Terrorism*, p. 86.
37. Astrid von Borcke, "Violence and Terror in Russian Revolutionary Populism: The *Narodnaya Volya*," in Mommsen and Hirschfeld (eds.), *Social Protest*, p. 48.
38. J. Browyer Bell, *Transnational Terror* (Washington, DC: American Enterprise Institute for Public Policy Research, 1975), p. 5.
39. Parry, *Terrorism*, p. 120.
40. Walther L. Bernecker, "The Strategies of 'Direct Action' and Violence in Spanish Anarchism," in Mommsen and Hirschfeld (eds.), *Social Protest*, pp. 88–111.
41. Walter Laqueur, *The New Terrorism: Fanaticism and the Arms of Mass Destruction* (New York: Oxford University Press, 1999), p. 18; and Maureen Perrie, "Political and Economic Terror in

the Tactics of the Russian Socialist-Revolutionary Party before 1914," in Mommsen and Hirschfeld (eds.), *Social Protest*, p. 72.
42. Gaucher, *The Terrorists*, p. 33; and Laqueur, *The New Terrorism*, p. 18.
43. Laqueur, *The New Terrorism*, p. 19.
44. Winn, *Exiles*, p. 227.
45. Laqueur, *The New Terrorism*, p. 21; and Jaqueur, *A History of Terrorism*, p. 16.
46. Gloria Jahoda, *The Trail of Tears: The Story of the American Indian Removals, 1813–1855* (New York: Wing Books, 1975), Chaps. 4 and 8.
47. Jahoda, *The Trail of Tears*, p. 43; and Dale van Every, *Disinherited: The Lost Birthright of the American Indians* (New York: William Morrow, 1966), p. 132.
48. Norman Finkelstein, "History's Verdict: The Cherokee Case," *Journal of Palestine Studies*, Vol. 24, No. 4 (1995), p. 37; Patricia Cleland Tracey, "Cherokee Gold in Georgia and California," *Journal of the West*, Vol. 39, No. 1 (2000), p. 50; and van Every, *Disinherited*, p. 132.
49. William G. McLoughlin, *Cherokee Renascence in the New Republic* (Princeton, NJ: Princeton University Press, 1986), pp. 432–33.
50. Tracey, "Cherokee Gold," p. 51.
51. Helen Fein, *Accounting for Genocide: National Responses and Jewish Victimization during the Holocaust* (Chicago: University of Chicago Press, 1979), pp. 12–17; and Hovannisian, "The Historical Dimensions," p. 29.
52. Rouben Adalian, "The Armenian Genocide: Context and Legacy," *Social Education: The Official Journal of the National Council for the Social Studies*, Vol. 55, No. 2 (1991), pp. 99–104; and Bell-Fialkoff, *Ethnic Cleansing*, p. 151.
53. Fein, *Accounting for Genocide*, p. 17.
54. Bell-Fialkoff, *Ethnic Cleansing*, p. 151.
55. Jean Chesneaux, "Secret Societies in China's Historical Evolution," in Chesneaux (ed.), *Popular Movements and Secret Societies*, p. 10.
56. Puyraimond, "The Ko-lao Hui," p. 113.
57. Etcheson, *Bleeding Kansas*, pp. 2–4.
58. Laqueur, *The New Terrorism*, p. 21.
59. Walter Laqueur, *Black Hand: The Rise of the Extreme Right in Russia* (New York: Harper Perennial, 1994), p. 26.
60. Duiker, *Cultures in Collision*, p. xvii.
61. Duiker, *Cultures in Collision*, p. 206.
62. Chesneaux, "Secret Societies," p. 10.
63. Laqueur, *Black Hand*, pp. 25–26.
64. Timothy Roberts, "Now the Enemy Is within Our Borders: The Impact of European Revolutions on American Perceptions of Violence before the Civil War," *American Transcendental Quarterly*, Vol. 17, No. 3 (2003), pp. 210–12.
65. Sinclair, *An Anatomy of Terror*, p. 140.
66. Paul Bradley Davis, "American Experiences and the Contemporary Perception of Terrorism," *Small Wars and Insurgencies*, Vol. 7, No. 2 (1996), p. 229; and Maurer, "The Ku Klux Klan," p. 146.
67. Hampshire, *Mormonism in Conflict*, pp. 275–76.
68. Hill, *Quest for Refuge*, p. 181.
69. Martha Crenshaw, "The Causes of Terrorism," in Kegley (ed.), *The New Global Terrorism*, p. 94.
70. Perry, *The Politics of Terror*, pp. 186–88.
71. Maurer, "The Ku Klux Klan," p. 145.
72. Abels, *Man on Fire*, pp. 76, 89.
73. Oates, *To Purge this Land*, p. 256.
74. Oates, *To Purge This Land*, p. 265.
75. Abels, *Man on Fire*, p. 89.
76. Oates, *To Purge This Land*, p. 361.

77. Heehs, "Terrorism in India."
78. von Borcke, "Violence and Terror," p. 49.
79. Alter, "Traditions of Violence," p. 144.
80. Huntington, "Political Development and Political Decay," pp. 95–139.

Chapter Seven Terrorist Groups between the Wars

1. Banac, *The National Question in Yugoslavia*, p. 309.
2. Banac, *The National Question*, p. 323; and Poulton, *Who Are the Macedonians?* p. 93.
3. Banac, *The National Question*, pp. 320, 367; and Poulton, *Who Are the Macedonians?* p. 92.
4. Banac, *The National Question*, pp. 303, 326; and Poulton, *Who Are the Macedonians?* p. 92.
5. Mark Biondich, " 'We Were Defending the State': Nationalism, Myth, and Memory in Twentieth-Century Croatia," in Lampe and Mazower (eds.), *Ideologies and National Identities*, p. 58.
6. Poulton, *Who Are the Macedonians?* p. 79.
7. Murray Clark Havens, Carl Leiden, and Karl P. Schmitt, *Assassination and Terrorism: Their Modern Dimensions*, rev. ed. (Manchaca, TX: Sterling Swift Publishing, 1975), pp. 80–90.
8. Michael Laffan, "Violence and Terror in Twentieth-Century Ireland: IRB and IRA," in Mommsen and Hirschfeld (eds.), *Social Protest, Violence and Terror in Nineteenth- and Twentieth-Century Europe* (New York: St. Martin's Press for the German Historical Society, 1982), p. 161.
9. Peter Taylor, *Behind the Mask: The IRA and Sinn Fein* (New York: TV Books, 1997), pp. 28–29.
10. Bell, *Transnational Terror*, p. 30; and Laffan, "Violence and Terror," p. 170.
11. Heehs, *Nationalism, Terrorism, Communalism*, p. 8; and Michael Silvestri, " 'The Sinn Fein of India': Irish Nationalism and the Policing of Revolutionary Terrorism in Bengal," *Journal of British Studies*, Vol. 39, No. 4 (2000), pp. 461–62.
12. Laqueur, *A History of Terrorism*, p. 46.
13. Michael J. Cohen, "Introduction," in Michael J. Cohen (ed.), *The Rise of Israel: Jewish Resistance to British Rule in Palestine 1944–1947*, Vol. 34 in The Rise of Israel: A Documentary Record from the Nineteenth Century to 1948 (New York: Garland Publishing, 1987), pp. v–vii; Gaucher, *The Terrorists*, p. 204; and David Schafer, "Origins of the Israeli/Palestinian Conflict: The Seeds of Enmity," *Humanist*, Vol. 62, No. 5 (2002), p. 12.
14. Caleb Carr, *The Lessons of Terror: A History of Warfare against Civilians, Why It Has Failed and Why It Will Fail Again* (New York: Random House, 2002), p. 211.
15. Ehud Sprinzak, "Extremism and Violence in Israeli Democracy," *Terrorism and Political Violence*, Vol. 12, No. 3/4 (2000), p. 213.
16. Schafer, "Origins of the Israeli/Palestinian Conflict," p. 13.
17. Richard K. Tucker, *The Dragon and the Cross: The Rise and Fall of the Ku Klux Klan in Middle America* (Hamden, CT: Archon Books, 1991), p. 5.
18. Sinclair, *An Anatomy of Terror*, p. 231.
19. Michael J. Schroeder, " 'To Induce a Sense of Terror': Caudillo Politics and Political Violence in Northern Nicaragua, 1926–34 and 1981–95," in Campbell and Brenner (eds.), *Death Squads in Global Perspective*, pp. 27–56.
20. Gaucher, *The Terrorists*, pp. 138–39.
21. Ford, *Political Murder*, pp. 256, 266–67; and Parry, *Terrorism*, p. 441.
22. Havens et al., *Assassination and Terrorism*, pp. 31, 40.
23. Adrian Lyttelton, "Fascism and Violence in Post-War Italy: Political Strategy and Social Conflict," in Mommsen and Hirschfeld (eds.), *Social Protest*, p. 266.
24. Lyttelton, "Fascism and Violence," p. 259.
25. Burton, *Urban Terrorism*, p. 69.

26. Lyttelton, "Fascism and Violence," p. 259.
27. Peter H. Merkl, "Approaches to Political Violence: The Stormtroopers," in Mommsen and Hirschfeld (eds.), *Social Protest*, p. 369.
28. Richard Bessel, "Violence as Propaganda: The Role of the Storm Troopers in the Rise of National Socialism," in Thomas Childers (ed.), *The Formation of the Nazi Constituency, 1919–1933* (Totowa, NJ: Barnes & Noble, 1986), p. 138.
29. Bessel, "Violence as Propaganda," p. 137; and Peter H. Merkl, *The Making of a Stormtrooper* (Boulder, CO: Westview, 1987), p. 171.
30. Benjamin Ziemann, "Germany after the First World War—A Violent Society?: Results and Implications of Recent Research on Weimar Germany," *Journal of European History*, Vol. 1, No. 1 (2003), p. 89.
31. Merkl, *Making of a Stormtrooper*, p. 181.
32. A. F. Upton, "Finland," in S. J. Woolf (ed.), *European Fascism* (New York: Vintage Books, 1968), p. 201.
33. Risto Alapuro and Erik Allardt, "The Lapua Movement: The Threat of Rightist Takeover in Finland," in Juan J. Linz and Alfred Stephan (eds.), *The Breakdown of Democratic Regimes: Europe* (Baltimore, MD: Johns Hopkins University Press, 1978), pp. 122–41.
34. Ludwig Jedlicka, "The Austrian Heimwehr," in Walter Laqueur and George L. Mosse (eds.), *International Fascism, 1920–1945*, Journal of Contemporary History 1 (New York: Harper and Row, 1966), p. 132; and Stadler, "Austria," in Woolf (ed.), *European Fascism*, p. 95.
35. Ivan T. Berend, *Decades of Crisis: Central and Eastern Europe before World War II* (Berkeley, CA: University of California Press, 1998), pp. 302–08; and Stadler, "Austria," p. 88.
36. Z. Barbu, "Rumania," in Woolf (ed.), *European Fascism*, pp. 152–53.
37. Laqueur, *A History of Terrorism*, p. 73.
38. Barbu, "Rumania," p. 157; and Constantin Iordachi, "Charisma, Religion, and Ideology: Romania's Interwar Legion of the Archangel Michael," in Lampe and Mazower (eds.), *Ideologies and National Identities*, p. 29.
39. Gaucher, *The Terrorists*, p. 145; and Barbu, "Rumania," p. 158.
40. Eugen Weber, "The Men of the Archangel," in Laqueur and Mosse (eds.), *International Fascism*, p. 103.
41. Joseph Baglieri, "Italian Fascism and the Crisis of Liberal Hegemony: 1901-1922," in Stein Ugelvik Larsen, Bernt Hagtvet, and Jan Petter Myklebust (eds.), *Who Were the Fascists: Social Roots of European Fascism* (Bergen: Universitetsforlaget, 1980), p. 327.
42. Anthony Read and David Fisher, *Kristallnacht: The Unleashing of the Holocaust* (New York: Peter Bedrick, 1989).
43. Arthur D. Brenner, "*Feme* Murder: Paramilitary 'Self-Justice' in Weimar Germany," in Campbell and Brenner (eds.), *Death Squads*, pp. 57–65, 77.
44. M. Ranier Lepsius, "From Fragmented Party Democracy to Government by Emergency Decree and National Socialist Takeover: Germany," in Linz and Stephan (eds.), *Breakdown of Democratic Regimes*, p. 68.
45. Bessel, "Violence as Propaganda," p. 135.
46. Schroeder, "To Induce a Sense of Terror," pp. 32–34.
47. Jens Petersen, "Violence in Italian Fascism," in Mommsen and Hirschfeld (eds.), *Social Violence*, p. 282.
48. Jedlicka, "The Austrian Heimwehr," p. 132.
49. Sheila Fitzpatrick, *Everyday Stalinism: Ordinary Life in Extraordinary Times: Soviet Russia in the 1930s* (New York: Oxford University Press, 1999), p. 209.
50. Paul B. Henze, "Russia and the Caucasus," *Studies in Conflict and Terrorism*, Vol. 19, No. 4 (1996), p. 390.
51. Fein, *Accounting for Genocide*; and Brenda D. Lutz and James M. Lutz, "Gypsies as Victims of the Holocaust," *Holocaust and Genocide Studies*, Vol. 9, No. 3 (1995), pp. 346–59.
52. Lutz and Lutz, "Gypsies as Victims," pp. 349, 353.
53. Biondich, "We Were Serving the State," p. 62.

54. Jedlicka, "The Austrian Heimwehr," p. 128; and Stadler, "Austria," p. 159.
55. Berend, *Decades of Crisis*, p. 306.
56. Walter Laqueur, *Terrorism* (Boston: Little Brown, 1977), p. 81.
57. Merkl, *Making of a Stormtrooper*, p. 171; and Bessel, "Violence as Propaganda," p. 137.
58. Ziemann, "Germany after the First World War," p. 81.
59. Juan J. Linz, "Political Space and Fascism as a Late-Comer," in Larsen et al. (eds.), *Who Were the Fascists*, p. 158.
60. S. J. Woolf, "Italy," in Woolf (ed.), *European Fascism*, pp. 48–49.
61. Schroeder, "To Induce a Sense of Terror," p. 32.
62. Taylor, *Behind the Mask*, p. 21.
63. Wolfgang J. Mommsen, "Non-Legal Violence and Terrorism in Western Industrial Societies: An Historical Analysis," in Mommsen and Hirschfeld (eds.), *Social Protest*, p. 395.
64. Berend, *Decades of Crisis*, pp. 200–01; and Lyttelton, "Fascism and Violence," p. 258.
65. Berend, *Decades of Crisis*, p. 188.
66. Iordachi, "Charisma, Religion, and Ideology," p. 22.
67. Banac, *The National Question*, p. 326; and Poulton, *Who Are the Macedonians?* p. 92.
68. Gaucher, *The Terrorists*, p. 205; and Schafer, "Origins of the Israeli/Palestinian Conflict," p. 12.
69. Gaucher, *The Terrorists*, p. 205.
70. Wilkinson, *Terrorism versus Democracy*, p. 22.
71. Upton, "Finland," p. 199.
72. Laqueur, *Terrorism*, p. 117.
73. V. Khoros, "The 'Crown'," p. 71.
74. Bruce Hoffman, "Rethinking Terrorism and Counter-Terrorism since 9/11," *Studies in Conflict and Terrorism*, Vol. 25, No. 5 (2002), p. 311.

Chapter Eight The End of Empires and Terrorism

1. Hoffman, *Inside Terrorism*, p. 46.
2. John Walton, *Reluctant Rebels: Comparative Studies of Revolution and Underdevelopment* (New York: Columbia University Press, 1984), p. 74.
3. Michael Laffan, "Violence and Terror in Twentieth-Century Ireland: IRB and IRA," in Mommsen and Hirschfeld (eds.), *Social Protest, Violence and Terror*, p. 171.
4. Alan O'Day, "Northern Ireland, Terrorism, and the British States," in Yonah Alexander, David Carlton, and Paul Wilkinson (eds.), *Terrorism: Theory and Practice* (Boulder, CO: Westview Press, 1979), pp. 125–26.
5. Cohen, "Introduction," p. vi.
6. Gaucher, *The Terrorists*, p. 220; and Hoffman, *Inside Terrorism*, p. 50.
7. Ian F.W. Beckett, *Modern Insurgencies and Counter-Insurgencies: Guerrillas and Their Opponents since 1750* (London: Routledge, 2001), pp. 88–89; and Cohen, "Introduction," p. vi.
8. Hoffman, *Inside Terrorism*, p. 51.
9. Wilfred Blythe, *The Impact of Chinese Secret Societies in Malaya: A Historical Study* (London: Oxford University Press, 1969), p. 419.
10. Robert Jackson, *The Malayan Emergency: The Commonwealth's Wars, 1948–1966* (London: Routledge, 1991), p. 14; and Sir Robert Thompson, *Defeating Communist Insurgency: The Lessons of Malaya and Vietnam*, Studies in International Security 10 (New York: Praeger, 1966), p. 24.
11. Peter Chalk, "Political Terrorism in South-East Asia," *Terrorism and Political Violence*, Vol. 10, No. 2 (1998), p. 120.

12. Beckett, *Modern Insurgencies*, p. 103; Jackson, *The Malayan Emergency*, p. 115; and Thompson, *Defeating Communist Insurgency*, p. 27.
13. Victor Purcell, *Malaysia* (New York: Walker, 1967), p. 113.
14. Beckett, *Modern Insurgencies*, p. 103.
15. Hoffman, *Inside Terrorism*, p. 58; and Brian M. Jenkins, "Defense against Terrorism," *Political Science Quarterly*, Vol. 101, No. 5 (1986), p. 776.
16. Beckett, *Modern Insurgencies*, p. 154.
17. Walton, *Reluctant Rebels*, p. 121.
18. Frank Furedi, *The Mau Mau War in Perspective*, East African Studies (London: James Currey, 1989), p. 110.
19. Beckett, *Modern Insurgencies*, p. 124; and Furedi, *Mau Mau War*, pp. 114–15.
20. Beckett, *Modern Insurgencies*, p. 128.
21. Hoffman, *Inside Terrorism*, pp. 62–64.
22. Beckett, *Modern Insurgencies*, p. 163; Gaucher, *The Terrorists*, p. 230; and Michael Stohl, "Demystifying the Mystery of International Terrorism," in Kegley (ed.), *International Terrorism*, p. 85.
23. Beckett, *Modern Insurgencies*, p. 165; and Hoffman, *Inside Terrorism*, p. 63.
24. Martha Crenshaw, "The Effectiveness of Terrorism in the Algerian War," in Martha Crenshaw (ed.), *Terrorism in Context* (University Park, PA: Pennsylvania University Press, 1995), p. 484.
25. Shaun Gregory, "France and the War on Terrorism," *Terrorism and Political Violence*, Vol. 15, No. 1 (2003), p. 128.
26. Laqueur, *A History of Terrorism*, p. 46.
27. Sinclair, *An Anatomy of Terror*, p. 269.
28. Bell-Fialkoff, *Ethnic Cleansing*, p. 41.
29. Gavin Williams and Terisa Turner, "Nigeria," in John Dunn (ed.), *West African States: Failure and Promise: A Study in Comparative Politics*, African Studies Series 23 (Cambridge: Cambridge University Press, 1978), p. 144.
30. Williams and Turner, "Nigeria," p. 144.
31. John Hatch, *Nigeria: The Seeds of Disaster* (Chicago: Henry Regnery, 1970), p. 284; and Williams and Turner, "Nigeria," p. 146.
32. Bell-Fialkoff, *Ethnic Cleansing*, p. 40.
33. Jeffrey M. Bale, "The May 1973 Terrorist Attack at Milan Police HQ: Anarchist 'Propaganda of the Deed' or 'False-Flag' Provocation," *Terrorism and Political Violence*, Vol. 8, No. 1 (1996), p. 154; and Leonard Weinberg, "Italian Neo-Fascist Terrorism: A Comparative Perspective," in Tore Bjorgo (ed.), *Terror from the Extreme Right* (London: Frank Cass, 1995), p. 232.
34. Robert F. Arnove, "Students in Politics," in John D. Martz and David J. Meyers (eds.), *Venezuela: The Democratic Experience* (New York: Praeger, 1977), p. 204.
35. Beckett, *Modern Insurgencies*, p. 177.
36. Gaucher, *The Terrorists*, p. 305.
37. Robert Cribb, "From *Petrus* to Ninja: Death Squads in Indonesia," in Campbell and Brenner (eds.), *Death Squads in Global Perspective*, p. 184.
38. Trouillot, *Haiti*, p. 156.
39. Elizabeth Abbott, *Haiti: The Duvaliers and Their Legacy* (New York: McGraw-Hill, 1988), p. 7.
40. Abbott, *Haiti*, p. 150; and Trouillot, *Haiti*, pp. 166–68, 189–90.
41. Donna M. Schlagheck, "The Superpowers, Foreign Policy, and Terrorism," in Kegley (ed.), *International Terrorism*, pp. 170–77.
42. Bale, "May 1973 Terrorist Attack," p. 134.
43. Asher Arian, *The Second Republic: Politics in Israel* (Chatham, NJ: Chatham House, 1998), p. 111.
44. Michael M. Harrison, "France and International Terrorism: Problem and Response," in Charters (ed.), *The Deadly Sin of Terrorism*, p. 105.
45. Beckett, *Modern Insurgencies*, p. 167.

46. Long, *Anatomy of Terrorism*, p. 95; and Karel A. Steenbrink, "Muslim-Christian Relations in the Pancasila State of Indonesia," *The Muslim World*, Vol. 88, No. 3/4 (1998), pp. 320–52.
47. Hatch, *Nigeria*, p. 284.
48. Marlye Gelin-Adams and David M. Malone, "Haiti: A Case of Endemic Weakness," in Robert I. Rotberg (ed.), *State Failure and State Weakness in a Time of Terror* (Cambridge, MA, and Washington, DC: World Peace Foundation and Brookings Institution Press, 2003), p. 301.
49. Trouillot, *Haiti*, p. 31.
50. Desai and Eckstein, "Insurgency," p. 463.
51. Hoffman, *Inside Terrorism*, p. 52.
52. Beckett, *Modern Insurgencies*, p. 165; and Martha Crenshaw, "The Effectiveness of Terrorism," p. 499.
53. Hoffman, *Inside Terrorism*, p. 59.
54. Walton, *Reluctant Rebels*, p. 130.
55. Richard Drake, *The Revolutionary Mystique and Terrorism in Contemporary Italy* (Bloomington, IN: Indiana University Press, 1989), p. 22.
56. Wilkinson, *Terrorism versus Democracy*, p. 22.

Chapter Nine The Rise of the New Left and the Failure of Communism: Increasing Terrorism on a Global Scale

1. Jeffrey Kaplan, *Radical Religion in America: Millenarian Movements from the Far Right to the Children of Noah* (Syracuse: Syracuse University Press, 1997), p. 13.
2. Hoffman, *Inside Terrorism*, p. 164; and Lutz and Lutz, *Global Terrorism*, pp. 163–64.
3. Philip Jenkins, "Strategy of Tension: The Belgium Terrorist Crisis 1982–1986," *Terrorism*, Vol. 13, No. 4/5 (1990), pp. 299–309.
4. Nadine Gurr and Benjamin Cole, *The New Face of Terrorism: Threats from Weapons of Mass Destruction* (London: I.B. Taurus, 2000), p. 148; and Kaplan, *Radical Religion in America*, p. 61.
5. Saul Landau, *The Guerrilla Wars of Central America: Nicaragua, El Salvador & Guatemala* (New York: St. Martin's, 1993), pp. 39–46.
6. Anderson and Sloan, *Terrorism: Assassins to Zealots*, pp. 8–9; and Christopher C. Harmon, "Five Strategies of Terrorism," *Small Wars and Insurgencies*, Vol. 12, No. 3 (2001), p. 40.
7. Cf. A. J. Jongman, "Trends in International and Domestic Terrorism in Western Europe, 1968–1988," *Terrorism and Political Violence*, Vol. 4, No. 4 (1992), pp. 26–76.
8. Martha Crenshaw, "Thoughts on Relating Terrorism to Historical Contexts," in Crenshaw (ed.), *Terrorism in Context*, p. 21.
9. Merkl, "West German Left-Wing Terrorism," in Crenshaw (ed.), *Terrorism in Context*, p. 166; and Dennis A. Pluchinsky, "An Organizational and Operational Analysis of Germany's Red Army Faction Terrorist Group (1972–1991)," in Yonah Alexander and Dennis A. Pluchinsky (eds.), *European Terrorism: Today and Tomorrow* (Washington, DC: Brassey's, 1992), p. 44.
10. Pluchinsky, "Organizational and Operational Analysis," p. 81.
11. Robert H. Evans, "Italy and International Terrorism," in Charters (ed.), *The Deadly Sin of Terrorism*, p. 74.
12. Richard Drake, "Red Brigades," in Martha Crenshaw and John Pimlott (eds.), *Encyclopedia of World Terrorism*, Vol. 3 (Armonk, NY: M. E. Sharpe, 1997), p. 561; and Marco Rimanelli, "Italian Terrorism and Society, 1940s–1980s: Roots, Ideologies, Evolution, and International Connections," *Terrorism*, Vol. 12, No. 4 (1989), p. 270.
13. Laqueur, *The New Terrorism*, p. 29.

14. Drake, "Red Brigades," p. 562.
15. Wilkinson, *Terrorism versus Democracy*, p. 98.
16. George Kassimeris, "Greece: Twenty Years of Political Terrorism," *Terrorism and Political Violence*, Vol. 7, No. 2 (1995), pp. 74–75.
17. Andrew Corsun, "Group Profile: The Revolutionary Organization 17 November in Greece (1975–1991)," in Alexander and Pluchinsky (eds.), *European Terrorism*, pp. 93, 116; Christopher C. Harmon, *Terrorism Today* (London: Frank Cass, 2000), p. 14; and George Kassimeris, *Europe's Last Red Terrorists: The Revolutionary Organization 17 November* (New York: New York University Press, 2001).
18. Corsun, "Group Profile," p. 102.
19. Tadashi Kuramatsu, "Japanese Terrorism," in Crenshaw and Pimlott (eds.), *Encyclopedia of World Terrorism*, Vol. 3, pp. 568–70.
20. Wilkinson, "Why Modern Terrorism?" p. 117.
21. Sumanta Banerjee, "Naxalbari and the Left Movement," in Ghanshyam Shah (ed.), *Social Movements and the State*, Readings in Indian Government and Politics, Vol. 4 (New Delhi: Sage, 2002), pp. 125–35.
22. Laqueur, *The New Terrorism*, p. 191.
23. Gamini Samaranayake, "Patterns of Political Violence and Responses of the Government in Sri Lanka, 1971–1996," *Terrorism and Political Violence*, Vol. 11, No. 1 (1999), p. 114.
24. Samaranayake, "Patterns of Political Violence," p. 114; and Gamini Samaranayake, "Political Violence in Sri Lanka: A Diagnostic Approach," *Terrorism and Political Violence*, Vol. 9, No. 2 (1997), p. 114.
25. Long, *Anatomy of Terrorism*, p. 57.
26. Samaranayake, "Political Violence in Sri Lanka," p. 114.
27. Beckett, *Modern Insurgencies and Counter-Insurgencies*, p. 205; and Harmon, "Five Strategies of Terrorism," p. 52.
28. Long, *Anatomy of Terrorism*, p. 85; and David Scott Palmer, "Peru, the Drug Business and Shining Path: Between Scylla and Charybdis?" *Journal of Interamerican Studies and World Affairs*, Vol. 34, No. 3 (1992), p. 78; and "The Revolutionary Terrorism of Peru's Shining Path," in Crenshaw (ed.), *Terrorism in Context*, p. 266.
29. William A. Hazelton and Sandra Woy-Hazelton, "Terrorism and the Marxist Left: Peru's Struggle against Sendero Luminoso," *Terrorism*, Vol. 11, No. 6 (1988), p. 482.
30. T. David Mason and Christopher Campany, "Guerrillas, Drugs and Peasants: The Rational Peasant and the War on Drugs," *Terrorism and Political Violence*, Vol. 7, No. 4 (1995), pp. 164–65.
31. Pamala L. Griset and Sue Mahan, *Terrorism in Perspective* (Thousand Oaks, CA: Sage Publications, 2003), p. 200.
32. Roman D. Ortiz, "Insurgent Strategies in the Post-Cold War: The Case of the Revolutionary Armed Forces of Colombia," *Studies in Conflict and Terrorism*, Vol. 25, No. 2 (2002), p. 131.
33. Laqueur, *The New Terrorism*, p. 214.
34. Long, *Anatomy of Terrorism*, p. 83.
35. Suzanne Bettina Danneskiold Lassen, "Drug Trafficking and Terrorism in Colombia," in Rubin (ed.), *Politics of Counterterrorism*, p. 133.
36. Kevin G. Barnhurst, "Contemporary Terrorism in Peru: Sendero Luminoso and the Media," *Journal of Communication*, Vol. 4, No. 4 (1991), p. 85; and Mason and Campany, "Guerrillas, Drugs, and Peasants," p. 166.
37. Hazelton and Hazelton-Woy, "Terrorism and the Marxist Left," p. 485; and Palmer, "Peru," p. 69.
38. Cindy C. Combs, *Terrorism in the Twenty-First Century*, 2nd ed. (Upper Saddle River, NJ: Prentice Hall, 2000), p. 100.
39. Lassen, "Drug Trafficking," pp. 113, 116; and Max G. Manwaring, "Non-State Actors in Colombia: Threats to the State and to the Hemisphere," *Small Wars and Insurgencies*, Vol. 13, No. 2 (2002), p. 70.

40. Chris Quillen, "A Historical Analysis of Mass Casualty Bombers," *Studies in Conflict and Terrorism*, Vol. 25, No. 5 (2002), p. 282.
41. David P. Thompson, "Pablo Escobar, Drug Baron: His Surrender, Imprisonment, and Escape," *Studies in Conflict and Terrorism*, Vol. 19, No. 1 (1996), p. 63.
42. Thompson, "Pablo Escobar," p. 55.
43. Beckett, *Modern Insurgencies*, pp. 175–76.
44. Richard Clutterbuck, *Living with Terrorism* (London: Faber and Faber, 1975), p. 36.
45. Jonathan R. White, *Terrorism: An Introduction*, 2nd ed. (Belmont, CA: Wadsworth, 1998), p. 76.
46. Richard Gillespie, "Political Violence in Argentina: Guerrillas, Terrorists, and Carapintadas," in Crenshaw (ed.), *Terrorism in Context*, p. 222.
47. Parry, *Terrorism*, p. 266; and Gary W. Wynia, *Argentina: Illusions and Realities* (New York: Holmes & Meier, 1986), p. 82.
48. Wynia, *Argentina*, p. 79.
49. Richard Gillespie, *Soldiers of Peron: Argentina's Montoneros* (Oxford: Clarendon Press, 1982), pp. 150–51.
50. Daniel Poneman, *Argentina: Democracy on Trial* (New York: Paragon House, 1987), p. 33.
51. Ihsan Bal and Sedat Laciner, "The Challenge of Revolutionary Terrorism to Turkish Democracy, 1960–80." *Terrorism and Political Violence*, Vol. 13, No. 4 (2001), p. 111.
52. Bal and Laciner, "Challenge of Revolutionary Terrorism," p. 101.
53. Jongman, "Trends," pp. 71–72.
54. Sabri Sayari and Bruce Hoffman, "Urbanisation and Insurgency: The Turkish Case, 1976–1980," *Small Wars and Insurgencies*, Vol. 5, No. 2 (1994), p. 171.
55. Bal and Laciner, "Challenge of Revolutionary Terrorism," p. 106; and Sayari and Hoffman, "Urbanisation and Insurgency," p. 162.
56. Cf. Jongman, "Trends," p. 72.
57. Jerrold D. Green, "Terrorism and Politics in Iran," in Crenshaw (ed.), *Terrorism in Context*, pp. 579–80.
58. James A. Bill and Carl Leiden, *Politics in the Middle East*, 2nd ed. (Boston: Little Brown, 1984), p. 388.
59. Green, "Terrorism and Politics," pp. 579–80.
60. Joseph Kostiner, "War, Terror, Revolution: The Iran–Iraq Conflict," in Rubin (ed.), *The Politics of Terrorism*, p. 125.
61. Jeffrey Ian Ross, "The Rise and Fall of Quebecois Separatist Terrorism: A Qualitative Application of Factors from Two Models," *Studies in Conflict and Terrorism*, Vol. 18, No. 5 (1995), pp. 285–97.
62. Michael M. Harrison, "France and International Terrorism: Problem and Response," in Charters (ed.), *The Deadly Sin of Terrorism*, p. 104; and Jongman, "Trends."
63. Parry, *Terrorism*, p. 111.
64. Gerhard Brunn, "Nationalist Violence and Terror in the Spanish Border Provinces: ETA," in Mommsen and Hirschfeld (eds.), *Social Protest, Violence and Terror*, p. 122; and Shabad and Ramo, "Political Violence in a Democratic State," p. 441.
65. Albin, "The Politics of Terrorism," p. 202; Brunn, "Nationalist Violence," p. 123; and Paddy Woodworth, "Why Do They Kill? The Basque Conflict in Spain," *World Policy*, Vol. 18, No. 1 (2001), p. 1.
66. Shabad and Ramo, "Political Violence in a Democratic State," p. 436.
67. O'Day, "Northern Ireland, Terrorism, and the British States," p. 126.
68. Coogan, *The IRA*, p. 261.
69. Chalk, *West European Terrorism and Counter-Terrorism*, p. 178.
70. Holland, *Hope against History*, pp. 120–22.
71. Bonner, "The United Kingdom's Response to Terrorism," p. 179.
72. Hoffman, *Inside Terrorism*, p. 182.
73. Chalk, "Political Terrorism in South-East Asia," *Terrorism and Political Violence*, pp. 118–34.

74. Krishna, "India and Sri Lanka," p. 270.
75. Joshi, "On the Razor's Edge," p. 21; and Long, *Anatomy of Terrorism*, p. 55.
76. Albin, "The Politics of Terrorism," p. 215; and Bruce Hoffman and Gordon McCormick, "Terrorism, Signaling, and Suicide Attack," *Studies in Conflict and Terrorism*, Vol. 27, No. 4 (2004), p. 258.
77. Joshi, "On the Razor's Edge," p. 19; and Long, *Anatomy of Terror*, p. 55.
78. Long, *Anatomy of Terrorism*, p. 55.
79. Samaramayake, "Political Violence in Sri Lanka," pp. 116–17.
80. Wallace, "Political Violence and Terrorism in India," p. 357.
81. Gossman, "India's Secret Armies," p. 263.
82. Hoffman, " 'Holy Terror'," p. 279.
83. Gossman, "India's Secret Armies," p. 264.
84. Narendra Subramanian, "Ethnicity and Pluralism," pp. 724–25.
85. Harrison, "France and International Terrorism," pp. 108–09; and Jongman, "Trends," p. 52.
86. Yezid Sayigh, "The Armed Struggle and Palestinian Nationalism," in Avraham Sela and Moshe Ma'oz (eds.), *The PLO and Israel: From Armed Conflict to Political Solution, 1964–1994* (New York: St. Martin's, 1997), pp. 251–52.
87. Carr, *The Lessons of Terror,* pp. 214–15.
88. Heinz Vetschera, "Terrorism in Austria: Experiences and Responses," *Terrorism and Political Violence*, Vol. 4, No. 4 (1992), pp. 214–15.
89. Vetschera, "Terrorism in Austria," pp. 214–15.
90. Noemi Gal-Or, "Countering Terrorism in Israel," in Charters (ed.), *The Deadly Sin of Terrorism*, p. 141.
91. Kuramatsu, "Japanese Terrorism," p. 570.
92. Hanauer, "The Path to Redemption," p. 263; and Shmuel Sandler, "Religious Zionism and the State: Political Accommodation and Religious Radicalism in Israel," in Bruce Maddy-Weitzman and Efraim Inbar (eds.), *Religious Radicalism in the Greater Middle East* (London: Frank Cass, 1997), p. 144.
93. Hoffman, *Inside Terrorism*, pp. 102–03.
94. Sandler, "Religious Zionism," p. 144.
95. Sprinzak, "Extremism and Violence in Israeli Democracy," pp. 223–24.
96. Gal-Or, "Countering Terrorism," pp. 150, 164–65.
97. Kostiner, "War, Terror, Revolution," p. 116.
98. Martha Crenshaw, "Why Is America the Primary Target? Terrorism as Globalized Civil War," in Kegley (ed.), *The New Global Terrorism*, pp. 163–64.
99. Ayla Schbley, "Defining Religious Terrorism: A Causal and Anthological Profile," *Studies in Conflict and Terrorism*, Vol. 26, No. 2 (2003), p. 109.
100. Oren Barak, "Lebanon: Failure, Collapse, and Resuscitation," in Rotberg (ed.), *State Failure and State Weakness*, p. 317.
101. Krishna, "India and Sri Lanka," p. 270.
102. Krishna, "India and Sri Lanka," p. 270; Joyce J. M. Pettigrew, *The Sikhs of the Punjab: Unheard Voices of State and Guerrilla Violence* (London: Zed Books, 1995); and Wallace, "Political Violence and Terrorism," p. 387.
103. Gal-Or, "Countering Terrorism," pp. 148, 165.
104. Cynthia J. Arnson, "Window on the Past: A Declassified History of Death Squads in El Salvador," in Campbell and Brenner (eds.), *Death Squads*, p. 89.
105. Frank M. Afflitto, "The Homogenizing Effects of State-Sponsored Terrorism: The Case of Guatemala," in Sluka (ed.), *Death Squad*, p. 116.
106. Parry, *Terrorism*, p. 271.
107. Patricia Weiss Fagen, "Repression and State Security," in Juan E. Corradi, Patricia Weiss Fagen, and Manuel Antonio Garreton (eds.), *Fear at the Edge: State Terror and Resistance in Latin America* (Berkeley, CA: University of California Press, 1992), p. 64.

108. Keith Gottschalk, "The Rise and Fall of Apartheid's Death Squads," in Campbell and Brenner (eds.), *Death Squads*, pp. 229–59; and David Welsh, "Right-Wing Terrorism in South Africa," in Bjorgo (ed.), *Terror from the Extreme Right*, pp. 239–64.
109. Peter Chalk, "The Response to Terrorism as a Threat to Liberal Democracy," *Australian Journal of Politics and History*, Vol. 44, No. 3 (1998), pp. 380–81.
110. Cline, "The Islamic Insurgency in the Philippines," p. 121; and Eva-Lotta Hedman, "State of Siege: Political Violence and Vigilante Mobilization in the Philippines," in Campbell and Brenner (eds.), *Death Squads*, pp. 133–37.
111. Samaranayake, "Patterns of Political Violence," p. 117.
112. George J. Aditjondro, "Ninjas, Nanggalas, Monuments, and Mossad Manuals: An Anthropology of Indonesian State Terror in East Timor," in Sluka (ed.), *Death Squad*, p. 158; and David Claridge, "State Terrorism? Applying a Definitional Model," *Terrorism and Political Violence*, Vol. 8, No. 3 (1994), pp. 95–106.
113. Aditjondro, "Ninjas," p. 171; and Claridge, "State Terrorism."
114. Matthew Jardine, "Power and Principle in East Timor," *Peace Review*, Vol. 10, No. 2 (1998), p. 195.
115. Gossman, "India's Secret Armies," p. 263; and Joyce Pettigrew, "Parents and Their Children in Situations of Terror: Disappearances and Special Police Activity in Punjab," in Sluka (ed.), *Death Squad*, p. 206.
116. Cline, "Islamic Insurgency," p. 133; Holland, *Hope Against History*, p. 141; and Long, *Anatomy of Terrorism*, p. 109.
117. Hoffman, *Inside Terrorism*, p. 194; and Laqueur, *The New Terrorism*, pp. 117–18.
118. Singh, "Kashmir, Pakistan and the War by Terror," pp. 81–94.
119. Pluchinsky, "Organizational and Operational Analysis," p. 81; and Rimanelli, "Italian Terrorism and Society," p. 280.
120. Joshi, "On the Razor's Edge," p. 22; and Laqueur, *The New Terrorism*, p. 194.
121. Gal-Or, "Countering Terrorism," p. 141; Harvey Kushner, *Terrorism in America: A Structural Approach to Understanding the Terrorist Threat* (Springfield, IL: Charles C. Thomas, 1998), p. 14.
122. Jae Taik Kim, "North Korean Terrorism: Trends, Characteristics, and Deterrence," *Terrorism*, Vol. 11, No. 4 (1988), p. 315; and Wilkinson, *Terrorism and the Liberal State*, p. 184.
123. Wilkinson, *Terrorism and the Liberal State*, p. 198.
124. Martha Crenshaw, "Democracy, Commitment Problems and Managing Ethnic Violence: The Case of India and Sri Lanka," *Terrorism and Political Violence*, Vol. 12, No. 3/4 (1998), p. 139; Erin K. Jenne, "Sri Lanka: A Fragmented State," in Rotberg (ed.), *State Failure and State Weakness*, p. 228; and Joshi, "On the Razor's Edge," pp. 22–23.
125. Brunn, "Nationalist Violence and Terror," p. 117.
126. Harmon, "Five Strategies of Terrorism," p. 54.
127. Kassimeris, *Europe's Last Red Terrorists*, p. 201; and Sayari and Hoffman, "Urbanisation and Insurgency," p. 163.
128. Greenway, "Hindu Nationalism Clouds the Face of India," p. 91; and Mark Juergensmeyer, "The Worldwide Rise of Religious Nationalism," *Journal of International Affairs*, Vol. 50, No. 1 (1996), p. 6.
129. Kassimeris, "Greece," p. 85.
130. Chalk, "The Response to Terrorism," p. 384.
131. Barnhurst, "Contemporary Terrorism in Peru," p. 82.
132. Bal and Laciner, "Challenge of Revolutionary Terrorism," p. 106.
133. McKenna, "Murdered or Martyred," pp. 196–97.
134. Barak, "Lebanon," p. 314.
135. Merkl, "West German Left-Wing Terrorism," pp. 172–73.
136. Donatella della Porta, "Left-Wing Terrorism in Italy," in Crenshaw (ed.), *Terrorism in Context*, p. 119; and Drake, "Red Brigades," pp. 564–65.
137. Kassimeris, *Europe's Last Red Terrorists*, p. 150.

138. Lutz and Lutz, *Global Terrorism*, pp. 140–41.
139. Vetschera, "Terrorism in Austria," p. 214.
140. Gal-Or, "Countering Terrorism," p. 143.
141. Kushner, *Terrorism in America*, pp. 21–22; and Gal-Or, "Countering Terrorism," p. 44.
142. Wilkinson, *Terrorism and the Liberal State*, p. 193; and *Terrorism versus Democracy*, p. 200.
143. Harrison, "France and International Terrorism," p. 107; and Jeremy Shapiro and Benedicte Suzan, "The French Experience of Counter-Terrorism," *Survival*, Vol. 45, No. 1 (2003), p. 69.
144. Shapiro and Suzan, "The French Experience," p. 74.
145. Evans, "Italy and International Terrorism," p. 88.
146. Michael Conroy and Manuel Pastor, Jr., "The Nicaraguan Experiment: Characteristics of a New Economic Model," in Hamilton et al. (eds.), *Crisis in Central America*, p. 220; and Landau, *Guerrilla Wars*, p. 52.
147. Pettigrew, "Parents and Their Children," p. 220.
148. Rapoport, "The Four Waves of Rebel Terror and September 11," pp. 36–52.
149. Wilkinson, "Why Modern Terrorism?" p. 119.

Chapter Ten From Marxism Back to Communalism

1. Peter Chalk, "The Evolving Dynamic of Terrorism in the 1990s," *Australian Journal of International Affairs*, Vol. 53, No. 2 (1999), p. 164.
2. Ortiz, "Insurgent Strategies in the Post-Cold War," pp. 136–37.
3. Laqueur, *The New Terrorism*, p. 214.
4. Harvey F. Kline, "Columbia: Lawlessness, Drug Trafficking, and Carving Up the State," in Robert I. Rotberg (ed.), *State Failure and State Weakness in a Time of Terror* (Cambridge, MA and Washington, DC: World Peace Foundation and Brookings Institution Press, 2003), p. 171.
5. Jurgen Brauer, Alejandro Gomez-Sorzano, and Sankara Sethuraman, "Decomposing Violence: Political Murder in Colombia, 1946–1999," *European Journal of Political Economy*, Vol. 20, No. 2 (2004), pp. 447–61; and Manwaring, "Non-State Actors in Colombia," p. 77.
6. Kline, "Colombia," p. 177; and Ortiz, "Insurgent Strategies," p. 134.
7. Gregory, "France and the War on Terrorism," p. 126.
8. Laqueur, *The New Terrorism*, p. 35; and Woodworth, "Why Do They Kill?" p. 11.
9. Bruce W. Warner, "Great Britain and the Response to International Terrorism," in Charters (ed.), *The Deadly Sin of Terrorism*, p. 16.
10. James Dingley, "The Bombing of Omagh, 15 August 1998: The Bombers, Their Tactics, Strategy, and Purpose behind the Incident," *Studies in Conflict and Terrorism*, Vol. 24, No. 6 (2001).
11. Dogu Ergil, "Suicide Terrorism in Turkey," *Civil Wars*, Vol. 3, No. 1 (2000), pp. 37–54.
12. Ergil, "Suicide Terrorism," p. 38.
13. Lawrence E. Cline, "From Ocalan to Al Qaida: The Continuing Terrorist Threat in Turkey," *Studies in Conflict and Terrorism*, Vol. 27, No. 4 (2004), p. 329; Adam Dolnik, "Die and Let Die: Exploring Links between Suicide Terrorism and Terrorist Use of Chemical, Biological, Radiological, and Nuclear Weapons," *Studies in Conflict and Terrorism*, Vol. 26, No. 1 (2003), p. 24; Ergil, "Suicide Terrorism," p. 46; and Radu, "Terrorism after the Cold War," pp. 280–81.
14. Cline, "From Ocalan to Al Qaida," p. 327.
15. Joshi, "On the Razor's Edge," pp. 19–42; Laqueur, *The New Terrorism*, pp. 193–94; and Chris Quillen, "A Historical Analysis of Mass Casualty Bombers," *Studies in Conflict and Terrorism*, Vol. 25, No. 5 (2002), p. 282.
16. Tore Bjorgo, "Extreme Nationalism and Violent Discourses in Scandinavia: 'The Resistance', 'Traitors', and 'Foreign Invaders'," in Bjorgo (ed.), *Terror from the Extreme Right*, p. 202; and

Leonard Weinberg, "On Responding to Right–Wing Terrorism," *Terrorism and Political Violence*, Vol. 8, No. 1 (1996), pp. 80–92.
17. Weinberg, "On Responding to Right–Wing Terrorism," p. 85.
18. Lauren M. McLaren, "Explaining Right–Wing Violence in Germany: A Time Series Analysis," *Social Science Quarterly*, Vol. 80, No. 1 (1999), p. 166; Peter H. Merkl, "Radical Right Parties in Europe and Anti–Foreign Violence: A Comparative Essay," in Bjorgo (ed.), *Terror from the Extreme Right*, pp. 102–06; Stephen M. Sobieck, "Democratic Responses to International Terrorism in Germany," in Charters (ed.), *The Deadly Sin of Terrorism*, p. 43; and Ehud Sprinzak, "Right-Wing Terrorism in a Comparative Perspective: The Case of Split Delegitimization," in Bjorgo (ed.), *Terror from the Extreme Right*, pp. 24–25.
19. Wilkinson, "Why Modern Terrorism?" p. 119.
20. Tore Bjorgo, "Extreme Nationalism and Violent Discourses," pp. 182–220; and *Racists and Right-Wing Violence in Scandinavia: Patterns, Perpetrators, and Responses* (Oslo: Tano Aschehoug, 1997); Weinberg, "On Responding to Right-Wing Terrorism"; and Paul Wilkinson, "Violence and Terror and the Extreme Right," *Terrorism and Political Violence*, Vol. 7, No. 4 (1995), p. 88.
21. Tore Bjorgo, "Introduction," pp. 9, 191; and Merkl, "Radical Right Parties," p. 102.
22. Bjorgo, *Racists and Right-Wing Violence*, pp. 313–14; Merkl, "Radical Right Parties," p. 110; and Sprinzak, "Right-Wing Terrorism," pp. 36–37.
23. Weinberg, "On Responding to Right-Wing Terrorism," p. 82.
24. Laszlo Kurti, "The Emergence of Postcommunist Youth Identities in Eastern Europe: From Communist Youth, to Skinheads, to National Socialists and Beyond," in Jeffrey Kaplan and Tore Bjorgo (eds.), *Nation and Race: The Developing Euro–American Racist Subculture* (Boston: Northeastern University Press, 1998), pp. 175–201.
25. Belinda Cooper, " 'We Have No Martin Luther King': Eastern Europe's Roma Minority," *World Policy Journal*, Vol. 18, No. 4 (2001/2002), p. 71; and Wilkinson, "Violence and Terror," pp. 89–90.
26. Gurr and Cole, *The New Face of Terrorism*, p. 144.
27. Mark S. Hamm, "Terrorism, Hate Crime, and Antigovernment Violence: A Review of the Research," in Harvey W. Kushner (ed.), *The Future of Terrorism: Violence in the New Millennium* (Thousand Oaks, CA: Sage Publications, 1998), p. 77; and Jeffrey Kaplan, "The Context of American Millenarian Revolutionary Theology: The Case of the 'Identity Christian' Church of Israel," *Terrorism and Political Violence*, Vol. 5, No. 1 (1993), pp. 30–82.
28. Gurr and Cole, *The New Face of Terrorism*, p. 144; Jeffrey Kaplan, "Right Wing Violence in North America," in Bjorgo (ed.), *Terror from the extreme Right*, p. 83; and Sprinzak, "Right-Wing Terrorism," p. 34.
29. Mark Pitcavage, "Camouflage and Conspiracy: The Militia Movement from Ruby Ridge to Y2K," *American Behavioral Scientist*, Vol. 44, No. 6 (2001), p. 959.
30. Gurr and Cole, *The New Face of Terrorism*, p. 61; and Jonathan B. Tucker and Jason Pate, "The Minnesota Patriots Council," in Jonathan B. Tucker (ed.), *Toxic Terror: Assessing Terrorist Use of Chemical and Biological Weapons* (Cambridge, MA: MIT Press, 2000), pp. 167–83.
31. Moorhead Kennedy, "The 21st Century Conditions Likely to Inspire Terrorism," in Kushner (ed.), *The Future of Terrorism*, p. 191; and Pitcavage, "Camouflage and Conspiracy," p. 961.
32. Brian M. Jenkins, "Terrorism and Beyond: A 21st Century Perspective," *Studies in Conflict and Terrorism*, Vol. 13, No. 4/5 (2001), p. 325; Harvey W. Kushner, *Terrorism in America: A Structural Approach to Understanding the Terrorist Threat* (Springfield, IL: Charles C. Thomas, 1998), pp. 82–83; and Brent L. Smith, "Moving to the Right: The Evolution of Modern American Terrorism," *Global Dialogue*, Vol. 2, No. 4 (2000), pp. 52–63.
33. Laqueur, *The New Terrorism*, p. 111.
34. Gary R. Perlstein, "Anti-Abortion Activists' Terror Campaign," in Crenshaw and Pimlott (eds.), *Encyclopedia of World Terrorism*, Vol. 3, pp. 542–44.
35. Chalk, "The Evolving Dynamic of Terrorism," p. 157; and Griset and Mahan, *Terrorism in Perspective*, pp. 113–15.

NOTES

36. Mark Juergensmeyer, *Terror in the Mind of God: The Global Rise of Religious Violence* (Berkeley: University of California Press, 2000), pp. 21–24.
37. Michael Malley, "Indonesia: The Erosion of State Capacity," in Rotberg (ed.), *State Failure*, p. 192.
38. Andrew Tan, "Armed Muslim Separatist Rebellion in Southeast Asia: Persistence, Prospects, and Implications," *Studies in Conflict and Terrorism*, Vol. 23, No. 4 (2000), p. 278.
39. Kirsten E. Schulze, "The Struggle for an Independent Aceh: The Ideology, Capacity, and Strategy of GAM," *Studies in Conflict and Terrorism*, Vol. 26, No. 4 (2003), p. 260.
40. Tan, "Armed Muslim Separatist Rebellion," p. 270.
41. Chalk, "Political Terrorism in South-East Asia," p. 123; and Schulze, "Struggle for an Independent Aceh," p. 261.
42. Malley, "Indonesia," p. 208.
43. Malley, "Indonesia."
44. Klare, "The New Face of Combat," p. 33.
45. Barry Desker, "Islam and Society in South-East Asia after 11 September," *Australian Journal of International Affairs*, Vol. 56, No. 5 (2002), p. 387.
46. Zachary Abuza, "Tentacles of Terror: Al Qaeda's Southeast Asian Network," *Contemporary Southeast Asia: A Journal of International and Strategic Affairs*, Vol. 24, No. 3 (2002), p. 447.
47. Steven L. Burg and Paul S. Shoup, *The War in Bosnia–Herzegovina* (Armonk, NY: M. E. Sharpe, 1999), p. 12; and Michael Moodie, "Tragedy in the Balkans: A Conflict Ended—or Interrupted?" *Small Wars and Insurgencies*, Vol. 9, No. 1 (1998), p. 15.
48. J. Andrew Slack and Roy R. Doyon, "Population Dynamics and Susceptibility for Ethnic Conflict: The Case of Bosnia and Herzegovina," *Journal of Peace Research*, Vol. 38, No. 2 (2001), pp. 139–61.
49. James Ron, "Territoriality and Plausible Deniability: Serbian Paramilitaries in the Bosnian War," in Campbell and Brenner (eds.), *Death Squads*, p. 286.
50. Taylor and Horgan, "Future Developments of Political Terrorism in Europe," pp. 87–88.
51. Burg and Shoup, *The War in Bosnia–Herzegovina*, p. 171; and Aleksander Pavkovic, *The Fragmentation of Yugoslavia: Nationalism and War in the Balkans*, 2nd ed. (New York: Longman, 2000), p. 168.
52. Tim Judah, *Kosovo: War and Revenge* (New Haven, CT: Yale University Press, 2000), p. 137; and Pavkovic, *Fragmentation of Yugoslavia*, pp. 189–91.
53. Chalk, "The Evolving Dynamic of Terrorism," p. 152; and Douglas Macgregor, "The Balkan Limits to Power and Principle," *Orbis*, Vol. 45, No. 1 (2001), p. 97.
54. Wilkinson, "Why Modern Terrorism," p. 124.
55. Abuza, "Tentacles of Terror," pp. 428–29; and Magnus Ranstorp, "Interpreting the Broader Context and Meaning of Bin–Laden's *Fatwa*," *Studies in Conflict and Terrorism*, Vol. 21, No. 4 (1998), p. 321.
56. Gavin Cameron, "Multi–Track Microproliferation: Lessons from Aum Shinrikyo and Al Qaida," *Studies in Conflict and Terrorism*, Vol. 22, No. 4 (1999), p. 282; and Jeffrey A. Nedoroscik, "Extremist Groups in Egypt," *Terrorism and Political Violence*, Vol. 14, No. 2 (2002), p. 72.
57. Kumar Ramakrishna, "Countering the New Terrorism of Al Qaeda without Generating Civilizational Conflict: The Need for an Indirect Strategy," in Tan and Ramakrishna (eds.), *The New Terrorism*, p. 209.
58. Simon Reeve, *The New Jackals: Ramzi Yousef, Osama bin Laden and the Future of Terrorism* (Boston: Northeastern University Press, 1999), p. 213.
59. Hoffman, "Rethinking Terrorism," p. 309.
60. Abuza, "Tentacles of Terror," p. 429; Ranstorp, "Interpreting the Broader Context," p. 321; and Reeve, *The New Jackals*, p. 3.
61. Abuza, "Tentacles of Terror," pp. 431–32.
62. Ranstorp, "Interpreting the Broader Context," p. 325.
63. Chalk, "Political Terrorism," p. 127.
64. Gregory, "France and the War on Terrorism," p. 133; and Nedoroscik, "Extremist Groups in Egypt," p. 62.

65. Lawrence Cline, "The Islamic Insurgency in the Philippines," *Small Wars and Insurgencies*, Vol. 11, No. 3 (2000), p. 125.
66. Abuza, "Tentacles of Terror," p. 440, Chalk, "Political Terrorism," p. 127; and Tan, "Armed Muslim Separatist Rebellion," pp. 273, 275.
67. Peter Chalk, "Al Qaeda and Its Links to Terrorist Groups in Asia," in Tan and Ramakrishna (eds.), *The New Terrorism*, p. 113; Reeve, *The New Jackals*, p. 237; Steven Rogers, "Beyond Abu Sayyaf: The Lessons of Failure in the Philippines," *Foreign Affairs*, Vol. 83, No. 1 (2004), p. 16; and Tan, "Armed Muslim Separatist Rebellion," p. 274.
68. Rogers, "Beyond Abu Sayyaf."
69. Martin Stone, *The Agony of Algeria* (New York: Columbia University Press, 1997), pp. 180–84.
70. David G. Kibble, "The Threat of Militant Islam: A Fundamental Reappraisal," *Studies in Conflict and Terrorism*, Vol. 19, No. 4 (1996), p. 357; O. Peter St. John, "Algeria: A Case Study of Insurgency in the New World Order," *Small Wars and Insurgencies*, Vol. 7, No. 2 (1996), p. 197; and Stone, *The Agony of Algeria*, p. 212.
71. Martha Crenshaw, "Political Violence in Algeria," *Terrorism and Political Violence*, Vol. 6, No. 3 (1994), p. 278.
72. St. John, "Algeria," p. 197; and Weinberg and Eubank, "Terrorism and the Shape of Things to Come," p. 103.
73. Jeremy Shapiro and Benedicte Suzan, "The French Experience of Counter-Terrorism," *Survival*, Vol. 45, No. 1 (2003), p. 80.
74. Hoffman, "The Emergence of the New Terrorism," p. 34; Shaipiro and Suzan, "The French Experience," p. 80; and St. John, "Algeria," p. 209. Israel recognized the possibility of such suicide attacks—it shot down a Libyan airliner in the 1970s in the Sinai and a small Lebanese plane near Tel Aviv in 2001. Cf. Ely Karmon "Countering NBC Terrorism," in Tan and Ramakrishna (eds.), *The New Terrorism*, p. 197.
75. Chalk, "The Evolving Dynamic of Terrorism," p. 160; and Stone, *The Agony of Algeria*, p. 91.
76. Jessica Stern, "Pakistan's Jihad Culture," *Foreign Affairs*, Vol. 79, No. 6 (2000), p. 118.
77. Alexander Evans, "The Kashmir Insurgency: As Bad As It Gets," *Small Wars and Insurgencies*, Vol. 11, No. 1 (2000), p. 78.
78. Laqueur, *The New Terrorism*, p. 151.
79. Princeton N. Lyman and F. Stephen Morrison, "The Terrorist Threat in Africa," *Foreign Affairs*, Vol. 83, No. 1 (2004), p. 79.
80. Assaf Moghadam, "Palestinian Suicide Terrorism in the Second Intifada: Motivations and Organizational Aspects," *Studies in Conflict and Terrorism*, Vol. 26, No. 2 (2003), p. 65; and Adam Dolnik and Anjali Bhattacharjee, "Hamas: Suicide Bombings, Rockets, or WMD?" *Terrorism and Political Violence*, Vol. 14, No. 3 (2002), p. 113.
81. Moghadam, "Palestinian Suicide Terrorism," and Radu, "Terrorism after the Cold War," pp. 280–81.
82. Gal Luft, "The Logic of Israel's Targeted Killing," *Middle East Quarterly*, Vol. 10, No. 1 (2003), pp. 3–7.
83. Magnus Ranstorp, "Terrorism in the Name of Religion," *Journal of International Affairs*, Vol. 50, No. 1 (1996), pp. 41–42.
84. Walter Laqueur, *No End to War: Terrorism in the Twenty–First Century* (New York: Continuum, 2003), p. 190; and Ahmed Rashid, *Jihad: The Rise of Militant Islam in Central Asia* (New Haven, CT: Yale University Press, 2002), pp. 9, 174.
85. Chalk, "The Evolving Dynamic of Terrorism," p. 153; Dolnik, "Die and Let Die," p. 26; and Wilkinson, *Terrorism versus Democracy*, p. 145.
86. Paul R. Pillar, *Terrorism and U. S. Foreign Policy* (Washington, DC: Brookings Institution, 2001), p. 43.
87. Laqueur, *No End to War*, p. 188.
88. Robert Jay Lifton, *Destroying the World To Save It: Aum Shinrikyo, Apocalyptic Violence, and the New Global Terrorism* (New York: Henry Holt, 2000), p. 203; and Manabu Watanabe, "Religion and

Violence in Japan Today: A Chronological and Doctrinal Analysis of Aum Shinrikyo," *Terrorism and Political Violence*, Vol. 10, No. 4 (1998), p. 95.
89. Ian Reader, "Spectres and Shadows: Aum Shinrikyo and the Road to Megiddo," *Terrorism and Political Violence*, Vol. 14, No. 1 (2002), p. 161.
90. Cameron, "Multi-Track Microproliferation," Christopher C. Harmon, *Terrorism Today* (London: Frank Cass, 2000), p. 97; and Lifton, *Destroying the World*, p. 41.
91. Lifton, *Destroying the World*, p. 210; and Reader, "Spectres and Shadows," p. 178.
92. David Claridge, "Exploding the Myths of Superterrorism," in Taylor and Horgan (eds.), *The Future of Terrorism*, p. 138.
93. Gary A. Ackerman, "Beyond Arson? A Threat Assessment of the Earth Liberation Front," *Terrorism and Political Violence*, Vol. 15, No. 4 (2003), pp. 143–70; Sean P. Eagan, "From Spikes to Bombs: The Rise of Eco–Terrorism," *Studies in Conflict and Terrorism*, Vol. 19, No. 1 (1995), pp. 1–18; and Luther Tweeten, *Terrorism, Radicalism, and Populism in Agriculture* (Ames, IA: Iowa State Press, 2003), p. 6.
94. Hamm, "Terrorism, Hate Crime, and Anti–Government Violence," p. 65.
95. Rachel Monaghan, "Animal Rights and Violent Protest," *Terrorism and Political Violence*, Vol. 9. No. 4 (1997), pp. 106–16; and "Terrorism in the Name of Animal Rights," in Taylor and Horgan (eds.), *The Future of Terrorism*, pp. 159–69.
96. Eagen, "From Spikes to Bombs," pp. 7, 10.
97. Iyabo Olojede, Banji Fajonyomi, Ighodalo Akhape, and Suraju O. Mudashiru, "Nigeria: Oil Pollution, Community Dissatisfaction and Threat to National Peace and Security," Occasional Paper Series, Vol. 4, No. 3 (Lagos: Department of Political Science, Lagos State University, 2000), p. 32.
98. Olojede et al., "Nigeria," p. 10.
99. Cf. Charles Ukeje, "Oil Communities and Political Violence: The Case of Ethnic Ijaws in Nigeria's Delta Region," *Terrorism and Political Violence*, Vol. 13, No. 4 (2001), pp. 15–36.
100. Laqueur, *The New Terrorism*, p. 151; and Jaideep Saikia, "The ISI Reaches East: Anatomy of a Conspiracy," *Studies in Conflict and Terrorism*, Vol. 25, No. 3 (2002), pp. 185–97.
101. Chalk, "The Evolving Dynamic of Terrorism," p. 155; and Ely Karmon, "Islamic Terrorist Activities in Turkey in the 1990s," *Terrorism and Political Violence*, Vol. 10, No. 4 (1998), p. 105.
102. Ortiz, "Insurgent Strategies," p. 139; and Radu, "Terrorism after the Cold War," p. 283.
103. Chalk, "Political Terrorism," p. 124.
104. Desker, "Islam and Society," pp. 387–88; Gershman, "Is Southeast Asia the Second Front?" pp. 70–71; Robert W. Hefner, "Global Violence and Indonesian Muslim Politics," *American Anthropologist*, Vol. 104, No. 3 (2002), p. 760; and Malley, "Indonesia," p. 206.
105. Gossman, "India's Secret Armies," pp. 262–63, 272–73; and Cynthia Keppley Mahmood, "Trials by Fire: Dynamics of Terror in Punjab and Kashmir," in Jeffrey A. Sluka (ed.), *Death Squad: The Anthropology of State Terror* (Philadelphia: University of Pennsylvania Press, 2000), p. 70.
106. Mahmood, "Trials by Fire."
107. Chetan Bhatt, *Hindu Nationalism: Origins, Ideologies, and Modern Myths* (Oxford: Berg, 2001), p. 196; and Sumit Ganguly, "The Crisis of Indian Secularism," *Journal of Democracy*, Vol. 14, No. 4 (2003), p. 20.
108. Peter Iadicola and Anson Shupe, *Violence, Inequality, and Human Freedom* (Lanham, MD: Rowman & Littlefield, 2003), p.179; and Mahmood, "Trials by Fire," p. 85.
109. Bhatt, *Hindu Nationalism*, pp. 197–201; Greenaway, "Hindu Nationalism Clouds the Face of India," pp. 89–93; and Mahmood, "Trials by Fire," p. 85.
110. Sikata Banerjee, *Warriors in Politics: Hindu Nationalism, Violence, and the Shiv Sena in India* (Boulder, CO: Westview Press, 2000), p. 35; Bhatt, *Hindu Nationalism*, p. 197; Greenaway, "Hindu Nationalism," p. 91; and Ganguly, "Crisis of Indian Secularism," p. 11.
111. Prem Shankar Jha, "The Fascist Impulse in Developing Countries: Two Case Studies," *Studies in Conflict and Terrorism*, Vol. 17, No. 3 (1994), pp. 229–74; and Mahmood, "Trials by Fire," p. 87.

112. JoAnn McGregor, "The Politics of Disruption: War Veterans and the Local State in Zimbabwe," *African Affairs*, Vol. 101, No. 402 (2002), pp. 9–37; Robert I. Rotberg, "Africa's Mess, Mugabe's Mayhem," *Foreign Affairs*, Vol. 79, No. 5 (2000), p. 48; Ian Taylor and Paul Williams, "The Limits of Engagement: British Foreign Policy and The Crisis in Zimbabwe," *International Affairs*, Vol. 78, No. 3 (2002), p. 551; and Wilkinson, *Terrorism versus Democracy*, p. 73.
113. Rotberg, "Africa's Mess," p. 50.
114. Manwaring, "Non-State Actors in Colombia," p. 72.
115. Edgar O'Ballance, *Sudan: Civil War and Terrorism, 1956–99* (New York: St. Martin's, 2000), p. 174.
116. Cooper, "'We Have No Martin Luther King'," p. 71; Judah, *Kosovo*, pp. 286–90; and Macgregor, "The Balkan Limits," p. 103.
117. Cooper, "'We Have No Martin Luther King'," pp. 71, 101, and Wilkinson, "Violence and Terror," pp. 89–90.
118. Merkl, "Radical Right Parties," p. 100.
119. Mahmood Mamdani, *When Victims Become Killers: Colonialism, Nativism, and the Genocide in Rwanda* (Princeton, NJ: Princeton University Press, 2001), p. 192; and Christian P. Scherrer, *Genocide and Crisis in Central Africa: Conflict Roots, Mass Violence, and Regional War* (Westport, CT: Praeger, 2002), p. 107.
120. Mamdani, *When Victims Become Killers*, pp. 190–91; and Stephen R. Shalom, "Genocide in Rwanda," in William Dudley (ed.), *Genocide* (San Diego: Greenhaven Press, 2001), p. 49.
121. John Mueller, "The Banality of 'Ethnic War'," *International Security*, Vol. 25, No. 1 (2000), p. 59.
122. Alan J. Kuperman, "Rwanda in Retrospect," *Foreign Affairs*, Vol. 79, No. 1 (2000), p. 98.
123. Cf. Kuperman, "Rwanda in Retrospect," p. 101; and Shalom, "Genocide in Rwanda," p. 56.
124. David Rieff, "Suffering and Cynicism in Burundi," *World Policy Journal*, Vol. 18, No. 3 (2001), pp. 61–67; and Shalom, "Genocide in Rwanda," p. 45.
125. Kline, "Colombia," and Manwaring, "Non–State Actors in Colombia."
126. Tan, "Armed Muslim Separatist Rebellion," p. 269.
127. Abuza, "Tentacles of Terror," p. 434; and Gershman, "Is Southeast Asia the Second Front?" p. 61.
128. McGregor, "The Politics of Disruption," p. 10.
129. Mark Juergensmeyer, "The Religious Roots of Contemporary Terrorism," in Kegley (ed.), *The New Global Terrorism*, pp. 185, 191.
130. Lifton, *Destroying the World*, p. 265; and Reader, "Spectres and Shadows," p. 163.
131. Sinclair, *Anatomy of Terror*, p. 339.
132. Arshin Adib–Moghaddam, "Global Intifadah? September 11th and the Struggle within Islam," *Cambridge Review of International Affairs*, Vol. 15, No. 2 (2002), p. 210; Pillar, *Terrorism and U.S. Foreign Policy*, p. 63; Magnus Ranstorp and Gus Xhudo, "A Threat to Europe? Middle East Ties with the Balkans and their Impact upon Terrorist Activity throughout the Region," *Terrorism and Political Violence*, Vol. 6, No. 2 (1994), p. 199; and Tan, "Armed Separatist Rebellion," p. 268.
133. Huntington, *The Clash of Civilizations and the Remaking of World Order*, p. 98; Juergensmeyer, "The Religious Roots," p. 185; Klare, "The New Face of Combat," p. 34; and Kumar Ramakrishna and Andrew Tan, "The New Terrorism: Diagnosis and Prescriptions," in Tan and Ramakrishna (eds.), *The New Terrorism*, p. 3.
134. James Dingley and Michael Kirk-Smith, "Symbolism and Sacrifice in Terrorism," *Small Wars and Insurgencies*, Vol. 13, No. 1 (2002), pp. 108–09, 123; and Woodworth, "Why Do They Kill?" p. 4.
135. Cline, "From Ocalan to Al Qaida," p. 329.
136. Shabad and Ramo, "Political Violence in a Democratic State," p. 468.
137. Timothy Garton Ash, "Is There a Good Terrorist?" in Kegley (ed.), *The New Global Terrorism*, p. 63.
138. Daniel Byman, "The Logic of Ethnic Terrorism," *Studies in Conflict and Terrorism*, Vol. 21, No. 2 (1998), p. 158.
139. Gurr and Cole, *The New Face of Terrorism*, p. 89; and Wilkinson, *Terrorism versus Democracy*, p. 11.
140. Byman, "The Logic of Ethnic Terrorism," p. 159.
141. Banerjee, *Warriors in Politics*, p. 120.

142. Ash, "Is There a Good Terrorist," pp. 68–69.
143. Robin Blackburn, "The Imperial Presidency, the War on Terrorism, and the Revolutions of Modernity," *Constellations: An International Journal of Critical and Democratic Theory*, Vol. 9, No. 1 (2002), p. 3; Don P. Chipman, "Osama bin Laden and Guerrilla War," *Studies in Conflict and Terrorism*, Vol. 26, No. 3 (2003), pp. 165–68; and Hoffman, "Rethinking Terrorism," p. 308.
144. Laqueur, *The New Terrorism*, p. 229; and Perlstein, "Anti–Abortion Activists' Terror Campaign," p. 544.
145. Merkl, "Radical Right Parties," p. 112.
146. Blackburn, "The Imperial Presidency," p. 14; Laqueur, *No End to War*, p. 181; Macgregor, "The Balkan Limits," pp. 97, 103; Abraham H. Miller and Nicholas A. Damask, "The Dual Myths of 'Narco-Terrorism': How Myths Drive Policy," *Terrorism and Political Violence*, Vol. 8, No. 1 (1996), p. 117; Radu, "Terrorism after the Cold War," p. 278; Rashid, *The Rise of Militant Islam*, p. 229; and Alex P. Schmid, "Terrorism and Democracy," *Terrorism and Political Violence*, Vol. 4, No. 4 (1992), p. 21.
147. Jasjit Singh, "Kashmir, Pakistan and the War by Terror," *Small Wars and Insurgencies*, Vol. 13, No. 2 (2002), p. 90.

Chapter Eleven   Conclusions

1. Anna Simons, "Making Sense of Ethnic Cleansing," *Studies in Conflict and Terrorism*, Vol. 22, No. 1 (1999), p. 14.
2. Gurr and Cole, *The New Face of Terrorism*, p. 200.
3. Cronin, "Behind the Curve," pp. 41–42; Daniel S. Gressang IV, "Terrorism in the 21st Century: Reassessing the Emerging Threat," *Terrorism and Political Violence*, Vol. 13, No. 3 (2001), p. 82; and Hoffman. "Holy Terror," pp. 272–73.
4. Gurr and Cole, *The New Face of Terrorism*, p. 31; John V. Parachini, "Comparing Motives and Outcomes of Mass Casualty Terrorism Involving Conventional and Unconventional Weapons," *Studies in Conflict and Terrorism*, Vol. 24, No. 5 (2001), p. 399; and Quillen, "A Historical Analysis of Mass Casualty Bombers," p. 290.
5. Jonathan Fox, "Religion and State Failure: An Examination of the Extent and Magnitude of Religious Conflict from 1950 to 1996," *International Political Science Review*, Vol. 25, No. 1 (2004), p. 66; and Mark Juergensmeyer, "Holy Orders: Religious Opposition to Modern States," *Harvard International Review*, Vol. 25, No. 4 (2004), p. 37.
6. Gurr, "Terrorism in Democracies," p. 206.
7. Cameron, "Multi-Track Microproliferation," p. 297; and Andrew O'Neill, "Terrorist Use of Weapons of Mass Destruction: How Serious Is the Threat?" *Australian Journal of International Affairs*, Vol. 57, No. 1 (2003), p. 107.
8. Jessica Stern, *The Ultimate Terrorists* (Cambridge, MA: Harvard University Press, 1999), pp. 10, 74–76.
9. Arpad Palfy, "Weapon System Selection and Mass-Casualty Outcomes," *Terrorism and Political Violence*, Vol. 15, No. 2 (2003), p. 92.
10. Claridge, "Exploding the Myths of Superterrorism," p. 143; Palfy, "Weapon System Selection"; Hoffman, "Change and Continuity in Terrorism," p. 417; and Wilkinson, "Why Modern Terrorism?" p. 134.
11. Cameron, "Multi-Track Microproliferation," p. 53.
12. Dolnik, "Die and Let Die," p. 20; and Hoffman and McCormick, "Terrorism, Signaling, and Suicide Attack," p. 249.
13. Ramakrishna and Tan, "The New Terrorism," pp. 3–4.
14. Peter Chalk, "Low Intensity Conflict in Southeast Asia: Piracy, Drug Trafficking and Political Terrorism," *Conflict Studies*, No. 305/306 (1998), p. 12.

15. Stohl, "Demystifying the Mystery of International Terrorism," pp. 95–96.
16. Byman, "The Logic of Ethnic Terrorism," p. 158.
17. Laqueur, *A History of Terrorism*, p. 143.
18. Gressang, "Terrorism in the 21st Century," p. 92.
19. Mark Basile, "Going to the Source: Why Al Qaeda's Financial Network Is Likely to Withstand the Current War on Terrorist Financing," *Studies in Conflict and Terrorism*, Vol. 27, No. 3 (2004), pp. 169–85; Jane Schneider and Peter Schneider, "The Mafia and al-Qaeda: Violent and Secretive Organizations in Comparative and Historical Perspective," *American Anthropologist*, Vol. 104, No. 3 (2002), pp. 776–82; and Sederberg, "Global Terrorism," pp. 280–81.
20. Rapoport, "The Four Waves of Rebel Terror and September 11," p. 50.

BIBLIOGRAPHY

Abbott, Elizabeth, *Haiti: The Duvaliers and Their Legacy* (New York: McGraw-Hill, 1988).
Abels, Jules, *Man on Fire: John Brown and the Cause of Liberty* (New York: Macmillan, 1971).
Abrahams, Ray, *Vigilant Citizens: Vigilantism and the State* (Cambridge: Polity Press, 1988).
Abuza, Zachary, "Tentacles of Terror: Al Qaeda's Southeast Asian Network," *Contemporary Southeast Asia: A Journal of International and Strategic Affairs*, Vol. 24, No. 3 (2002), pp. 427–65.
Ackerman, Gary A., "Beyond Arson? A Threat Assessment of the Earth Liberation Front," *Terrorism and Political Violence*, Vol. 15, No. 4 (2003), pp. 143–70.
Adalian, Rouben, "The Armenian Genocide: Context and Legacy," *Social Education: The Official Journal of the National Council for the Social Studies*, Vol. 55, No. 2 (1991), pp. 99–104.
Adib-Moghaddam, Arshin, "Global Intifadah? September 11th and the Struggle within Islam," *Cambridge Review of International Affairs*, Vol. 15, No. 2 (2002), pp. 203–16.
Aditjondro, George J., "Ninjas, Nanggalas, Monuments, and Mossad Manuals: An Anthropology of Indonesian State Terror in East Timor," in Jeffrey A. Sluka (ed.), *Death Squad: The Anthropology of State Terror* (Philadelphia: University of Pennsylvania Press, 2000), pp. 158–88.
Afflitto, Frank M., "The Homogenizing Effects of State-Sponsored Terrorism: The Case of Guatemala," in Jeffrey A. Sluka (ed.), *Death Squad: The Anthropology of State Terror* (Philadelphia: University of Pennsylvania Press, 2000), pp. 114–26.
Africa, Thomas W., "Urban Violence in Imperial Rome," *Journal of Interdisciplinary History*, Vol. 2, No. 1 (1971), pp. 3–21.
Alapuro, Risto and Erik Allardt, "The Lapua Movement: The Threat of Rightist Takeover in Finland," in Juan J. Linz and Alfred Stephan (eds.), *The Breakdown of Democratic Regimes: Europe* (Baltimore, MD: Johns Hopkins University Press, 1978), pp. 122–41.
Albin, Ceclia, "The Politics of Terrorism: A Contemporary Survey," in Barry Rubin (ed.), *The Politics of Terrorism: Terror as a State and Revolutionary Strategy* (Washington, DC: Foreign Policy Institute, 1989), pp. 183–234.
Allegro, John M., *The Chosen People: A Study of Jewish History from the Time of the Exile until the Revolt of Bar Kocheba, Sixth Century B. C. to Second Century A. D.* (Garden City, NY: Doubleday, 1972).
Alter, Peter, "Traditions of Violence in the Irish National Movement," in Wolfgang J. Mommsen and Gerhard Hirschfeld (eds.), *Social Protest, Violence and Terror in Nineteenth- and Twentieth-Century Europe* (New York: St. Martin's Press for the German Historical Institute, 1982), pp. 137–54.
Anderson, Sean Kendall and Stephen Sloan, *Terrorism: Assassins to Zealots* (Lanham, MD: Scarecrow Press, 2003).
Andriolo, Karin, "Murder by Suicide: Episodes from Muslim History," *American Anthropologist*, Vol. 104, No. 3 (2002), pp. 736–42.

Applebaum, Shimon, "The Zealots: The Case for Revaluation," *Journal of Roman Studies*, Vol. 61 (1971), pp. 155–70.
Arian, Asher, *The Second Republic: Politics in Israel* (Chatham, NJ: Chatham House, 1998).
Arnove, Robert F., "Students in Politics," in John D. Martz and David J. Meyers (eds.), *Venezuela: The Democratic Experience* (New York: Praeger, 1977), pp. 195–214.
Arnson, Cynthia J., "Window on the Past: A Declassified History of Death Squads in El Salvador," in Bruce B. Campbell and Arthur D. Brenner (eds.), *Death Squads in Global Perspective: Murder with Deniability* (New York: Palgrave Macmillan, 2000), pp. 85–124.
Ash, Timothy Garton, "Is There a Good Terrorist?" in Charles W. Kegley, Jr. (ed.), *The New Global Terrorism: Characteristics, Causes, Controls* (Upper Saddle River, NJ: Prentice Hall, 2003), pp. 60–70.
Badey, Thomas J., "Defining International Terrorism: A Pragmatic Approach," *Terrorism and Political Violence*, Vol. 10, No. 1 (1998), pp. 90–107.
Baglieri, Joseph, "Italian Fascism and the Crisis of Liberal Hegemony: 1901–1922," in Stein Ugelvik Larsen, Bernt Hagtvet and Jan Petter Myklebust (eds.), *Who Were the Fascists: Social Roots of European Fascism* (Bergen: Universitetsforlaget, 1980), pp. 318–36.
Bal, Ihsan and Sedat Laciner, "The Challenge of Revolutionary Terrorism to Turkish Democracy, 1960–1980," *Terrorism and Political Violence*, Vol. 13, No. 4 (2001), pp. 90–115.
Bale, Jeffrey M., "The May 1973 Terrorist Attack at Milan Police HQ: Anarchist 'Propaganda of the Deed' or 'False-Flag' Provocation," *Terrorism and Political Violence*, Vol. 8, No. 1 (1996), pp. 132–66.
Banac, Ivo, *The National Question in Yugoslavia: Origins, History, Politics* (Ithaca: Cornell University Press, 1984).
Banerjee, Sikata, *Warriors in Politics: Hindu Nationalism, Violence, and the Shiv Sena in India* (Boulder, CO: Westview Press, 2000).
Banerjee, Sumanta, "Naxalbari and the Left Movement," in Ghanshyam Shah (ed.), *Social Movements and the State*, Readings in Indian Government and Politics, Vol. 4 (New Delhi: Sage, 2002), pp. 125–92.
Barak, Oren, "Lebanon: Failure, Collapse, and Resuscitation," in Robert I. Rotberg (ed.), *State Failure and State Weakness in a Time of Terror* (Cambridge, MA and Washington, DC: World Peace Foundation and Brookings Institution Press, 2003), pp. 305–09.
Barbu, Z., "Rumania," in S. J. Woolf (ed.), *European Fascism* (New York: Vintage Books, 1968), pp. 146–66.
Barker, John W., *Justinian and the Later Roman Empire* (Madison: University of Wisconsin Press, 1966).
Barnhurst, Kevin G., "Contemporary Terrorism in Peru: Sendero Luminoso and the Media," *Journal of Communication*, Vol. 41, No. 4 (1991), pp. 75–89.
Basile, Mark, "Going to the Source: Why Al Qaeda's Financial Network Is Likely to Withstand the Current War on Terrorist Financing," *Studies in Conflict and Terrorism*, Vol. 27, No. 3 (2004), pp. 169–85.
Becker, Marvin B., *Florence in Transition: Volume I, The Decline of the Commune* (Baltimore: Johns Hopkins Press, 1967).
Beckett, Ian F. W., *Modern Insurgencies and Counter-Insurgencies: Guerrillas and Their Opponents since 1750* (London: Routledge, 2001).
Bell, J. Browyer, *Transnational Terror* (Washington, DC: American Enterprise Institute, 1975).
Bell-Fialkoff, Andrew, *Ethnic Cleansing* (New York: St. Martin's Griffin, 1999).
Berend, Ivan T., *Decades of Crisis: Central and Eastern Europe before World War II* (Berkeley, CA: University of California Press, 1998).
Bernecker, Walther L., "The Strategies of 'Direct Action' and Violence in Spanish Anarchism," in Wolfgang J. Mommsen and Gerhard Hirschfeld (eds.), *Social Protest, Violence and Terror in Nineteenth- and Twentieth Century Europe* (New York: St. Martin's Press for the German Historical Institute, 1982), pp. 88–111.

Bessel, Richard, "Violence as Propaganda: The Role of the Storm Troopers in the Rise of National Socialism," in Thomas Childers (ed.), *The Formation of the Nazi Constituency, 1919–1933* (Totowa, NJ: Barnes & Noble, 1986), pp. 131–46.
Bhatt, Chetan, *Hindu Nationalism: Origins, Ideologies, and Modern Myths* (Oxford: Berg, 2991).
Bill, James A. and Carl Leiden, *Politics in the Middle East*, 2nd ed. (Boston: Little Brown, 1984).
Biondich, Mark, " 'We Were Defending the State': Nationalism, Myth, and Memory in Twentieth-Century Croatia," in John R. Lampe and Mark Mazower (eds.), *Ideologies and National Identities: The Case of Twentieth Century Southeastern Europe* (Budapest: Central European University Press, 2004), pp. 54–81.
Bjorgo, Tore, "Extreme Nationalism and Violent Discourses in Scandinavia: 'The Resistance', 'Traitors', and 'Foreign Invaders',", in Tore Bjorgo (ed.), *Terror from the Extreme Right* (London: Frank Cass, 1995), pp. 182–220.
——— "Introduction," in Tore Bjorgo (ed.), *Terror from the Extreme Right* (London: Frank Cass, 1995), pp. 1–16.
——— *Racist and Right-Wing Violence in Scandinavia: Patterns, Perpetrators, and Responses* (Oslo: Tano Ascheoug, 1997).
Blackburn, Robin, "The Imperial Presidency, the War on Terrorism, and the Revolution of Modernity," *Constellations: An International Journal of Critical and Democratic Theory*, Vol. 9, No. 1 (2002), pp. 3–33.
Blythe, Wilfred, *The Impact of Chinese Secret Societies in Malaya: A Historical Study* (London: Oxford University Press, 1969).
Bobrick, Benson, *Angel in the Whirlwind: The Triumph of the American Revolution* (New York: Simon and Schuster, 1977).
Bonner, David, "The United Kingdom's Response to Terrorism," *Terrorism and Political Violence*, Vol. 4, No. 4 (1992), pp. 171–205.
Bratchel, Michael E., "Lucca, 1430–94: The Politics of the Restored Republic," in Thomas W. Blomquist and Maureen F. Mazzaoui (eds.), *The "Other Tuscany": Essays in the History of Lucca, Pisa, and Siena during the Thirteenth, Fourteenth, and Fifteenth Centuries*, Studies in Medieval Culture 34 (Kalamazoo, MI: Medieval Institute Publications, Western Michigan University, 1994), pp. 19–40.
Brauer, Jurgen, Alejandro Gomez-Sorzano, and Sankara Sethuraman, "Decomposing Violence: Political Murder in Colombia, 1946–1999," *European Journal of Political Economy*, Vol. 20, No. 2 (2004), pp. 447–61.
Brenner, Arthur D., "*Feme* Murder: Paramilitary 'Self-Justice' in Weimar Germany," in Bruce B. Campbell and Arthur D. Brenner (eds.), *Death Squads in Global Perspective: Murder with Deniability* (New York: Palgrave Macmillan, 2000), pp. 57–83.
Brunn, Gerhard, "Nationalist Violence and Terror in the Spanish Border Provinces: ETA," in Wolfgang J. Mommsen and Gerhard Hirschfeld (eds.), *Social Protest, Violence, and Terror in Nineteenth- and Twentieth-Century Europe* (New York: St. Martin's Press for the German Historical Institute, 1982), pp. 112–36.
Burg, Steven L. and Paul S. Shoup, *The War in Bosnia-Herzegovina* (Armonk, NY: M. E. Sharpe, 1999).
Burton, Anthony M., *Urban Terrorism: Theory, Practice, & Response* (New York: The Free Press, 1975).
Byman, Daniel (1998), "The Logic of Ethnic Terrorism," *Studies in Conflict and Terrorism*, Vol. 21, No. 2 (1998), pp. 149–69.
Cameron, Gavin, "Multi-Track Microproliferation: Lessons from Aum Shinrikyo and Al Qaida," *Studies in Conflict and Terrorism*, Vol. 22, No. 4 (1999), pp. 277–309.
Campbell, Bruce B., "Death Squads: Definition, Problems, and Historical Context," in Bruce B. Campbell and Arthur D. Brenner (eds.), *Death Squads in Global Perspective: Murder with Deniability* (New York: Palgrave Macmillan, 2000), pp. 1–26.

Carr, Caleb, *The Lessons of Terror: A History of Warfare against Civilians, Why It Has Failed and Why It Will Fail Again* (New York: Random House, 2002).

Chalk, Frank and Kurt Jonassohn, *The History and Sociology of Genocide: Analyses and Case Studies* (New Haven: Yale University Press, 1990).

Chalk, Peter, *West European Terrorism and Counter-Terrorism: The Evolving Dynamic* (Houndsmill, Basingstoke: Macmillan, 1996).

——— "Political Terrorism in South-East Asia," *Terrorism and Political Violence*, Vol. 10, No. 2 (1998), pp. 118–34.

——— "The Response to Terrorism as a Threat to Liberal Democracy," *Australian Journal of Politics and History*, Vol. 44, No. 3 (1998), pp. 373–88.

——— "Low Intensity Conflict in Southeast Asia: Piracy, Drug Trafficking and Political Terrorism," *Conflict Studies*, No. 305/306 (1998).

——— "The Evolving Dynamic of Terrorism in the 1990s," *Australian Journal of International Affairs*, Vol. 53, No. 2 (1999), pp. 151–68.

——— "Al Qaeda and Its Links to Terrorist Groups in Asia," in Andrew Tan and Kumar Ramakrishna (eds.), *The New Terrorism: Anatomy, Trends and Counter-Strategies* (Singapore: Eastern University Press, 2002), pp. 107–28.

Charters, David A., "Introduction," in David A. Charters (ed.), *The Deadly Sin of Terrorism: Its Effect on Democracy and Civil Liberty in Six Countries* (Westport, CT: Greenwood Press, 1994), pp. 1–4.

Chesneaux, Jean, "Secret Societies in China's Historical Evolution," in Jean Chesneaux (ed.), *Popular Movements and Secret Societies in China 1840–1950* (Stanford, CA: Stanford University Press, 1972), pp. 1–21.

Chipman, Don P., "Osama bin Laden and Guerrilla War," *Studies in Conflict and Terrorism*, Vol. 26, No. 3 (2003), pp. 163–70.

Claridge, David, "State Terrorism? Applying a Definitional Model," *Terrorism and Political Violence*, Vol. 8, No. 3 (1996), pp. 47–63.

——— "Exploding the Myths of Superterrorism," in Max. Taylor and John Horgan (eds.), *The Future of Terrorism* (London: Frank Cass, 2000), pp. 133–48.

Cline, Lawrence E., "The Islamic Insurgency in the Philippines," *Small Wars and Insurgencies*, Vol. 11, No. 3 (2000), pp. 115–38.

——— "From Ocalan to Al Qaida: The Continuing Terrorist Threat in Turkey," *Studies in Conflict and Terrorism*, Vol. 27, No. 4 (2004), pp. 321–35.

Clutterbuck, Richard, *Living with Terrorism* (London: Faber and Faber, 1975).

Cohen, Michael J., "Introduction," in Michael J. Cohen (ed.), *The Rise of Israel: Jewish Resistance to British Rule in Palestine 1944–1947*, Vol. 34 in The Rise of Israel: A Documentary Record from the Nineteenth Century to 1948 (New York: Garland Publishing, 1987), pp. v–vii.

Comber, Leon, *Chinese Secret Societies in Malaya: A Survey of the Triad Society from 1800 to 1900*, Monographs of the Association for Asian Studies No. 6 (Locust Valley, NY: J. J. Augustin, 1959).

Combs, Cindy C., *Terrorism in the Twenty-First Century*, 2nd ed. (Upper Saddle River, NJ: Prentice Hall, 2000).

Conroy, Michael E. and Manuel Pastor, Jr., "The Nicaraguan Experiment: Characteristics of a New Economic Model," in Nora Hamilton, Jeffrey A. Frieden, Linda Fuller, and Manuel Pastor, Jr. (eds.), *Crisis in Central America: Regional Dynamics and U.S. Policy in the 1980s* (Boulder, CO: Westview, 1988), pp. 207–25.

Coogan, Tim Pat, *The IRA: A History* (Niwot, CO: Roberts Rinehart, 1993).

Cooley, John K., "Terrorism: Continuity and Change in the New Century," *Global Dialogue*, Vol. 2, No. 4 (2000), pp. 7–18.

Cooper, Belinda, " 'We Have No Martin Luther King': Eastern Europe's Roma Minority," *World Policy Journal*, Vol. 18, No. 4 (2001/02), pp. 69–78.

Corsun, Andrew, "Group Profile: The Revolutionary Organization 17 November in Greece (1975–1991)," in Yonah Alexander and Dennis A. Pluchinsky (eds.), *European Terrorism: Today and Tomorrow* (Washington: Brassey's, 1992), pp. 93–125.

Crenshaw, Martha, "Political Violence in Algeria," *Terrorism and Political Violence*, Vol. 6, No. 3 (1994), pp. 261–80.

——— "The Effectiveness of Terrorism in the Algerian War," in Martha Crenshaw (ed.), *Terrorism in Context* (University Park, PA: Pennsylvania State University Press, 1995), pp. 473–513.

——— "Thoughts on Relating Terrorism to Historical Contexts," in Martha Crenshaw (ed.), *Terrorism in Context* (University Park, PA: Pennsylvania State University Press, 1995), pp. 3–24.

——— "Democracy, Commitment Problems and Managing Ethnic Violence: The Case of India and Sri Lanka," *Terrorism and Political Violence*, Vol. 12, No. 3/4 (2000), pp. 135–59.

——— "The Causes of Terrorism," in Charles W. Kegley, Jr. (ed.), *The New Global Terrorism: Characteristics, Causes, Controls* (Upper Saddle River, NJ: Prentice Hall, 2003), pp. 92–105.

——— "Why Is America the Primary Target? Terrorism as Globalized Civil War," in Charles W. Kegley, Jr. (ed.), *The New Global Terrorism: Characteristics, Causes, Controls* (Upper Saddle River, NJ: Prentice Hall, 2003), pp. 160–72.

Cribb, Robert, "From Petrus to Ninja: Death Squads in Indonesia," in Bruce B. Campbell and Arthur D. Brenner (eds.), *Death Squads in Global Perspective: Murder with Deniability* (New York: Palgrave Macmillan, 2000), pp. 181–202.

Cronin, Audrey Kurth, "Behind the Curve: Globalization and International Terrorism," *International Security*, Vol. 27, No. 3 (2002/03), pp. 30–58.

Daftary, Farhad, *The Assassin Legends: Myths of the Isma'ilis* (London: I. B. Tauris, 1991).

Dale, Stephen Frederic, "Religious Suicide in Islamic Asia: Anticolonial Terrorism in India, Indonesia, and the Philippines," *Journal of Conflict Resolution*, Vol. 32, No. 1 (1988), pp. 37–59.

Dartnell, Michael, "A Legal Inter-Network for Terrorism: Issues of Globalization, Fragmentation, and Legitimacy," in Max Taylor and John Horgan (eds.), *The Future of Terrorism* (London: Frank Cass, 2000), pp. 197–208.

Davis, Paul Bradley, "American Experiences and the Contemporary Perception of Terrorism," *Small Wars and Insurgencies*, Vol. 7, No. 2 (1996), pp. 220–42.

DeCaro, Louis A., Jr., *"Fire from the Midst of You": A Religious Life of John Brown* (New York: New York University Press, 2002).

della Porta, Donatella (1995), "Left-Wing Terrorism in Italy," in Martha Crenshaw (ed.), *Terrorism in Context* (University Park, PA: Pennsylvania State University Press, 1995), pp. 105–59.

Desai, Raj and Harry Eckstein, "Insurgency: The Transformation of Peasant Rebellion," *World Politics*, Vol. 42, No. 4 (1990), pp. 441–65.

Desker, Barry, "Islam and Society in South-East Asia after 11 September," *Australian Journal of International Affairs*, Vol. 56, No. 5 (2002), pp. 383–94.

Deutch, John, "Terrorism," *Foreign Policy*, No. 109 (1997), pp. 10–22.

Dingley, James, "The Bombing of Omagh, 15 August 1998: The Bombers, Their Tactics, Strategy, and Purpose behind the Incident," *Studies in Conflict and Terrorism*, Vol. 24, No. 6 (2001), pp. 451–65.

Dingley, James and Michael Kirk-Smith, "Symbolism and Sacrifice in Terrorism," *Small Wars and Insurgencies*, Vol. 13, No. 1 (2002), pp. 102–28.

Division of Archives and History (State of New York), *The American Revolution in New York: Its Political, Social and Economic Significance* (Albany: The University of the state of New York, 1926).

Dolnik, Adam, "Die and Let Die: Exploring Links between Suicide Terrorism and Terrorist Use of Chemical, Biological, Radiological, and Nuclear Weapons," *Studies in Conflict and Terrorism*, Vol. 26, No. 1 (2003), pp. 17–35.

Dolnik, Adam and Anjali Bhattacharjee, "Hamas: Suicide Bombings, Rockets, or WMD?" *Terrorism and Political Violence*, Vol. 14, No. 3 (2002), pp. 109–28.

Drake, Richard, *The Revolutionary Mystique and Terrorism in Contemporary Italy* (Bloomington, IN: Indiana University Press, 1989).
——— "Red Brigades," in Martha Crenshaw and John Pimlott (eds.), *Encyclopedia of World Terrorism*, Vol. 3 (Armonk, NY: M. E. Sharpe, 1997), pp. 561–65.
Dubois, Laurent, *Avengers of the New World: The Story of the Haitian Revolution* (Cambridge: Belknap Press of Harvard University Press, 2004).
Duiker, William J., *Cultures in Collision: The Boxer Rebellion* (San Rafael, CA: Presidio Press, 1978).
Duyvesteyn, Isabelle, "How New Is the New Terrorism?" *Studies in Conflict and Terrorism*, Vol. 27, No. 5 (2004), pp. 439–54.
Eagan, Sean P., "From Spikes to Bombs: The Rise of Eco-Terrorism," *Studies in Conflict and Terrorism*, Vol. 19, No. 1 (1996), pp. 1–18.
Earl, D. C., *Tiberius Gracchus: A Study in Politics*, Collection Latomus, Vol. 66 (Bruxelles-Bercham: Latomus Revue d'Etudes Latines, 1963).
Eck, Werner, "The Bar Kokhba Revolt: The Roman Point of View," *Journal of Roman Studies*, Vol. 89 (1999), pp. 76–89.
Ellis, Peter Berresford, *Hell or Connaught! The Cromwellian Colonisation of Ireland 1652–1660* (New York: St. Martin's, 1975).
Endres, Rudolf, "The Peasant War in Franconia," in Bob Scribner and Gerhard Benecke (eds.), *The German Peasant War 1525—New Viewpoints* (London: George Allen and Unwin, 1979), pp. 63–83.
Epstein, Steven A., *Genoa & the Genoese, 958–1528* (Chapel Hill: University of North Carolina Press, 1996).
Ergil, Dogu, "Suicide Terrorism in Turkey," *Civil Wars*, Vol. 3, No. 1 (2000), pp. 37–54.
Etcheson, Nicole, *Bleeding Kansas: Contested Liberty in the Civil War Era* (Lawrence: University Press of Kansas, 2004).
Evans, Alexander, "The Kashmir Insurgency: As Bad As It Gets," *Small Wars and Insurgencies*, Vol. 11, No. 1 (2000), pp. 69–81.
Evans, Robert H., "Italy and International Terrorism," in David A. Charters (ed.), *The Deadly Sin of Terrorism: Its Effect on Democracy and Civil Liberty in Six Countries* (Westport, CT: Greenwood Press, 1994), pp. 73–102.
Fagen, Patricia Weiss, "Repression and State Security," in Juan E. Corradi, Patricia Weiss Fagen, and Manuel Antonio Garreton (eds.), *Fear at the Edge: State Terror and Resistance in Latin America* (Berkeley, CA: University of California Press, 1992), pp. 39–71.
Fein, Helen, *Accounting for Genocide: National Responses and Jewish Victimization during the Holocaust* (Chicago: University of Chicago Press, 1979).
Finkelstein, Norman, "History's Verdict: The Cherokee Case," *Journal of Palestine Studies*, Vol. 24, No. 4 (1995), pp. 32–45.
Fisher, Nick, "*Hybris*, Revenge and *Stasis* in the Greek City-States," in Hans van Wees (ed.), *War and Violence in Ancient Greece* (London: Duckworth and the Classical Press of Wales, 2000), pp. 83–123.
Fitzpatrick, Sheila, *Everyday Stalinism: Ordinary Life in Extraordinary Times: Soviet Russia in the 1930s* (New York: Oxford University Press, 1999).
Ford, Franklin L., *Political Murder: From Tyrannicide to Terrorism* (Cambridge, MA: Harvard University Press, 1985).
Fox, Jonathan, "Religion and State Failure: An Examination of the Extent and Magnitude of Religious Conflict from 1950 to 1996," *International Political Science Review*, Vol. 25, No. 1 (2004), pp. 55–76.
Fuks, Alexander, "Aspects of the Jewish Revolt in A.D. 115–117," *Journal of Roman Studies*, Vol. 51, No. 1/2 (1961), pp. 98–104.

BIBLIOGRAPHY

Furedi, Frank, *The Mau Mau War in Perspective*, East African Studies (London: James Currey, 1989).
Furet, Francois, "Terror," in Francois Furet and Mona Ozouf (eds.), *A Critical Dictionary of the French Revolution*, Arthur Goldhammer, trans. (Cambridge, MA: Belknap Press, 1989), pp. 137–50.
Gal-Or, Noemi, "Countering Terrorism in Israel," in David A. Charters (ed.), *The Deadly Sin of Terrorism: Its Effect on Democracy and Civil Liberty in Six Countries* (Westport, CT: Greenwood Press, 1994), pp. 137–72.
Ganguly, Sumit, "The Crisis of Indian Secularism," *Journal of Democracy*, Vol. 14, No. 4 (2003), pp. 11–25.
Gaucher, Roland, *The Terrorists: From Tsarist Russia to the O.A.S.*, Paula Spurlin, trans. (London: Secker & Warburg, 1968).
Gelin-Adams, Marlye and David M. Malone, "Haiti: A Case of Endemic Weakness," in Robert I. Rotberg (ed.), *State Failure and State Weakness in a Time of Terror* (Cambridge, MA and Washington, DC: World Peace Foundation and Brookings Institution Press, 2003), pp. 287–304.
Gershman, John, "Is Southeast Asia the Second Front?" *Foreign Affairs*, Vol. 81, No. 4 (2002), pp. 60–74.
Gillespie, Richard, *Soldiers of Peron: Argentina's Montoneros* (Oxford: Clarendon Press, 1982).
——— "Political Violence in Argentina: Guerillas, Terrorists, and Carapintadas," in Martha Crenshaw (ed.), *Terrorism in Context* (University Park, PA: Pennsylvania State University Press, 1995), pp. 211–48.
Glick, Carl and Hong Sheng-Hwa, *Swords of Silence: Chinese Secret Societies—Past and Present* (New York: Whittlesey House, 1947).
Gossman, Patricia, "India's Secret Armies," in Bruce B. Campbell and Arthur D. Brenner (eds.), *Death Squads in Global Perspective: Murder with Deniability* (New York: Palgrave Macmillan, 2000), pp. 261–86.
Gottschalk, Keith, "The Rise and Fall of Apartheid's Death Squads," in Bruce B. Campbell and Arthur D. Brenner (eds.), *Death Squads in Global Perspective: Murder with Deniability* (New York: Palgrave Macmillan, 2000), pp. 229–59.
Grant, Michael, *Julius Caesar: A Biography* (New York: M. Evans & Co., 1992).
Green, Jerrold D., "Terrorism and Politics in Iran," in Martha Crenshaw (ed.), *Terrorism in Context* (University Park, PA: Pennsylvania State University Press, 1995), pp. 553–94.
Greenway, H. D. S., "Hindu Nationalism Clouds the Face of India," *World Policy Journal*, Vol. 18, No. 1 (2001), pp. 89–93.
Greer, Donald, *The Incidence of Terror during the French Revolution: A Statistical Interpretation* (Cambridge: Harvard University Press, 1935).
Gregory, Shaun, "France and the War on Terrorism," *Terrorism and Political Violence*, Vol. 15, No. 1 (2003), pp. 124–47.
Gressang, Daniel S., IV, "Terrorism in the 21st Century: Reassessing the Emerging Threat," *Terrorism and Political Violence*, Vol. 13, No. 3 (2001), pp. 72–97.
Griffith, Paddy, *The Art of War of Revolutionary France, 1789–1802* (London: Greenhill Books, 1998).
Griset, Pamala L. and Sue Mahan, *Terrorism in Perspective* (Thousand Oaks, CA: Sage Publications, 2003).
Gross, Feliks, *Violence in Politics: Terror and Assassination in Eastern Europe and Russia*, Studies in the Social Sciences 13 (The Hague: Mouton, 1972).
Gurr, Nadine and Benjamin Cole, *The New Face of Terrorism: Threats from Weapons of Mass Destruction* (London: I. B. Tauris, 2000).
Gurr, Ted Robert, "Terrorism in Democracies: When It Occurs, Why It Fails," in Charles W. Kegley, Jr. (ed.), *The New Global Terrorism: Characteristics, Causes, Controls* (Upper Saddle River, NJ: Prentice Hall, 2003), pp. 202–15.
Hale, J. R., *Florence and the Medici: The Pattern of Control* (London: Thames and Hudson, 1977).

Hamm, Mark S., "Terrorism, Hate Crime, and Antigovernment Violence: A Review of the Research," in Harvey W. Kushner (ed.), *The Future of Terrorism: Violence in the New Millennium* (Thousand Oaks, CA: Sage Publications, 1998), pp. 59–96.

Hampshire, Annette P., *Mormonism in Conflict: The Nauvoo Years*, Studies in Religion and Society, Vol. 11 (New York: Edwin Mellen Press, 1985).

Hanauer, Laurence S., "The Path to Redemption: Fundamentalist Judaism, Territory, and Jewish Settler Violence in the West Bank," *Studies in Conflict and Terrorism*, Vol. 18, No. 4 (1995), pp. 245–70.

Harmon, Christopher C., *Terrorism Today* (London: Frank Cass, 2000).

——— "Five Strategies of Terrorism," *Small Wars and Insurgencies*, Vol. 12, No. 3 (2001), pp. 39–66.

Harrison, Michael M., "France and International Terrorism: Problems and Response," in David A. Charters (ed.), *The Deadly Sin of Terrorism: Its Effect on Democracy and Civil Liberty in Six Countries* (Westport, CT: Greenwood Press, 1994), pp. 103–35.

Hatch, John, *Nigeria: The Seeds of Disaster* (Chicago: Henry Regnery, 1970).

Havens, Murray Clark, Carl Leiden, and Karl M. Schmitt, *Assassination and Terrorism: Their Modern Dimensions*, rev. ed. (Manchaca, TX: Sterling Swift, 1975).

Hazleton, William A. and Sandra Woy-Hazleton, "Terrorism and the Marxist Left: Peru's Struggle against Sendero Luminoso," *Terrorism*, Vol. 11, No. 6 (1988), pp. 471–90.

Head, Constance, *Justinian II of Byzantium* (Madison: University of Wisconsin Press, 1972).

Hedman, Eva-Lotta, "State of Siege: Political Violence and Vigilante Mobilization in the Philippines," in Bruce B. Campbell and Arthur D. Brenner (eds.), *Death Squads in Global Perspective: Murder with Deniability* (New York: Palgrave Macmillan, 2000), pp. 125–51.

Heehs, Peter, "Terrorism in India during the Freedom Struggle," *Historian*, Vol. 55, No. 3 (1993), pp. 469–82.

——— *Nationalism, Terrorism, Communalism: Essays in Modern Indian History* (Delhi: Oxford University Press, 1998).

Hefner, Robert W., "Global Violence and Indonesian Muslim Politics," *American Anthropologist*, Vol. 104, No. 3 (2002), pp. 766–75.

Henze, Paul B., "Russia and the Caucasus," *Studies in Conflict and Terrorism*, Vol. 19, No. 4 (1996), pp. 389–402.

Hill, Marvin S., *Quest for Refuge: The Mormon Flight from American Pluralism* (Salt Lake City: Signature Books, 1989).

Hoffman, Bruce, " 'Holy Terror': The Implications of Terrorism Motivated by a Religious Imperative," *Studies in Conflict and Terrorism*, Vol. 18, No. 4 (1995), pp. 271–84.

——— *Inside Terrorism* (New York: Columbia University Press, 1998).

——— "Change and Continuity in Terrorism," *Studies in Conflict and Terrorism*, Vol. 24, No. 5 (2001), pp. 417–28.

——— "The Emergence of the New Terrorism," in Andrew Tan and Kumar Ramakrishna (eds.), *The New Terrorism: Anatomy, Trends and Counter-Strategies* (Singapore: Eastern Universities Press, 2002), pp. 30–49.

——— "Rethinking Terrorism and Counterterrorism since 9/11," *Studies in Conflict and Terrorism*, Vol. 25, No. 5 (2002), pp. 303–16.

Hoffman, Bruce and Gordon H. McCormick, "Terrorism, Signaling, and Suicide Attack," *Studies in Conflict & Terrorism*, Vol. 27, No. 4 (2004), pp. 243–81.

Hoffmann, Stanley, "Clash of Globalizations," *Foreign Affairs*, Vol. 81, No. 4 (2002), pp. 104–15.

Holland, Jack, *Hope against History: The Course of Conflict in Northern Ireland* (New York: Henry Holt, 1999).

Holmes, George, *Florence, Rome, and the Origins of the Renaissance* (Oxford: Clarendon Press, 1986).

Hook, Judith, *Siena: A City and Its History* (London: Hamish Hamilton, 1979).

Bibliography

Hovannisian, Richard G., "The Historical Dimensions of the Armenian Question, 1878–1923," in Richard G. Hovannisian (ed.), *The Armenian Genocide in Perspective* (New Brunswick, NJ: Transaction Books, 1986), pp. 19–42.

Hoyer, Siegfried, "Arms and Military Organisation in the German Peasant War," in Bob Scribner and Gerhard Benecke (eds.), *The German Peasant War 1525—New Viewpoint* (London: George Allen and Unwin, 1979), pp. 98–108.

Huntington, Samuel, "Political Development and Political Decay," *World Politics*, Vol. 17, No. 3 (1965), pp. 95–139.

——— "The Clash of Civilizations?" *Foreign Affairs*, Vol. 72, No. 3 (1993), pp. 22–49.

——— *The Clash of Civilizations and the Remaking of World Order* (New York: Simon & Schuster, 1996).

Iadicola, Peter and Anson Shupe, *Violence, Inequality, and Human Freedom*, 2nd ed. (Lanham, MD: Rowman and Littlefield, 2003).

Iordachi, Constantin, "Charisma, Religion, and Ideology: Romania's Interwar Legion of the Archangel Michael," in Michael R. Lampe and Mark Mazower (eds.), *Ideologies and National Identities: The Case of Twentieth Century Southeastern Europe* (Budapest: Central European University Press, 2004), pp. 19–53.

Jackson, Robert, *The Malayan Emergency: The Commonwealth's Wars, 1948–1966* (London: Routledge, 1991).

Jahoda, Gloria, *The Trail of Tears: The Story of the American Indian Removals, 1813–1855* (New York: Wing Books, 1975).

James, C. L. R., *The Black Jacobins: Toussaint L'Ouverture and the Santo Domingo Revolution*, 2nd ed. (New York: Vintage Books, 1963).

Jardine, Matthew, "Power and Principle in East Timor," *Peace Review*, Vol. 10, No. 2 (1998), pp. 195–202.

Jedlicka, Ludwig, "The Austrian Heimwehr," in Walter Laqueur and George L. Mosse (eds.), *International Fascism, 1920–1945*, Journal of Contemporary History 1 (New York: Harper and Row, 1966), pp. 127–44.

Jenkins, Brian M., "Defense Against Terrorism," *Political Science Quarterly*, Vol. 101, No. 5 (1986), pp. 773–86.

——— "Terrorism and Beyond: A 21st Century Perspective," *Studies in Conflict and Terrorism*, Vol. 24, No. 5 (2001), pp. 321–27.

——— "International Terrorism: The Other World War," in Charles W. Kegley, Jr. (ed.), *The New Global Terrorism: Characteristics, Causes, Controls* (Upper Saddle River, NJ: Prentice Hall, 2003), pp. 15–26.

Jenkins, Philip, "Strategy of Tension: The Belgian Terrorist Crisis 1982–1986," *Terrorism*, Vol. 13, No. 4/5 (1990), pp. 299–309.

Jenne, Erin K., "Sri Lanka: A Fragmented State," in Robert I. Rotberg (ed.), *State Failure and State Weakness in a Time of Terror* (Cambridge, MA and Washington, DC: World Peace Foundation and Brookings Institution Press, 2003), pp. 219–44.

Jha, Prem Shankar, "The Fascist Impulse in Developing Countries: Two Case Studies," *Studies in Conflict and Terrorism*, Vol. 17, No. 3 (1994), pp. 229–74.

Jongman, A. J., "Trends in International and Domestic Terrorism in Western Europe, 1968–1988," *Terrorism and Political Violence*, Vol. 4, No. 4 (1992), pp. 26–76.

Josephus, *The Jewish War*, G. A. Williamson, trans., rev. ed. (New York: Dorset Press, 1981).

Joshi, Manoj, "On the Razor's Edge: The Liberation Tigers of Tamil Eelam," *Studies in Conflict and Terrorism*, Vol. 19, No. 1 (1996), pp. 19–42.

Judah, Tim, *Kosovo: War and Revenge* (New Haven: Yale University Press, 2000).

Juergensmeyer, Mark, "The Worldwide Rise of Religious Nationalism," *Journal of International Affairs*, Vol. 50, No. 1 (1996), pp. 1–20.

Juergensmeyer, Mark, *Terror in the Mind of God: The Global Rise of Religious Violence* (Berkeley: University of California Press, 2000).
——— "The Religious Roots of Contemporary Terrorism," in Charles W. Kegley, Jr. (ed.), *The New Global Terrorism: Characteristics, Causes, Controls* (Upper Saddle River, NJ: Prentice Hall, 2003), pp. 185–93.
——— " 'Holy Orders': Religious Opposition to Modern States," *Harvard International Review*, Vol. 25, No. 4 (2004), pp. 34–38.
Kaplan, Jeffrey, "The Context of American Millenarian Revolutionary Theology: The Case of the 'Identity Christian' Church of Israel," *Terrorism and Political Violence*, Vol. 5, No. 1 (1993), pp. 30–82.
——— "Right Wing Violence in North America," in Tore Bjorgo (ed.), *Terror from the Extreme Right* (London: Frank Cass, 1995), pp. 44–95.
——— *Radical Religion in America: Millenarian Movements from the Far Right to the Children of Noah* (Syracuse: Syracuse University Press, 1997).
Karmon, Ely, "Islamic Terrorist Activities in Turkey in the 1990s," *Terrorism and Political Violence*, Vol. 10, No. 4 (1998), pp. 101–21.
——— "Countering NBC Terrorism," in Andrew Tan and Kumar Ramakrishna (eds.), *The New Terrorism: Anatomy, Trends and Counter-Strategies* (Singapore: Eastern Universities Press, 2002), pp. 193–206.
Kassimeris, George, *Europe's Last Red Terrorists: The Revolutionary Organization 17 November* (New York: New York University Press, 2001).
——— "Greece: Twenty Years of Political Terrorism," *Terrorism and Political Violence*, Vol. 7, No. 2 (1995), pp. 74–92.
Kegley, Charles W., Jr., "The Causes of Terrorism," in Charles W. Kegley, Jr. (ed.), *International Terrorism: Characteristics, Causes, Controls* (New York: St. Martin's, 1990), pp. 97–112.
Kennedy, Moorhead, "The 21st Century Conditions Likely to Inspire Terrorism," in Harvey W. Kushner (ed.), *The Future of Terrorism: Violence in the New Millennium* (Thousand Oaks, CA: Sage, 1988), pp. 185–94.
Khoros, V., " 'The Crown', the 'Roots,' and the 'Climate' of Terrorism," *Russian Politics and Law*, Vol. 41, No. 2 (2003), pp. 70–6.
Kibble, David G., "The Threat of Militant Islam: A Fundamental Reappraisal," *Studies in Conflict and Terrorism*, Vol. 19, No. 4 (1996), pp. 353–64.
Kim, Jae Taik, "North Korean Terrorism: Trends, Characteristics, and Deterrence," *Terrorism*, Vol. 11, No. 4 (1988), pp. 309–322.
Klare, Michael T., "The New Face of Combat: Terrorism and Irregular Warfare in the 21st Century," in Charles W. Kegley, Jr. (ed.), *The New Global Terrorism: Characteristics, Causes, Controls* (Upper Saddle River, NJ: Prentice Hall, 2003), pp. 27–35.
Kline, Harvey F., "Colombia: Lawlessness, Drug Trafficking, and Carving Up the State," in Robert I. Rotberg (ed.), *State Failure and State Weakness in a Time of Terror* (Cambridge, MA and Washington, DC: World Peace Foundation and Brookings Institution Press, 2003), pp. 161–82.
Knecht, R. J., *The French Wars of Religion, 1559–1598*, 2nd ed., Seminar Studies in History (Harlow, Essex: Longman, 1996).
Kostiner, Joseph, "War, Terror, Revolution: The Iran–Iraq Conflict," in Barry Rubin (ed.), *The Politics of Terrorism: Terror as a State and Revolutionary Strategy* (Washington, DC: Foreign Policy Institute, 1989), pp. 95–128.
Krishna, Sankaran, "India and Sri Lanka: A Fatal Convergence," *Studies in Conflict and Terrorism*, Vol. 15, No. 4 (1992), pp. 267–81.
Kuperman, Alan J., "Rwanda in Retrospect," *Foreign Affairs*, Vol. 79, No. 1 (2000), pp. 94–118.
Kuramatsu, Tadashi, "Japanese Terrorism," in Martha Crenshaw and John Pimlott (eds.), *Encyclopedia of World Terrorism*, Vol. 3 (Armonk, NY: M. E. Sharpe, 1997), pp. 568–70.

Kurti, Laszlo, "The Emergence of Postcommunist Youth Identities in Eastern Europe: From Communist Youth to Skinheads, to National Socialists and Beyond," in Jeffrey Kaplan and Tore Bjorgo (eds.), *Nation and Race: The Developing Euro-American Racist Subculture* (Boston: Northeastern University Press, 1998), pp. 175–201.

Kushner, Harvey W., "The New Terrorism," in Harvey W. Kushner (ed.), *The Future of Terrorism: Violence in the New Millennium* (Thousand Oaks, CA: Sage, 1988), pp. 3–20.

——— *Terrorism in America: A Structural Approach to Understanding the Terrorist Threat* (Springfield, IL: Charles C. Thomas, 1998).

Laffan, Michael, "Violence and Terror in Twentieth-Century Ireland: IRB and IRA," in Wolfgang J. Mommsen and Gerhard Hirschfeld (eds.), *Social Protest: Violence and Terror in Nineteenth- and Twentieth-Century Europe* (New York: St. Martin's Press for the German Historical Institute, 1982), pp. 155–74.

Landau, Saul, *The Guerrilla Wars of Central America: Nicaragua, El Salvador & Guatemala* (New York: St. Martin's, 1993).

Laqueur, Walter, *Terrorism* (Boston: Little Brown, 1977).

——— "The Futility of Terrorism," in Charles W. Kegley, Jr. (ed.), *International Terrorism: Characteristics, Causes, Controls* (New York: St. Martin's, 1990), pp. 69–73.

——— *Black Hand: The Rise of the Extreme Right in Russia* (New York: Harper Perennial, 1994).

——— *The New Terrorism: Fanaticism and the Arms of Mass Destruction* (New York: Oxford University Press, 1999).

——— *A History of Terrorism* (New Brunswick, NJ: Transaction Publishers, 2001).

——— *No End to War: Terrorism in the Twenty-First Century* (New York: Continuum, 2003).

Lassen, Suzanne Bettina Danneskiold, "Drug Trafficking and Terrorism in Colombia," in Barry Rubin (ed.), *The Politics of Counterterrorism: The Ordeal of Democratic States* (Washington, DC: Foreign Policy Institute, 1990), pp. 107–36.

Leckie, Robert, *George Washington's War: The Saga of the American Revolution* (New York: Harper Collins, 1992).

Lepsius, M. Ranier (1978), "From Fragmented Party Democracy to Government by Emergency Decree and National Socialist Takeover: Germany," in Juan L. Linz and Alfred Stephan (eds.), *The Breakdown of Democratic Regimes: Europe* (Baltimore: Johns Hopkins University Press, 1978), pp. 34–79.

LeVine, Victor T., "The Logomachy of Terrorism: On the Political Uses and Abuses of Definition," *Terrorism and Political Violence*, Vol. 7, No. 4 (1995), pp. 45–59.

Lewis, Bernard, *The Assassins: A Radical Sect in Islam* (New York: Basic Books, 1968).

Lifton, Robert Jay, *Destroying the World To Save It: Aum Shinrikyo, Apocalyptic Violence, and the New Global Terrorism* (New York: Henry Holt, 2000).

Lintott, A. W., "Cicero and Milo," *Journal of Roman Studies*, Vol. 64 (1974), pp. 62–78.

Linz, Juan J., "Political Space and Fascism as a Late-Comer," in Stein Ugelvik Larsen, Bernt Hagtvet and Jan Petter Myklebust (eds.), *Who Were the Fascists: Social Roots of European Fascism* (Bergen: Universitetsforlaget, 1980), pp. 153–89.

Long, David E., *The Anatomy of Terrorism* (New York: Free Press, 1990).

Luft, Gal, "The Logic of Israel's Targeted Killing," *Middle East Quarterly*, Vol. 10, No. 1 (2003), pp. 3–7.

Lutz, Brenda Davis and James M. Lutz, "Gypsies as Victims of the Holocaust," *Holocaust and Genocide Studies*, Vol. 9, No. 3 (1995), pp. 346–59.

Lutz, James M. and Brenda J. Lutz, *Global Terrorism* (London: Routledge, 2004).

Lyman, Princeton N. and F. Stephen Morrison, "The Terrorist Threat in Africa," *Foreign Affairs*, Vol. 83, No. 1 (2004), pp. 75–86.

Lyttelton, Adrian, "Fascism and Violence in Post-War Italy: Political Strategy and Social Conflict," in Wolfgang J. Mommsen and Gerhard Hirschfeld (eds.), *Social Protest, Violence and Terror in*

Nineteenth- and Twentieth-Century Europe (New York: St. Martin's Press for the German Historical Institute, 1982), pp. 257–74.

McGregor, JoAnn, "The Politics of Disruption: War Veterans and the Local State in Zimbabwe," *African Affairs*, Vol. 101, No. 402 (2002), pp. 9–37.

McKenna, Thomas M., "Murdered or Martyred? Popular Evaluations of Violent Death in the Muslim Separatist Movement in the Philippines," in Jeffrey A. Sluka (ed.), *Death Squad: The Anthropology of State Terror* (Philadelphia: University of Pennsylvania Press, 2000), pp. 189–203.

McLaren, Lauren M., "Explaining Right-Wing Violence in Germany: A Time Series Analysis," *Social Science Quarterly*, Vol. 80, No. 1 (1999), pp. 166–80.

McLoughlin, William G., *Cherokee Renascence in the New Republic* (Princeton, NJ: Princeton University Press, 1986).

Macgregor, Douglas A., "The Balkan Limits to Power and Principle," *Orbis*, Vol. 45, No. 1 (2001), pp. 93–110.

Mahmood, Cynthia Keppley, "Trials by Fire: Dynamics of Terror in Punjab and Kashmir," in Jeffrey A. Sluka (ed.), *Death Squad: The Anthropology of State Terror* (Philadelphia: University of Pennsylvania Press, 2000), pp. 70–90.

Malley, Michael, "Indonesia: The Erosion of State Capacity," in Robert I. Rotberg (ed.), *State Failure and State Weakness in a Time of Terror* (Cambridge, MA and Washington, DC: World Peace Foundation and Brookings Institution Press, 2003), pp. 183–218.

Mamdani, Mahmood, *When Victims Become Killers: Colonialism, Nativism, and the Genocide in Rwanda* (Princeton, NJ: Princeton University Press, 2001).

Manwaring, Max G., "Non-State Actors in Colombia: Threats to the State and to the Hemisphere," *Small Wars and Insurgencies*, Vol. 13, No. 2 (2002), pp. 68–80.

Martines, Lauro, "Political Conflict in the Italian City States," *Government and Opposition*, Vol. 3, No. 1 (1967–1968), pp. 69–91.

Mason, T. David and Christopher Campany, "Guerrillas, Drugs and Peasants: The Rational Peasant and the War on Drugs in Peru," *Terrorism and Political Violence*, Vol. 7, No. 4 (1995), pp. 140–70.

Maurer, Marvin, "The Ku Klux Klan and the National Liberation Front: Terrorism Applied to Achieve Diverse Goals," in Marius H. Livingston with Lee Bruce Kress and Marie G. Wanek (eds.), *International Terrorism in the Contemporary World*, Contributions in Political Science No. 3 (Westport, CT: Greenwood. 1978), pp. 131–52.

Merkl, Peter H., "Approaches to Political Violence: The Stormtroopers," in Wolfgang J. Mommsen and Gerhard Hirschfeld (eds.), *Social Protest, Violence and Terror in Nineteenth- and Twentieth-Century Europe* (New York: St. Martin's Press for the German Historical Institute, 1982), pp. 367–83.

——— *The Making of a Stormtrooper* (Boulder, CO: Westview Press, 1987).

——— "Radical Right Parties in Europe and Anti-Foreign Violence: A Comparative Essay," in Tore Bjorgo, *Terror from the Extreme Right* (London: Frank Cass, 1995), pp. 96–118.

——— "West German Left-Wing Terrorism," in Martha Crenshaw (ed.), *Terrorism in Context* (University Park, PA: Pennsylvania State University Press, 1995), pp. 160–210.

Millar, Fergus, "The Political Character of the Classical Roman Republic, 200–151 B.C.," *Journal of Roman Studies*, Vol. 74 (1984), pp. 1–19.

——— *The Crowd in Rome in the Late Republic*, Thomas Spencer Jerome Lectures 22 (Ann Arbor: University of Michigan Press, 1998).

Miller, Abraham and Nicholas A. Damask, "The Dual Myths of 'Narco-Terrorism': How Myths Drive Policy," *Terrorism and Political Violence*, Vol. 8, No. 1 (1996), pp. 114–31.

Moghadam, Assaf, "Palestinian Suicide Terrorism in the Second Intifada: Motivations and Organizational Aspects," *Studies in Conflict and Terrorism*, Vol. 26, No. 2 (2003), pp. 203–16.

Mommsen, Wolfgang J., "Non-Legal Violence and Terrorism in Western Industrial Societies: An Historical Analysis," in Wolfgang J. Mommsen and Gerhard Hirschfeld (eds.), *Social Protest,*

Violence and Terror in Nineteenth- and Twentieth-Century Europe (New York: St. Martin's Press for the German Historical Institute, 1982), pp. 384–403.
Monaghan, Rachel, "Animal Rights and Violent Protest," *Terrorism and Political Violence*, Vol. 9, No. 4 (1997), pp. 106–16.
——— "Terrorism in the Name of Animal Rights," in Max. Taylor and John Horgan (eds.), *The Future of Terrorism* (London: Frank Cass, 2000), pp. 159–69.
Moodie, Michael, "Tragedy in the Balkans: A Conflict Ended—or Interrupted?" *Small Wars and Insurgencies*, Vol. 9, No. 1 (1998), pp. 12–31.
Mousseau, Michael, "Market Civilization and Its Clash with Terror," *International Security*, Vol. 27, No. 3 (2002/03), pp. 5–29.
Mueller, John, "The Banality of 'Ethnic War'," *International Security*, Vol. 25, No. 1 (2000), pp. 42–70.
Muller, Edward N. and Mitchell A. Seligson, "Inequality and Insurgency," *American Political Science Review*, Vol. 81, No. 2 (1987), pp. 425–51.
Nedoroscik, Jeffrey A., "Extremist Groups in Egypt," *Terrorism and Political Violence*, Vol. 14, No. 2 (2002), pp. 47–76.
Nippel, Wilfried, "Policing Rome," *Journal of Roman Studies*, Vol. 74 (1984), pp. 20–29.
Noor, Farish A., "Globalization, Resistance and the Discursive Politics of Terror, Post-September 11," in Andrew Tan and Kumar Ramakrishna (eds.), *The New Terrorism: Anatomy, Trends and Counter-Strategies* (Singapore: Eastern Universities Press, 2002), pp. 155–77.
O'Ballance, Edgar, *Sudan: Civil War and Terrorism, 1956–99* (New York: St. Martin's, 2000).
O'Day, Alan, "Northern Ireland, Terrorism, and the British State," in Yonah Alexander, David Carlton and Paul Wilkinson (eds.), *Terrorism: Theory and Practice* (Boulder, CO: Westview, 1979), pp. 121–35.
O'Neill, Andrew, "Terrorist Use of Weapons of Mass Destruction: How Serious Is the Threat?" *Australian Journal of International Affairs*, Vol. 57, No. 1 (2003), pp. 99–112.
Oates, Stephen B., *To Purge This Land with Blood: A Biography of John Brown*, 2nd ed. (Amherst: University of Massachusetts Press, 1984).
Oberman, Heiko A., "The Gospel of Social Unrest," in Bob Scribner and Gerhard Benecke (eds.), *The German Peasant War of 1525—New Viewpoints* (London: George Allen & Unwin, 1979), pp. 39–51.
Olojede, Iyabo, Banji Fajonyomi, Ighodalo Akhape, and Suraju O. Mudashiru, "Nigeria: Oil Pollution, Community Dissatisfaction and Threat to National Peace and Security," Occasional Paper Series, Vol. 4, No. 3 (Lagos: Department of Political Science, Lagos State University, 2000).
Ortiz, Roman D., "Insurgent Strategies in the Post-Cold War: The Case of the Revolutionary Armed Forces of Colombia," *Studies in Conflict and Terrorism*, Vol. 25, No. 2 (2002), pp. 127–43.
Ownby, David, *Brotherhoods and Secret Societies in Early and Mid-Qing China: The Formation of a Tradition* (Stanford, CA: Stanford University Press, 1966).
Palfy, Arpad, "Weapon System Selection and Mass-Casualty Outcomes," *Terrorism and Political Violence*, Vol. 15, No. 2 (2003), pp. 81–95.
Palmer, David Scott, "Peru, the Drug Business and Shining Path: Between Scylla and Charybdis?" *Journal of Interamerican Studies and World Affairs*, Vol. 34, No. 3 (1992), pp. 65–88.
——— "The Revolutionary Terrorism of Peru's Shining Path," in Martha Crenshaw (ed.), *Terrorism in Context* (University Park, PA: Pennsylvania State University Press, 1995), pp. 249–308.
Parachini, John V., "Comparing Motives and Outcomes of Mass Casualty Terrorism Involving Conventional and Unconventional Weapons," *Studies in Conflict and Terrorism*, Vol. 24, No. 5 (2001), pp. 389–406.
Parry, Albert, *Terrorism: From Robespierre to Arafat* (New York: Vanguard Press, 1976).
Pavkovic, Aleksander, *The Fragmentation of Yugoslavia: Nationalism and War in the Balkans*, 2nd ed. (New York: Longman, 2000).
Perlstein, Gary R., "Anti-Abortion Activists' Terror Campaign," in Martha Crenshaw and John Pimlott (eds.), *Encyclopedia of World Terrorism*, Vol. 3 (Armonk, NY: M. E. Sharpe, 1997), pp. 542–44.

Perrie, Maureen, "Political and Economic Terror in the Tactics of the Russian Socialist-Revolutionary Party before 1914," in Wolfgang Mommsen and Gerhard Hirschfeld (eds.), *Social Protest, Violence and Terror in Nineteenth- and Twentieth-Century Europe* (New York: St. Martin's Press for the German Historical Institute, 1982), pp. 63–79.

Perry, Duncan M., *The Politics of Terror: The Macedonian Liberation Movements 1893–1903* (Durham, NC: Duke University Press, 1988).

Petersen, Jens, "Violence in Italian Fascism," in Wolfgang J. Mommsen and Gerhard Hirschfeld (eds.), *Social Protest, Violence and Terror in Nineteenth- and Twentieth-Century Europe* (New York: St. Martin's Press for the German Historical Institute, 1982), pp. 275–99.

Pettigrew, Joyce, *The Sikhs of the Punjab: Unheard Voices of State and Guerrilla Violence* (London: Zed Books, 1995).

——— "Parents and Their Children in Situations of Terror: Disappearances and Special Police Activity in Punjab," in Jeffrey A. Sluka (ed.), *Death Squad: The Anthropology of State Terror* (Philadelphia: University of Pennsylvania Press, 2000), pp. 204–25.

Pillar, Paul R., *Terrorism and U.S. Foreign Policy* (Washington, DC: Brookings Institutions, 2001).

Pitcavage, Mark, "Camouflage and Conspiracy: The Militia Movement from Ruby Ridge to Y2K," *American Behavioral Scientist*, Vol. 44, No. 6 (2001), pp. 957–81.

Pluchinsky, Dennis A, "An Organizational and Operational Analysis of Germany's Red Army Faction Terrorist Group (1972–1991)," in Yonah Alexander and Dennis A. Pluchinsky (eds.), *European Terrorism: Today and Tomorrow* (Washington, DC: Brassey's, 1992), pp. 3–92.

Poneman, Daniel, *Argentina: Democracy on Trial* (New York: Paragon House, 1987).

Poulton, Hugh, *Who Are the Macedonians?* 2nd ed. (Bloomington: Indiana University Press, 2000).

Purcell, Victor, *Malaysia* (New York: Walker, 1967).

Puyraimond, Guy, "The Ko-lao Hui and the Anti-Foreign Incidents of 1891," in Jean Chesneaux (ed.), *Popular Movements and Secret Societies in China 1840–1950* (Stanford, CA: Stanford University Press, 1972), pp. 113–24.

Quillen, Chris, "A Historical Analysis of Mass Casualty Bombers," *Studies in Conflict and Terrorism*, Vol. 25, No. 5 (2002), pp. 279–92.

Raaflaub, Kurt A., "From Protection and Defense to Offense and Participation: Stages in the Conflict of Orders," in Kurt A. Raaflaub (ed.), *Social Struggles in Archaic Rome: New Perspectives on the Conflict of the Orders* (Berkeley: University of California Press, 1986), pp. 198–243.

Radu, Michael, "Terrorism after the Cold War," *Orbis*, Vol. 46, No. 2 (2002), pp. 275–87.

Rajendram, Lavina, "Does the Clash of Civilizations Paradigm Provide a Persuasive Explanation of International Politics after September 11th?" *Cambridge Review of International Affairs*, Vol. 15, No. 2 (2002), pp. 217–32.

Ramakrishna, Kumar, "Countering the New Terrorism of Al Qaeda without Generating Civilizational Conflict: The Need for an Indirect Strategy," in Andrew Tan and Kumar Ramakrishna (eds.), *The New Terrorism: Anatomy, Trends and Counter-Strategies* (Singapore: Eastern Universities Press, 2002), pp. 207–32.

Ramakrishna, Kumar and Andrew Tan, "The New Terrorism: Diagnosis and Prescriptions," in Andrew Tan and Kumar Ramakrishna (eds.), *The New Terrorism: Anatomy, Trends and Counter-Strategies* (Singapore: Eastern Universities Press, 2002), pp. 3–29.

Ranstorp, Magnus, "Terrorism in the Name of Religion," *Journal of International Affairs*, Vol. 50, No. 1 (1996), pp. 42–62.

——— "Interpreting the Broader Context and Meaning of Bin-Laden's *Fatwa*," *Studies in Conflict and Terrorism*, Vol. 21, No. 4 (1998), pp. 321–30.

Ranstorp, Magnus and Gus Xhudo, "A Threat to Europe? Middle East Ties with the Balkans and Their Impact upon Terrorist Activity throughout the Region," *Terrorism and Political Violence*, Vol. 6, No. 2 (1994), pp. 196–223.

Rapoport, David C., "Fear and Trembling: Terrorism in Three Religious Traditions," *American Political Science Review*, Vol. 78, No. 3 (1984), pp. 658–77.
——— "Religion and Terror: Thugs, Assassins, and Zealots," in Charles W. Kegley, Jr. (ed.), *International Terrorism: Characteristics, Causes, Controls* (New York: St. Martin's, 1990), pp. 146–57.
——— "The Four Waves of Rebel Terror and September 11," in Charles W. Kegley, Jr. (ed.), *The New Global Terrorism: Characteristics, Causes, Controls* (Upper Saddle River, NJ: Prentice Hall, 2003), pp. 36–52.
Rashid, Ahmed, *Jihad: The Rise of Militant Islam in Central Asia* (New Haven, CT: Yale University Press, 2002).
Raymond, Gregory A., "The Evolving Strategies of Political Terrorism," in Charles W. Kegley, Jr. (ed.), *The New Global Terrorism: Characteristics, Causes, Controls* (Upper Saddle River, NJ: Prentice Hall, 2003), pp. 71–83.
Read, Anthony and David Fisher, *Kristallnacht: The Unleashing of the Holocaust* (New York: Peter Bedrick Books, 1989).
Reader, Ian, "Spectres and Shadows: Aum Shinrikyo and the Road to Megiddo," *Terrorism and Political Violence*, Vol. 14, No. 1 (2002), pp. 147–86.
Reeve, Simon, *The New Jackals: Ramzi Yousef, Osama bin Laden and the Future of Terrorism* (Boston: Northeastern University Press, 1999).
Renovard, Yves, *The Avignon Papacy: The Popes in Exile, 1305–1403*, Denis Bethell, trans. (New York: Barnes and Noble, 1994 reprint, originally published in translation in 1970).
Rieff, David, "Suffering and Cynicism in Burundi," *World Policy Journal*, Vol. 18, No. 3 (2001), pp. 61–67.
Rimanelli, Marco, "Italian Terrorism and Society, 1940s–1980s: Roots, Ideologies, Evolution, and International Connections," *Terrorism*, Vol. 12, No. 4 (1989), pp. 249–96.
Roberts, Timothy, "Now the Enemy is Within Our Borders: The Impact of European Revolutions on American Perceptions of Violence before the Civil War," *American Transcendental Quarterly*, Vol. 17, No. 3 (2003), pp. 197–214.
Robins, Nicholas A., *Genocide and Millennialism in Upper Peru: The Great Rebellion of 1780–1782* (Westport, CT: Praeger, 2002).
Rogers, Steven, "Beyond Abu Sayyaf: The Lessons of Failure in the Philippines," *Foreign Affairs*, Vol. 83, No. 1 (2004), pp. 15–20.
Ron, James, "Territoriality and Plausible Deniability: Serbian Paramilitaries in the Bosnian War," in Bruce B. Campbell and Arthur D. Brenner (eds.), *Death Squads in Global Perspective: Murder with Deniability* (New York: Palgrave Macmillan, 2000), pp. 286–312.
Ros, Martin, *Night of Fire: The Black Napoleon and the Battle for Haiti*, Karin Ford-Treep, trans. (New York: Sarpedon, 1994).
Ross, Jeffrey Ian, "The Rise and Fall of Quebecois Separatist Terrorism: A Qualitative Application of Factors from Two Models," *Studies in Conflict and Terrorism*, Vol. 18, No. 5 (1995), pp. 285–97.
Rotberg, Robert I., "Africa's Mess, Mugabe's Mayhem," *Foreign Affairs*, Vol. 79, No. 5 (2000), pp. 47–61.
Rude, George, *The Crowd in the French Revolution* (Oxford: The Clarendon Press, 1959).
Runciman, W. G., "Capitalism without Classes: The Case of Classical Rome," *British Journal of Sociology*, Vol. 34, No. 2, (1983), pp. 157–81.
Saikia, Jaideep, "The ISI Reaches East: Anatomy of a Conspiracy," *Studies in Conflict and Terrorism*, Vol. 25, No. 3 (2002), pp.185–97.
St. John, O. Peter, "Algeria: A Case Study of Insurgency in the New World Order," *Small Wars and Insurgencies*, Vol. 7, No. 2 (1996), pp. 196–219.
Samaranayake, Gamini, "Political Violence in Sri Lanka: A Diagnostic Approach," *Terrorism and Political Violence*, Vol. 9, No. 2 (1997), pp. 99–119.

Samaranayake, Gamini, "Patterns of Political Violence and Responses of the Government in Sri Lanka, 1971–1996," *Terrorism and Political Violence*, Vol. 11, No. 1 (1999), pp. 110–22.

Sandler, Shmuel, "Religious Zionism and the State: Political Accommodation and Religious Radicalism in Israel," in Bruce Maddy-Weitzman and Efraim Inbar (eds.), *Religious Radicalism in the Greater Middle East* (London: Frank Cass, 1997), pp. 133–54.

Sayari, Sabri and Bruce Hoffman, "Urbanisation and Insurgency: The Turkish Case, 1976–1980," *Small Wars and Insurgencies*, Vol. 5, No. 2 (1994), pp. 162–79.

Sayigh, Yezid, "The Armed Struggle and Palestinian Nationalism," in Avraham Sela and Moshe Ma'oz (eds.), *The PLO and Israel: From Armed Conflict to Political Solution, 1964–1994* (New York: St. Martin's, 1997), pp. 23–35.

Schafer, David, "Origins of the Israeli/Palestinian Conflict: The Seeds of Enmity," *Humanist*, Vol. 62, No. 5 (2002), pp. 9–14.

Schbley, Ayla, "Defining Religious Terrorism: A Causal and Anthological Profile," *Studies in Conflict and Terrorism*, Vol. 26, No. 2 (2003), pp. 105–34.

Scherrer, Christian P., *Genocide and Crisis in Central Africa: Conflict Roots, Mass Violence, and Regional War* (Westport, CT: Praeger, 2002).

Schlagheck, Donna M., "The Superpowers, Foreign Policy, and Terrorism," in Charles W. Kegley, Jr. (ed.), *International Terrorism: Characteristics, Causes, Controls* (New York: St. Martin's, 1990), pp. 170–77.

Schmid, Alex P., *Political Terrorism: A Research Guide to Concepts, Theories, Data Bases, and Literature* (New Brunswick, NJ: Transaction Books, 1983).

——— "The Response Problem as a Definition Problem," *Terrorism and Political Violence*, Vol. 4, No. 4 (1992), pp. 7–13.

——— "Terrorism and Democracy," *Terrorism and Political Violence*, Vol. 4, No. 4 (1992), pp. 14–25.

Schneider, Jane and Peter Schneider, "The Mafia and al-Qaeda: Violent and Secretive Organizations in Comparative and Historical Perspective," *American Anthropologist*, Vol. 104, No. 3 (2002), pp. 776–82.

Schroeder, Michael J., " 'To Induce a Sense of Terror': Caudillo Politics and Political Violence in Northern Nicaragua, 1926–34 and 1981–95," in Bruce B. Campbell and Arthur D. Brenner (eds.), *Death Squads in Global Perspective: Murder with Deniability* (New York: Palgrave Macmillan, 2000), pp. 27–56.

Schulze, Kirsten E., "The Struggle for an Independent Aceh: The Ideology, Capacity, and Strategy of GAM," *Studies in Conflict and Terrorism*, Vol. 26, No. 4 (2003), pp. 241–71.

Sederberg, Peter C., "Global Terrorism: Problems of Challenge and Response," in Charles W. Kegley, Jr. (ed.), *The New Global Terrorism: Characteristics, Causes, Controls* (Upper Saddle River, NJ: Prentice Hall, 2003), pp. 267–84.

Serulnikov, Sergio, *Subverting Colonial Authority* (Durham, NC: Duke University Press, 2003).

Shabad, Goldie and Francisco Jose Llera Ramo, "Political Violence in a Democratic State: Basque Terrorism in Spain," in Martha Crenshaw (ed.), *Terrorism in Context* (University Park, PA: Pennsylvania State University Press, 1995), pp. 410–69.

Shalom, Stephen R., "Genocide in Rwanda," in William Dudley (ed.), *Genocide* (San Diego, CA: Greenhaven Press, 2001), pp. 43–58.

Shapiro, Jeremy and Benedicte Suzan, "The French Experience of Counter-Terrorism," *Survival*, Vol. 45, No. 1 (2003), pp. 67–98.

Sheldon, Rose Mary, "Taking on Goliath: The Jews against Rome, AD 66–73," *Small Wars and Insurgencies*, Vol. 5, No. 1 (1994), pp. 1–28.

Sherwin-White, A. N., "Violence in Roman Politics," *Journal of Roman Studies*, Vol. 46, No. 1/2 (1956), pp. 1–9.

Shubik, Martin, "Terrorism, Technology, and the Socioeconomics of Death," *Comparative Strategy*, Vol. 16, No. 4 (1997), pp. 399–414.

Sick, Gary G., "The Political Underpinnings of Terrorism," in Charles W. Kegley, Jr. (ed.), *International Terrorism: Characteristics, Causes, Controls* (New York: St. Martin's, 1990), pp. 51–54.
Sicker, Martin, *Between Rome and Jerusalem: 300 Years of Roman–Judean Relations* (Westport, CT: Praeger, 2001).
Silvestri, Michael, " 'The Sinn Fein of India': Irish Nationalism and the Policing of Revolutionary Terrorism in Bengal," *Journal of British Studies*, Vol. 39, No. 4 (2000), pp. 454–86.
Simons, Anna, "Making Sense of Ethnic Cleansing," *Studies in Conflict and Terrorism*, Vol. 22, No. 1 (1999), pp. 1–20.
Sinclair, Andrew, *An Anatomy of Terror: A History of Terrorism* (London: Macmillan, 2003).
Singh, Jasjit, "Kashmir, Pakistan and the War by Terror," *Small Wars and Insurgencies*, Vol. 13, No. 2 (2002), pp. 81–94.
Slack, J. Andrew and Roy R. Doyon, "Population Dynamics and Susceptibility for Ethnic Conflict: The Case of Bosnia and Herzegovina," *Journal of Peace Research*, Vol. 38, No. 2 (2001), pp. 139–61.
Smith, Brent L. (2000), "Moving to the Right: The Evolution of Modern American Terrorism," *Global Dialogue*, Vol. 2, No. 4 (2000), pp. 52–63.
Sobieck, Steven M., "Democratic Responses to International Terrorism in Germany," in David A. Charters (ed.), *The Deadly Sin of Terrorism: Its Effect on Democracy and Civil Liberty in Six Countries* (Westport, CT: Greenwood Press, 1994), pp. 43–72.
Sprinzak, Ehud, "Right-Wing Terrorism in a Comparative Perspective: The Case of Split Delegitmization," in Tore Bjorgo (ed.), *Terror from the Extreme Right* (London: Frank Cass, 1995), pp. 17–43.
——— "Extremism and Violence in Israeli Democracy," *Terrorism and Political Violence*, Vol. 12, No. 3/4 (2002), pp. 209–36.
Sproat, Peter A. "Can the State be Terrorist?" *Terrorism*, Vol. 14, No. 1 (1991), pp. 19–29.
Stadler, K. R., "Austria," in S. J. Woolf (ed.), *European Fascism* (New York: Vintage Books, 1968), pp. 88–110.
Stavig, Ward, *The World of Tupac Amaru: Conflict, Community, and Identity in Colonial Peru* (Lincoln: University of Nebraska Press, 1999).
Steenbrink, Karel A., "Muslim-Christian Relations in the *Pancasila* State of Indonesia," *The Muslim World*, Vol. 87, No. 3/4 (1998), pp. 320–52.
Stern, Jessica, "Pakistan's Jihad Culture," *Foreign Affairs*, Vol. 79, No. 6 (2000), pp. 115–126.
——— *The Ultimate Terrorists* (Cambridge, MA: Harvard University Press, 1999).
Stohl, Michael, "Demystifying the Mystery of International Terrorism," in Charles W. Kegley, Jr. (ed.), *International Terrorism: Characteristics, Causes, Controls* (New York: St. Martin's, 1990), pp. 81–96.
——— "The Mystery of the New Global Terrorism: Old Myths, New Realities?" in Charles W. Kegley, Jr. (ed.), *The New Global Terrorism: Characteristics, Causes, Controls* (Upper Saddle River, NJ: Prentice Hall, 2003), pp. 84–91.
Stone, Martin, *The Agony of Algeria* (New York: Columbia University Press, 1997).
Subramanian, Narendra, "Ethnicity and Pluralism: An Exploration with Reference to Indian Cases," *Canadian Journal of Political Science*, Vol. 32, No. 4 (1999), pp. 715–44.
Tan, Andrew, "Armed Muslim Separatist Rebellion in Southeast Asia: Persistence, Prospects, and Implications," *Studies in Conflict and Terrorism*, Vol. 23, No. 4 (2000), pp. 267–88.
Taylor, Ian and Paul Williams, "The Limits of Engagement: British Foreign Policy and the Crisis in Zimbabwe," *International Affairs*, Vol. 78, No. 3 (2002), pp. 547–65.
Taylor, Max. and John Horgan, "Future Developments of Political Terrorism in Europe," in Max. Taylor and John Horgan (eds.), *The Future of Terrorism* (London: Frank Cass, 2000), pp. 83–93.
Taylor, Peter, *Behind the Mask: The IRA and Sinn Fein* (New York: TV Books, 1997).
Thompson, David P., "Pablo Escobar, Drug Baron: His Surrender, Imprisonment, and Escape," *Studies in Conflict and Terrorism*, Vol. 19, No. 1 (1996), pp. 55–91.

Thompson, Sir Robert, *Defeating Communist Insurgency: The Lessons of Malaya and Vietnam*, Studies in International Security 10 (New York: Praeger, 1966).

Thomson, Sinclair, *We Alone Will Rule: Native Andean Politics in the Age of Insurgency* (Madison: University of Wisconsin Press, 2002).

Thornton, Thomas Perry, "Terror as a Weapon of Political Agitation," in Harry Eckstein (ed.), *Internal War: Problems and Approaches* (Glencoe, IL: The Free Press, 1964), pp. 71–99.

Tracey, Patricia Cleland, "Cherokee Gold in Georgia and California," *Journal of the West*, Vol. 39, No. 1 (2000), pp. 49–55.

Trouillot, Michel-Rolph, *Haiti: State against Nation—The Origins and Legacy of Duvalierism* (New York: Monthly Review Press, 1990).

Tucker, Jonathan B. and Jason Pate, "The Minnesota Patriots Council," in Jonathan B. Tucker (ed.), *Toxic Terror: Assessing Terrorist Use of Chemical and Biological Weapons* (Cambridge, MA: MIT Press, 2000), pp. 159–83.

Tucker, Richard K., *The Dragon and the Cross: The Rise and Fall of the Ku Klux Klan in Middle America* (Hamden, CT: Archon Books, 1991).

Tweeten, Luther, *Terrorism, Radicalism, and Populism in Agriculture* (Ames, IA: Iowa State Press, 2003).

Ukeje, Charles, "Oil Communities and Political Violence: The Case of Ethnic Ijaws in Nigeria's Delta Region," *Terrorism and Political Violence*, Vol. 13, No. 4 (2001), pp. 15–36.

Upton, A. F., "Finland," in S. J. Woolf (ed.), *European Fascism* (New York: Vintage Books, 1968), pp. 184–216.

van Every, Dale, *Disinherited: The Lost Birthright of the American Indian* (New York: William Morrow, 1996).

Veness, David, "Low Intensity and High Impact Conflict," in Max Taylor and John Horgan (eds.), *The Future of Terrorism* (London: Frank Cass, 2000), pp. 8–14.

Vetschera, Heinz, "Terrorism in Austria: Experiences and Responses," *Terrorism and Political Violence*, Vol. 4, No. 4 (1992), pp. 210–33.

von Borcke, Astrid, "Violence and Terror in Russian Revolutionary Populism: The *Narodnaya Volya*," in Wolfgang J. Mommsen and Gerhard Hirschfeld (eds.), *Social Protest, Violence and Terror in Nineteenth- and Twentieth-Century Europe* (New York: St. Martin's Press for the German Historical Institute, 1982), pp. 48–62.

von Ungern-Sternberg, Jurgen, "The End of the Conflict of the Orders," in Kurt A. Raaflaub (ed.), *Social Struggles in Archaic Rome: New Perspectives on the Conflict of the Orders* (Berkeley: University of California Press, 1986), pp. 353–77.

Waley, Daniel, *The Papal State in the Thirteenth Century* (London: Macmillan, 1961).

Wallace, Paul, "Political Violence and Terrorism in India: The Crisis of Identity," in Martha Crenshaw (ed.), *Terrorism in Context* (University Park, PA: Pennsylvania State University Press, 1995), pp. 352–409.

Walton, John, *Reluctant Rebels: Comparative Studies of Revolution and Underdevelopment* (New York: Columbia University Press, 1984).

Warner, Bruce W., "Great Britain and the Response to International Terrorism," in David A. Charters (ed.), *The Deadly Sin of Terrorism: Its Effect on Democracy and Civil Liberty in Six Countries* (Westport, CT: Greenwood Press, 1994), pp. 13–42.

Watanabe, Manabu, "Religion and Violence in Japan Today: A Chronological and Doctrinal Analysis of Aum Shinrikyo," *Terrorism and Political Violence*, Vol. 10, No. 4 (1998), pp. 80–100.

Weber, Eugen, "The Men of the Archangel," in Walter Laqueur and George L. Mosse (eds.), *International Fascism, 1920–1945*, Journal of Contemporary History 1 (New York: Harper and Row, 1966), pp. 101–26.

Weinberg, Leonard, "Italian Neo-Fascist Terrorism: A Comparative Perspective," in Tore Bjorgo (ed.), *Terror from the Extreme Right* (London: Frank Cass, 1995), pp. 221–38.

BIBLIOGRAPHY

—— "On Responding to Right-Wing Terrorism," *Terrorism and Political Violence*, Vol. 8, No. 1 (1996), pp. 80–92.

Weinberg, Leonard B. and William L. Eubank, "Terrorism and the Shape of Things to Come," in Max. Taylor and John Horgan (eds.), *The Future of Terrorism* (London: Frank Cass, 2000), pp. 83–93.

Welsh, David, "Right-Wing Terrorism in South Africa," in Tore Bjorgo (ed.), *Terror from the Extreme Right* (London: Frank Cass, 1995), pp. 239–64.

Whitby, Michael, "The Violence of the Circus Factions," in Keith Hopwood (ed.), *Organised Crime in Antiquity* (London: Duckworth with the Classical Press of Wales, 1999), pp. 229–53.

White, Jonathan R., *Terrorism: An Introduction*, 2nd ed. (Belmont, CA: Wadsworth, 1988).

Wilkinson, Paul, *Terrorism and the Liberal State* (London: Macmillan, 1977).

—— "Violence and Terror and the Extreme Right," *Terrorism and Political Violence*, Vol. 7, No. 4 (1995), pp. 82–93.

—— *Terrorism versus Democracy: The Liberal State Response* (London: Frank Cass, 2000).

—— "Politics, Diplomacy and Peace Processes: Pathways out of Terrorism," in Max. Taylor and John Horgan (eds.), *The Future of Terrorism* (London: Frank Cass, 2000), pp. 66–82.

—— "Why Modern Terrorism? Differentiating Types and Distinguishing Ideological Motivations," in Charles W. Kegley, Jr. (ed.), *The New Global Terrorism: Characteristics, Causes, Controls* (Upper Saddle River, NJ: Prentice Hall, 2003), pp. 106–38.

Williams, Gavin and Terisa Turner, "Nigeria," in John Dunn (ed.), *West African States: Failure and Promise: A Study in Comparative Politics*, African Studies Series 23 (Cambridge: Cambridge University Press, 1978), pp. 132–72.

Winn, Kenneth H., *Exiles in a Land of Liberty* (Chapel Hill, NC: University of North Carolina Press, 1989).

Woodworth, Paddy, "Why Do They Kill? The Basque Conflict in Spain," *World Policy Journal*, Vol. 18, No. 1 (2001), pp. 1–12.

Woolf, S. J., "Italy," in S. J. Woolf (ed.), *European Fascism* (New York: Vintage Books, 1968), pp. 39–60.

Wynia, Gary W., *Argentina: Illusions and Realities* (New York: Holmes & Meier, 1986).

Yakobson, Alexander, *Elections and Electioneering in Rome: A Study in the Political System of the Later Republic* (Stuttgart: Franz Steiner Verlag, 1999).

Ziemann, Benjamin, "Germany after the First World War—A Violent Society?: Results and Implications of Recent Research on Weimar Germany," *Journal of European History*, Vol. 1, No. 1 (2003), pp. 80–95.

INDEX

Page numbers in italics refer to items in the tables at the end of the chapters

abortion, opposition to, 133–4, 146, 151, *154*, 171
Abu Nidal Organization, 111, 122
Abu Sayyaf, 138, *156*
Aceh, 39, 134, 146, 147, 150, *154*
Aceh Sumatra National Liberation Front (GAM), 134
Aden, 137
Afghanistan, 1, 115, 135, 137–8, 139, 140, 143, 153
Albanians, 67, 136, 144–5, 146, 149, *155*
Alexander I, King of Yugoslavia, 68
Alexander II, Tsar, 53–4
Alexander III, Tsar, 54
ALF, *see* Animal Liberation Front
Algeria, 87–8, 94, 95, 138–9, 143, 146, 147, 150, 152, *156*, 162, 164
  independence struggle, 87, 93, 95, 97, 162
  OAS, 87–8, 91–2, *97*
Al-Qaeda, 3, 136–8, 140, 141, 143, 146, 147, 150–1, 152, 153, *155*, 161, 162, 164, 166, 168
  in Afghanistan, 137–8, 140, 143, 166
  and Madrid attacks, 132, 137
  and September 11th, 2, 132, 137, 150, 162
  and weapons of mass destruction, 164
Ambion, 135, 146, 148, *155*
American Civil War, 50–1, 59, 159, 161

American Revolution, 36, 37, 40, 43, 44, 45, *46*, 161–2, 166
anarchists, 1, 47, 51, 52–4, 57, 61, 62, *64*, 72–3, 108, 160, 161, 167
Animal Liberation Front (ALF), 142, 148, *156*
Animal Rights Militia (ARM), 142
anthrax, 163
Antiterrorist Liberation Groups (GAL), 114, 123, *127*
April 19 Movement (M-19), 105
Arabs, 69, 78, *82*, 85
Arab terrorism, 80, *82*
Arafat, Yassir, 111
Archduke Franz Ferdinand, 52, 60, 176n31
Argentina, 106, 116, 119, 121, *126*
  and death squads, 114, 121, 122, 124, *128*, 162
Argentine Anti-Communist Alliance, 114
ARM, *see* Animal Rights Militia
Armenian Secret Army for the Liberation of Armenia (ASALA), 111, *127*
Armenians, 48, 52–3, 56, 57, 61, 62, *64*, 160
  genocide, 48, 56, 57, *64*, 74, 111, 161, 162
  Ottoman massacres, 53, 56, *64*
  post World War II attacks against Turkey, 111, 117, 118, 121, *127*

Index

Army of God, 134
Asahara, Shoko, 141
ASALA, *see* Armenian Secret Army for the Liberation of Armenia
assassination, 8, 9, 10, 28, 29, 30, 52
  and anarchists, 53–4, 61, 108
  in Argentina, 106, 114
  attempts on (Charles) DeGaulle, 88
  attempt on (Islam) Karimov, 140
  of (Julius) Caesar, 21
  in Colombia, 105, *126*, 130
  and ETA, 108
  of Franz Ferdinand, 52, 60, 176n31
  of (Indira) Gandhi, 110, 113
  of (Mahatma) Gandhi, 88
  of (Rajiv) Gandhi, 116
  in India, 51, 88, 110, 113, 116
  in Iran, 107
  in Ireland, 51, 109
  in Japan, 70, 76
  and Jewish Zealots, 22
  of King Alexander I, 68
  of Lord Moyne, 69
  in Nicaragua, 100
  of Rabin, 140
  in Rumania, 73
  and Sikhs, 110
  and Social Revolutionaries, 54–5
  in Sri Lanka, 103, 110, 116, 131
  of Tsar Alexander II, 54, 108
  in Weimar Germany, 70, 76
Assassins, 28–9, 31–2, 33, 34, *34*, 161
Assyria, 3
Athens, 20, 23
Aum Shinrikyo, 141, 146, 147, 150, *156*, 162, 163, 164
Austria, 72, 74, 75, 121
  and OPEC meeting, 112
Austria-Hungary, 52, 53, 60
AUS, *see* Self Defense Forces of Colombia
authoritarianism, 9–10, 12, 15, 16, 25, 72, 73, 75, 78, 80, 89, 91, 92, 100, 108, 121, 144, 159
Avignon Papacy, 31

Ayodhya, 143
Aztecs, 2

Baader-Meinhof Gang; 101, *125*; *see also* Red Army Faction
Bali, 137, 147
Balkans, 51, 52, 57, 59, 61, 62, 66, 149, 153
Bar Kokhba, 22
Belgium, 84, 93, 100, 101, *124*
Bengal, 47, 51, 61, *64*, 68–9, 74, 78, 91, 103
Biafra, 89
bin Laden, Osama, 137, 159
biological weapons, 163, 164
Black Hand, 47, 52, 57, 60, 62, *64*
Black Hundred, 47, 54, 58, 61, 62
Black International, 91
Black September, 111
Bolivia, 37
Borneo, 134–5, *154*
Bosnia and Herzegovina, 67, 74, 135–6, 146, 147, 148, 149, 152, *155*, 161, 163
Boston Tea Party, 37, 44
Boxers, 47, 48, 57, 58, 59, 61, 62, *63*, 159, 160, 161
Branch Davidians, 133
Brazil, 106, 114, 120, *126*
Britain, 39, 42, 47, 51, 53, 56, 68, 69, 76, 77, 79, 80, 92, 102, 109, 132, 142, 147
  and American Revolution, 43–4, 45, *46*
  and Cyprus, 86, *96*
  and declining empire, 84, 93
  and India, 47, 51, 61, *64*, 68–9, 79, *81*, 95
  and Ireland, 51, 61, 68, 76, 77, *81*, 85, 92, *97*, 99, 108–09, 131, 149, *154*
  and Kenya, 86–7, 94, *97*
  and Malaya, 49, 85–6, 92, *97*
  and Palestine, 69, 78, 80, *82*, 85, 94, *96*, 161
Brown, John, 50, 60
  and Harpers Ferry raid, 50, 60
Bulgaria, 67, 68, *82*, 132
  and IMRO, 51, 52, 67, 75

Burundi, 145, 146, *157*
Byzantine Empire, 19, 23, 24, 25, 26, 27, 159, 161

Camp David Accords, 112
capitalism, opposition to, 58, 78, 92, 99, 100, 102, 104, 112, 117, 120, *125*
Castro, Fidel, 90, 91
CCC, *see* Communist Combat Cells
Chechens, 140–1, 148, 150, 153, *156*, 164
chemical weapons, 141, 150, 163–4
Cherokees, 55–6, 61, *63*, 160
China, 48, 57, 58, *63*, 161
  ancient, 3, 19, 28
Christian Identity movement, 133
Christianity, 17, 39, 46, 48, 138, 148, 161
  fundamentalism, 69–70, 133
Christian Patriot organizations, 133
Christians, 113, 117, 135
  Chinese, 48, 57, *63*, 161
  in India, 144, *155*
  in Indonesia, 135, 143, 146, 149–50, *155*
  in Nigeria, 88–9, 92, 139–40, 146, 147
  in Ottoman Empire, 47, 51–3, 57, 60, 61, *64*, 149
  in Philippines, 48, 138, 143, 161
  in Singapore, 49
CIA, 91, 112
Civil Rights Act of, 1964, 89
clash of civilizations, 17, 33, 42, 58, 92, 118, 148, 150, 163, 164
Codreanu, Corneliu, 72, 73
Cold War, 84, 91, 99, 115, 118, 123, 129, 159, 160, 165
Colombia, 84, 119, 121, 130, 151, 162, 166
  and death squads, 114, 144, 146, 152, *157*
  and drug cartels, 117, 124, *126*, 130, 146, 153, 160, 166
  and left, 105, 116, 121, 130, 143, 145, 146, 151, 153, *153*

colonialism, 11, 37, 38, 39, 42, 43, 44, 45, 46, 78, 79, 84, 85–6, 88–9, 92, 95, 96, 112, 124, 166, 168
Communist Combat Cells (CCC), 101, *125*
Communist Party of Indonesia (PKI), 89, 90, *97*
Continuity IRA, 131
Contras, 100, 115, 117, 122, *125*
Corsican nationalists, 108, 115, 117–18, 121, *127*, 130, 146, 147, 148, 149
Croatia, 67–8, 74, 75, 79, *82*, 161
Cromwell, Oliver, 36, 41, 42, 43, *45*
Cuba, 90, 91, 115
cultural genocide, 13
Cyprus, 22, 24, 26, 86, 93, 94, 95, *96*, 163
Czechoslovakia, 75

Darfur, 144
Dayaks, 135, 146, 149, *154*
death squads, 10, 113–15, 117, 119, 124, 160, 162
  and Argentina, 114, 121, 122, 124, *128*, 162
  and Colombia, 114, 144, 146, 152, *157*
  and East Timor, 114–15, 119–20, 123, *128*, 161, 162
  and El Salvador, 113–14
  and Guatemala, 114, 122, *128*, 162
  and India, 115, 117, 122–3, *127*, 143, 151, *156*
  and Philippines, 114, 117, 119, 123, *128, 157*
  and Rumania, 73
  and Rwanda, 145
  and South Africa, 114, 117, 123, *128*
  and Spain, 114, 123, *127*
  and Sri Lanka, 114, 117, 123, *128*
DeGaulle, Charles, 88, 94
Dessalines, 38
diaspora populations, 62, 75, 94, 115, 118, 143
Direct Action, 101, *125*

drug cartels/dealers, 105, 124, 153, 160, 166, 168
  in Colombia, 105–6, 117, 123, 124, *126*, 130, 144, 146, 153, *153*, 160
  in Peru, 105, 124, 153
Dutch East Indies, 41, 58, 59, 134, 161; see also Indonesia,
Duvalier, Francois, 90, 92, 93, 96, *98*
dynamite, 3, 18, 167

Earth Liberation Front (ELF), 142, 148, *156*
Easter Rising, 68
East Timor, 114, 118, 119–20, *128*, 134, 146–7, 161, 162, 163
  and death squads, 114, 120, 123, *128*, 161, 162
Egypt, 91, 99, 138, 150, *155*, 164
  ancient, 3, 19, 22, 24, 26
  and, 1967 War, 99
ELF, see Earth Liberation Front
ELN, see National Liberation Army
El Salvador, 103, 113, 115, 119, 121, *126*
empires, breakup, 4, 16, 84, 88, 93, 95, 129, 146, 166, 167
Entebbe, Uganda, 112
environmental groups, 142, 148, *156*
EOKA, see Organization of Cypriot Fighters
EPL, see Popular Liberation Army
ERP, see People's Revolutionary Army
ETA, see Euzkadi ta Askatasuna
ethnic cleansing, 12–13, 18, 61, 66, 110, 134, 151, 153, 160, 167, 168
  Armenians, 56, 57, 61, *64*
  Borneo, 134–5, 149, *154*
  Bosnia, 135–6, 144, 146, 147, *155*, 161, 163
  Croatia, 74–75, 161
  East Timor, 163
  Haiti, 38, 44
  India, 88, 96, *97*, 100–1, 139, 151, 163
  Indonesia, 89, 96, *97*, 134, 135, *155*
  Ireland, 36, 41, *45*

Kosovo, 136, 144–5, 147, 152, *155*, 163
Nigeria, 96, 88–9, *106*, 139–40
Rwanda, 145
Sudan, 144, 152, 163
ethnocide, 13
Euzkadi ta Askatasuna, 108, 114, 115, 117–18, *127*, 130, 146, 149, *154*, 162, 164

FALN, see Forces for National Liberation
false flag attacks, 89, 91, 100
Farabundo Marti National Liberation Front (FMLN), 104, *126*
FARC, see Revolutionary Armed Forces of Colombia
fascism, 67, 71, 72, 73, 77, 78, 79, 81, *83*, 123, 132, 144, 161
Fascist Party (Italy), 71, 72, 73, 74, 76, 77, 80, *83*, 89
Finland, 72, 80
First of October Anti-Fascist Popular Forces, (GRAPO), 101, *125*
FLN, see National Liberation Front (Algeria)
Florence, 31, 32–3
FMLN, see Farabundo Marti National Liberation Front
Forces for National Liberation (FALN) (Venezuela), 90, 92, 93, 96, *98*
France, 31, 36, 41, 42, 43, 45, 47, 53, 56, 68, 84, 88, 91–2, 93, 101, 114, 122, 130, 147
  and Algeria, 87, 88, 92, 94, *97*, 139
  and Corsica, 108, *127*, 130, 147, 148
  and French Revolution, 43, 44, 46, 166
  and Haiti, 38, 43
French Revolution, 1, 35, 38, 39, 41–2, 43, *46*, 161, 166
Front for the National Liberation of Corsica, 108
Fujimoro, Alberto, 104

GAL, *see* Antiterrorist Liberation Groups
GAM, *see* Aceh Sumatra National Liberation Front
Gandhi, Indira, 100, 113
Gandhi, Mahatma, 88
Gandhi, Rajiv, 116
Genoa, 31
genocide, 12–13, 18, 66, 75, 152, 162
    against Armenians, 56, 57, *64*, 111, 121, 152, 161, 162
    against Gypsies, 74, *82*, 162
    against Jews, 74, *83*, 152, 161, 162
    in Rwanda, 145, 146, 152, *157*, 162
Georgia Guard, 55
German Peasant War of 1525, 28, 31, 32
Germany, 15, 28, 32, 33, 52, 53, 56, 68, 69, 75, 76, *82*, 101, 112, *125*, 152
    and Nazis, 71, 73, 74, 75, *83*, 162
    and right-wing groups, 70, 71, 72, 80, *83*, 132, 145
    and Weimar Republic, 70, 71, 73, 76, *82*
GIA, *see* Islamic Army Group
Girondins, 40, 44
globalization, 16, 17, 25, 27, 42, 58, 62, 78–9, 92, 117–18, 147–8, 152, 166–7, 168
Glorious Revolution, 35
Gracchus, Gaius, 21, 24
Gracchus, Tiberius, 21, 24
GRAPO, *see* First of October Anti-Fascist Popular Forces
Great Britain, *see* Britain
Great Depression, 66, 77
Greece, 86, 91, 94, *96*, *102*, 118
    ancient, 19, 23, 25
    and 17 November Organization, 102, 120, *125*, 129
Guatemala, 114, 119, 123
    and death squads, 114, 122, *128*, 162
guerrilla warfare, 9, 18, 38, 39, 84, 95–6, 137, 140, 159, 162, 163, 166
    in Afghanistan, 115
    in Algeria, 87, 94, 95, *97*, 138, 139, 162
    in American Revolution, 36
    in Brazil, 106
    in Colombia, 105, 116, 124, *126*, 130, 151, *153*, 162
    in Cyprus, 86, 113
    in El Salvador, 103–4, 121, *126*
    in Guatemala, 114, 123
    and IMRO, 67
    in India, 110, 111, *156*, 162
    in Indonesia, 134
    in Ireland, 68, 79
    in Jewish revolts, 22, 26
    in Kenya, 87, 95, *97*
    in Malaya, 86, 95, *97*, 163
    in Nicaragua, 100, 123, *125*
    in Ottoman Empire, 61
    and Palestinians, 111, 162, 163
    in Peru, 104, 105, *126*, 162
    in the Philippines, 107, 119, 162
    Russia and Chechens, 140, 150, *156*, 162
    in Sri Lanka, 103, 110, *128*, 131, *154*, 162
    Turkey and Kurds, 131, *151*
    in Venezuela, 90
Gypsies, 74, 76, *82*, 132, 144–5, *155*, 162,

Haiti, 35, 38, 40, 41, 42, 43, 44, 45, *46*, 90, 92, 93, 94, 96, *98*, 162
Hamas, 140, 156
Hijackings, 103, 111, 112, 139
Hindus, 39, 69, 79, 81, 88, 91, 92, 94, *97*, 110–11, 117, 118, 139, 143, 144, 149
Hinduvata, 118, 143, 147, *155*, 161
Hitler, Adolf, 71–2, 73–4, 80, 81, *83*
Hizballah, 113, 115
Holocaust, 74, 80, 83, 161; *see also* genocide
Hungary, 67, 68, 75
Hutu, 145, 152, *157*

INDEX

Ibo (Igbo), 88–9, 90, 92, 93, 94, *97*
IMRO, *see* Internal Macedonian Revolutionary Organization
IMU, *see* Islamic Movement of Uzbekistan
India, 38, 39, 46, 51, 57, 61, *64*, 68–9, 75, 78, 81, *81*, 88, 91, 92, 93, 94, 95, 96, *97*, 103, 110, 115, 116, 117, 129, 143–4, 148, 150, 153, *155*
 ancient, 28
 and death squads, 115, 122–3, *127*, 151, *156*
 and Kashmir, 111, 139, 151, *156*, 162
 partition, 88, 96, *97*, 163
 and Sikhs, 110–11, 113, 115, 117, *127*, 162
 and Sri Lanka, 116
Indians (Americas), 37, 38, 40, 47, 55–6, 57, 58, 63, *63*, 104, 114, 117, 159
Indonesia, 88, 89, 90, 91, 92, 93, 94, 95, 96, *97*, 134, 143, 146–7, 149–50
 and Aceh, 134, 150, *154*
 and Borneo, 134–5, *154*
 and East Timor, 114–15, 119–20, 123, *128*, 134, 146–7
 and Malakus, 135, 143, 149, *155*
INLA, *see* Irish National Liberation Army
Inquisition, 35, 41, 42, 43, *45*
instrumental terrorism, 35, 48, 62, 76–7, 81, 91, 92, 96, 117, 146, 159, 160, 161, 165, 167, 168
Internal Macedonian Revolutionary Organization (IMRO), 51–2, 66–7, 75, 79, *82*, 160
IRA, *see* Irish Republican Army
Iran, 107–8, 113, 115, 119, 120, *127*, 143, 162
Iraq, 1, 15, 107–8, 111, 115, 163, 168
Ireland, 36, 41, 42–3, *45*, 47, 51, 57, 61, 62, 64, 68, 75, 76, 77–8, 79, *81*, 84–5, 92, *97*, 148
Irgun, 69, 80, 85, 94, 111
Irish National Liberation Army (INLA), 109

Irish Republican Army, 68, 75, 77, *81*, 84–5, 91, 95, 96, *97*, 108–9, 115, 117, 121, 130–1, 143, 146, 149, *154*, 164
Irish Republican Brotherhood, 62, *64*
Iron Guard, 72–3, 79, *83*, 161
Islam, 17, 28, 39, 43, 52, 92, 132, 134, 136, 140, 148
Islamic Army Group (GIA) (Algeria), 138, *156*
Islamic Group (Egypt), 138, 150, *155*
Islamic Jihad (Palestine), 140
Islamic Movement Army (MIA) (Algeria), 138, *156*
Islamic Movement of Uzbekistan (IMU), 140, 150, *156*
Israel, 1, 81, 94, *96*, 11–12, 115, 118–19, 121–2, 137, 138, 140, 146, 147, 150, 161, 162, 190n74
 ancient, 21
 and 1967 War, 99, 111
Italy, 28, 30, 32, 33, *34*, 53, 57, 67–8, 69, 73, 75, 76, 77, 79, 93, 95, 99, 111, 118, 120, 122, 159, 161
 and Fascists, 70–1, 72, 73, 74, 77, *83*, 162
 and neo-fascists, 89, 91, 92, 95, 96, *98*, 100, *124*
 and Red Brigades, 101, 118, 120, *125*

Jammu and Kashmir, *see* Kashmir
Janatha Vimukthi Peramuna (JVP), 103, 114, *126*
Japan, 48, 70, 76, 78, 80, *82*, 103, 118, *125*, 141, 147, *156*
Japanese Red Army (JRA), 103, 112, 116, *125*, 143
JCAG, *see* Justice Commandos of the Armenian Genocide
Jewish terrorists, 69, 80, *82*, 85, 94, 95, *96*, 112, 113, 122, *127*, 140, 146, 147, 150, 161

Jews, 54–5, 57, 58–9, 69, 70, 72, 73, 74, 75, 76, 78, *82, 83*, 85, 94, 121, 132, 133, 162
  in ancient world, 19, 21–2, 24, 26–7; *see also* Maccabees and Zealots
JRA, *see* Japanese Red Army
Judaism, 43
Julius Caesar, 21
juramentado, 39
Justice Commandos of the Armenian Genocide (JCAG), 111, *127*
JVP, *see* Janatha Vimukthi Peramuna

Kansas, 47, 50, 54, 57–8, 59, 60, 62, *63*, 159, 160, 161, 165
Karimov, Islam, 140
Kashmir, 111, 115, 117, 121, *127*, 139, 143, 146, 148, 150, 151, *156*, 162
Kenya, 86–7, 93, 94, 95, *97*, 137
  embassy attack, 137, 138, 162
KGB, 91
kidnapping, 7, 22, 72, 85, 102, 103, 105, 106, 108, 113, 120, 138, 141
KKK, *see* Ku Klux Klan
Kosovo, 67, 136, 144, 147, 148, 149, 152, 153, *155*, 163
Kosovo Liberation Army (KLA), 136, 149, 153, *155*
Ku Klux Klan, 50–1, 57, 59, 60, 62, *63*, 70, 74, 76, 78, 79, 80, *82*, 89, 91, 93, 94–5, 96, *98*, 99–100, 118, 122, *124*, 159, 160, 161
Kurdish Workers Party (PKK), 107, 129–30, 131, 149, 153, *153*, 162
Kutari, Tomas, 37

Lapua Movement, 72, 80
Laskar Jihad, 135, 143
Lavon Affair, 91
leaderless resistance, 9, 39, 43, 53, 133, 134, 142, 168
Lebanon, 112–13, 115, 117, 120, *128*, 148, 153
Legion of the Archangel Michael, 72–3, 76, 77, 78, 161
Lenin, 54, 62, 100

Liberation Tigers of Tamil Eelam (LTTE), 110, 116, 121, 131, 146, 153, *154*
Libya, 115, 190n74
LTTE, *see* Liberation Tigers of Tamil Eelam

M-19, *see* April 19 Movement
Maccabees, 22, 26, 27, 166
Macedonia, 24, 25, 51–2, 66–7, 75, 78, 79, 81, *82*, 136, 148, 149, *155*
Madrid train bombings, 132, 137, 151
Madurese, 135, 149, *154*
Malabar, 39, 41, 161
Malakus, 135, 146, *155*
Malaya, 48–9, 59, 60, 62, 85–6, 91, 92, 93, 95, 96, *97*, 163
Malayan Communist Party (MCP), 86, *97*
Mau Mau, 86–7, 94, 95–6, *97*
McVeigh, Timothy, 133
Medellín Cartel, 105, *126*, 130, 160
MEK, *see* Mujahedin-e-Khlaq
MIA, *see* Islamic Movement Army
militia movement (United States), 133, *154*
Milosevic, Slobodan, 135, 136
MIR, *see* Movement of the Revolutionary Left (Venezuela)
MNLF, *see* Moro National Liberation Front
modernization, 4, 16–18, 25, 58, 62, 63, 78–9, 92, 117, 118, 136, 147–8
Mongols, 29–30, 33
Montagnards, 40, 44
Montoneros, 106–7, 114, 119, 121, *126*, 162
Mormons, 47, 49–50, 54, 57, 59, 60, 61, 63, *63*, 159, 160, 161
Moro, Aldo, 102, 122
Morocco, 94
Moro National Liberation Front (MNLF), 109, *156*
Movement of the Revolutionary Left (MIR) (Venezuela), 90, 92, 93, *98*
MRTA, *see* Tupac Amaru Revolutionary Army

Mugabe, Robert, 144, 146, 147, 151–2, *157*
Mujahedin-e-Khlaq (MEK), 107–8, 115, *127*
Munich Olympics, 1, 111
Muslims, 38–9, 41, 42, *46*, 48, 59, 62, 87, 88, 91–2, 94, 109, 114, 115, 119, 121, 134, 135, 137–38, 139, 140–1, 143–4, 149, 150, 161
Muslim terrorists, 2, 22, *128*, 135, 138, 139, 141, 147, 150, *157*, 160, 161, 164
Mussolini, Benito, 71, *83*, 89

Napoleon, 42, 57, 166
Narodnaya Volya, *see* People's Will
National Liberation Army (ELN) (Colombia), 105, *126*
National Liberation Front (FLN) (Algeria), 87, 94, 95, *97*
nationalism, 15, 47, 62, 77, 78, 79, 92, 163
Naxalites, 103
Nazi Party, 71–2, 73, 74, 75, 76, 80, 81, *83*, 152, 162
neo-fascists, 89, 91, 92, 95, 96, *98*, 100, 122, *124*, 131
neo-Nazis, 129, 131–32, 145, 148, 151, *154*
Netherlands, 39, 84, 93, 134
Nicaragua, 70, 74, 76, 77, 80, 81, *82*, 100, 117, 122, 123, *125*
Nigeria, 139, 142, 146, 147, 148, 149
 crisis of 1966, 88–9, 90, 91, 92, 93, 94, 95, 96, *97*
Night of the Long Knives, 72
Nivelles Group, 100, *124*
Nizari, *see* Assassins
North Korea, 115–16
Northern Ireland, 36, 68, 85, 90, *97*, 99, 108, 130–31, 147, 149, *154*
nuclear weapons, 4, 141, 161

OAS, *see* Secret Army Organization
Oklahoma City, 1, 133, *154*
Optimates, 21, 24, 25, *27*
Order, The, 100, 116–17, 122, *125*, 133

Organization of Cypriot Fighters (EOKA), 86, 94, *96*
Oslo Accords, 121–22, *127*, 140
Ottoman Empire, 57, 61, 63, *64*, 149, 152

pagsabil, 39, 42, 43, 45, *46*, 57, 160, 174; *see also* suicide attacks,
Pakistan, 88, 93, 94, *97*, 111, 115, 137, 139, 143, 153, *156*, 163
Palestine Mandate, 69, 85, 86, 94, 95, *96*, 161, 162–63
Palestinian Liberation Organization (PLO), 99, 111–12, 115, 118, 121–22, *127*, 140
Palestinians, 118, 121, *127*, 140, *156*, 164
Patricians, 20–1, *26*
Pavelic, Ante, 67, 74, 76
peasant uprisings, 28, 31–2, 33, 34, *34*, 165
Peloponnesian Wars, 20, 23
Peninsulares, 37, 40–1
People's Revolutionary Army (ERP) (Argentina), 106–7, 114, 119
People's Will, 53, 61
Persia, 21–2, 26, 28, 29
Peru, 37, 40–1, 104, 105, 116, 119, 120–21, *126*, 162
 and drug cartels, 105, 124, 153
PFLP, *see* Popular Front for the Liberation of Palestine
Philippines, 39, 41, 48, 109, 114, 117, 123, 138, 143, 146, 148, *156*, 161, 162
 and death squads, 123, *128*, 143, *157*, 161, 162
 and Muslim separatists, 109, 114, 115, 117, 118, 119, 120, 138, 143, 146, 148, 150, *156*
PKI, *see* Communist Party of Indonesia
PKK, *see* Kurdish Workers Party
Plebeians, 20–1, 23–4, 26, *27*
PLO, *see* Palestinian Liberation Organization
poison, 3, 133, 164
Poland, 56, 77
Popular Front for the Liberation of Palestine (PFLP), 111, 112

Popular Liberation Army (EPL) (Colombia), 105
Populares, 21, 24, 25
Portugal, 39, 42, 80, 91, 95, 101, 114
propaganda of the deed, 53, 73
propaganda of the word, 53
Puerto Rico, 108
Puritan Revolution, 35, 36, 41

Quebec, 108, 117, *127*

Rabin, Yitzak, 140
RAF, *see* Red Army Faction
rape as terrorism, 114, 135, 143
Rashtriya Swayamsevak Sangh (RSS), 88
Real IRA, 131
Red Army Faction (RAF), 101, 112, *125*
Red Brigades, 3, 101–2, 116, 118, 120, 162
Reformation, 4, 28, 32, 35
Reign of Terror, 35, 38, 40, *46*
religion, 2, 4, 11, 13, 14, 16–17, 35–6, 41, 123–24, 129, 133–34, 146, 147–48, 152, *154*, 159–60, 161, 163, 166; *see also* specific religions
Revolutionary Armed Forces of Colombia (FARC), 105, 118, 121, 123, *126*, 130, 143, 151, *153, 157*
  and drug cartels, 105, 123, *126*, 139, 146, *153*, 160
Robespierre, 40, 44
Rome, 31, 71
  empire, 19, 20, 22–3, 24, 25–6
  republic, 19, 20–1, 23–4, 25, *27*, 159, 161
Ruby Ridge, 133
Rumania, 72–3, 76, 77, 78, *83*, 161
Russia, 47, 52–4, 56, 57, 58, 59, 61–2, 63, *65*, 66, 108, 140–41, 147, 150, *156*, 176n31
Rwanda, 145, 146, 152, *157*

sans-culottes, 38, 40
Saudi Arabia, 137
Secret Army Organization (OAS), 88, 91–2, 93, 94, 96, *97*

secret societies, 19, 47, 48–9, 57, 58, 59, 62, *63*
Sejluk Turks, 29
Seleucid Greeks, 19, 21–2, 24, 25, 26, *27*
Self Defense Forces of Colombia (AUS), 144, 146, 152, *157*
September 11th, 1, 2, 129, 132, 137, 162, 164
Serbia, 47, 52, 57, 60, *64*, 67, 77, 135, 136, *155*
Serbs, 52, 67–8, 74–5, *82*, 135–36, 144, 149, 152, *155*, 161
17 November Organization, 102, 120, *125*, 129
Shia, 28–9, 33, 113
Shining Path, 104, 105, 117, 119, 121, 153
Sikhs, 92, 110–11, 113, 115, 117, 118, 121, 122–23, *127*, 143, 160
Singapore, 49, 85, *97*, 112
skinheads, 129, 132, 145
SLA, *see* Symbionese Liberation Army (SLA)
slavery, 38, 42, 47, 50, 54, 57–8, 59, 60, 62, 63, *63*, 165
Smith, Joseph, 49, 54
Social Revolutionaries, 54, 62, *64*, 161
Somalia, 137
Sons of Liberty, 36, 43
South Africa, 114
  and death squads, 114, 117, 123, *128*
Southeast Asia, 35, 38–9, 42, 43, 45, 48, 57, 58, 62, 84, 138, 166
Soviet Union, 15, 72, 74, 75, *83*, 89, 90, 91, 115, 120, 129, 140, 166
  and Cold War, 84, 91, 115
Spain, 37–8, 39, 43, 53, 54, 91, 95, 101, 106, *127*, 137, 151, *154*
  and Basques, 108, 114, 118, 123, 130, 149, *154*, 162, 164
  and death squads, 114, 123, *127*
  and Madrid train bombings, 132, 137, 151
Spanish America, 35, 37, 40–1, 42, 43, 44, 45, *46*

Index

Sparta, 20, 23
Sri Lanka, 103, 109–10, 113, 115, 116, 117, 118, 120, *126*, 131, 148, 149, 152, 153, *154*, 161, 162
  and death squads, 114, 117, 123, *128*
Stalin, 15, 74, 76, 80, 81, *83*, 90, 162
St. Bartholomew's Day Massacre, 36, 41, *45*
Stern Gang, 69, 85
street violence, 21, 30, 40, 42, 70–2, 73–4, 75, 76, 80, 96, 162
Sturmabteilunger (SA), 71–2, 73, *83*
Sudan, 143, 152, 163
suicide attacks, 39, 42, 43, 45, *46*, 48, 57, 58, 59–60, *83*, 107, 113, 116, 131, 137, 140, 141, 152, *156*, 160, 161, 164, 168, 190n74
Sun Yat-sen, 48
Sunni, 28–9, 30, 31–2, 34, 107
Symbionese Liberation Army (SLA), 103
Syria, 21, 29, 99, 115

Taliban, 1, 137–38, 162
Tanzania
  embassy bombing, 137, 138, 162
tarring and feathering, 36
terrorism
  definition, 6–11
Time of Troubles (Ireland), 68
Tokyo subway attacks, 141, 150
totalitarian states, 9–10, 15, 158
Tunisia, 94
Tupac Amaru (II), 37, 40–1, 45, *46*, 104, 106, 162
Tupac Amaru Revolutionary Army (MRTA), 104, 105, 117, 119, 121, *126*, 153
Tupameros, 106, 121, *126*
Turkey, 51–2, 56, 74, 107, 111, 118, 119, 120, 121, 122, *124, 125, 127*, 129–30, 131, 149, 162
Tutsi, 145, 152, *157*, 162

Ulster, *see* Northern Ireland
United Kingdom, *see* Britain
United Nations, 85

United States, 1, 40, 48, 50, 53, 59, 62, 63, *63*, 75, *82*, 90, 91, 92, 94, *98*, 100, 101, 102–3, 108, 111, 112, 113, 116–17, *124, 125*, 131, 132–33, 137, 138, 142, 147, 148, 150, 151, 152, 159, 161, 163, 164, 168
  and abortion, 133–34, 146, 151, 161
  "Bleeding" Kansas, 50, 59, *63*, 159
  and Cold War, 84, 91, 115, 159
  and Contras, 115, 122
  and Indians, 47, 55–6, 57, 63, *63*, 159
  KKK in, 57, 59–60, 69–70, 74, 76, 78, 89, 92, 94–5, 99–100, 159
  and Mormon persecutions, 49–50, 57, 63, *63*, 159
  Vietnam War, 99, 100, 102–3, *125*
Uruguay, 106, 114, 119, 121, *126*
Uruguayan Movement of National Liberation, *see* Tupameros
Utashe, 67–8, 74–5, *82*, 161
Uzbekistan, 140, 146, 147, 150, 153, *156*

Venezuela, 90, 91, 92, 93, 95, *98*, 103
Venice, 30–1
Vietnam War, 99, 100, 102–3, *125*, 166
vigilantes, 11, 21, 114, 143, 161
Voting Rights Act of 1965, 89

weak states, 10–11, 15–16, 23, 25, 26, 31, 33, 42–3, 48–9, 59, 61, 62–3, 77–8, 93, 106, 118–20, 134, 146–47, 165, 166, 167, 168
weapons of mass destruction, 17, 163–64, 168
Weathermen, 102–3, *125*
World War I, 47, 52, 56, 60, 62, *64*, 66, 72, 77, 121, 166
World War II, 69, 84, 85–6, 93, 95

Yugoslavia, 60, 66–8, 75–6, 77, 79, 129, 135–36, 144

Zealots, 22–3, 166
Zimbabwe, 144, 146, 147, 151–52, *157*
Zionist Occupation Government, 133